IMAGES
of America

EAST VILLAGE

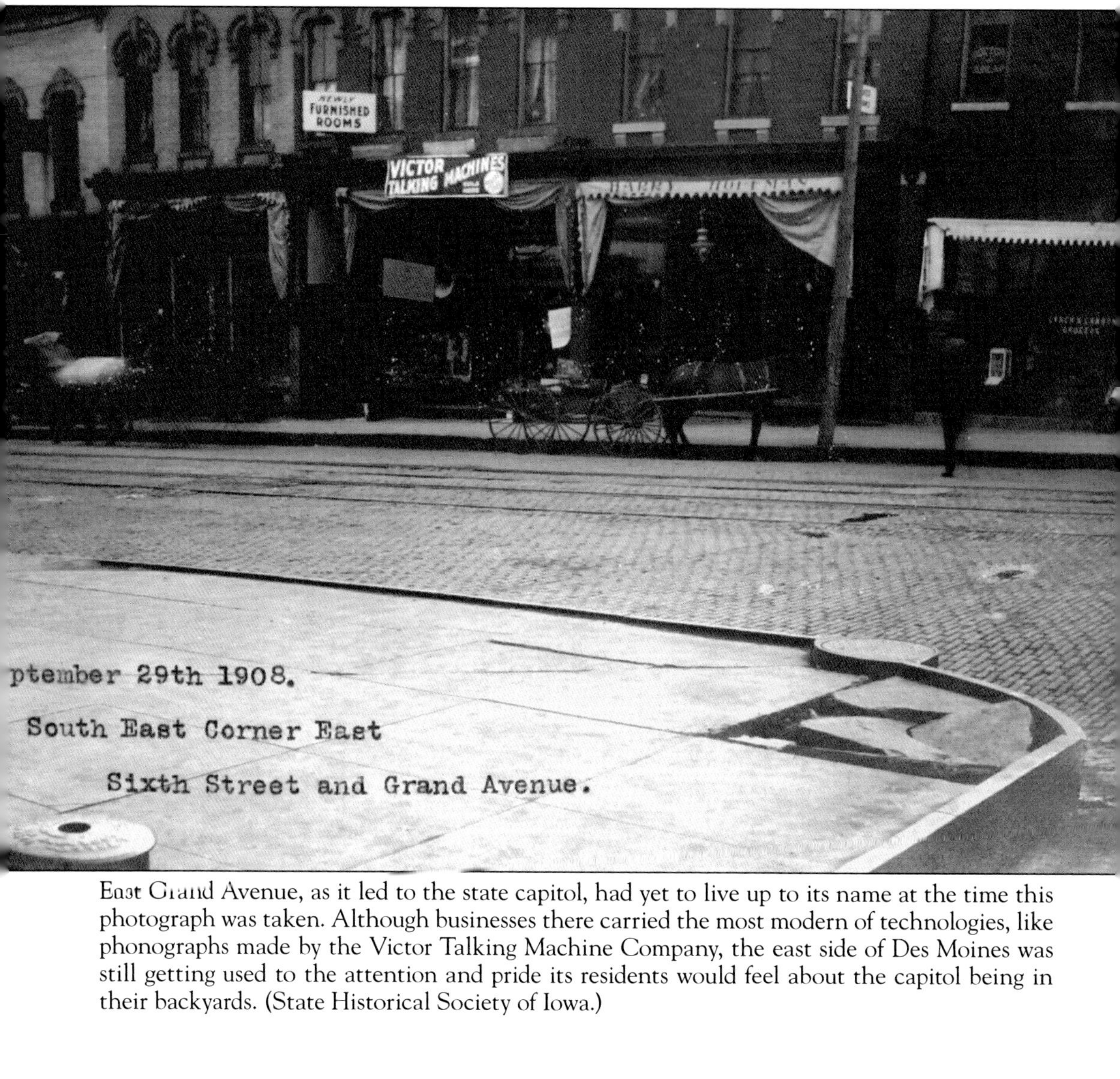

East Grand Avenue, as it led to the state capitol, had yet to live up to its name at the time this photograph was taken. Although businesses there carried the most modern of technologies, like phonographs made by the Victor Talking Machine Company, the east side of Des Moines was still getting used to the attention and pride its residents would feel about the capitol being in their backyards. (State Historical Society of Iowa.)

On the Cover: Passengers board a curb liner on East Locust at East Sixth Streets in February 1953. It was the year the city of Des Moines introduced one-way streets on both sides of the river to make it easier for cars to pass through downtown. East Village returned to two-way streets in 2003 to better improve traffic circulation as a result of the Capitol Gateway East Urban Design plan. (State Historical Society of Iowa.)

IMAGES
of America

EAST VILLAGE

Sarah C. Oltrogge

ARCADIA
PUBLISHING

ISBN 978-0-7385-7742-5

Published by Arcadia Publishing
Charleston SC, Chicago IL, Portsmouth NH, San Francisco CA

Printed in the United States of America

Library of Congress Control Number: 2009934372

For all general information contact Arcadia Publishing at:
Telephone 843-853-2070
Fax 843-853-0044
E-mail sales@arcadiapublishing.com
For customer service and orders:
Toll-Free 1-888-313-2665

Visit us on the Internet at www.arcadiapublishing.com

For my family, who encourages me to be a better person, and especially my mother, Nada, who nudges me "gently" along life's road.

Contents

ACKNOWLEDGMENTS

I am deeply indebted to the staff at the State Historical Society of Iowa, who is entrusted with the care of Iowa's history. I particularly wish to thank Becki Plunkett, Susan Jellinger, Shari Stelling, Bruce Kreuger, and other library and archives staff and volunteers who assisted me in my research. This book would not have been possible without their helpfulness. There were many individuals who guided my journey: Ted Gerstle, my editor, who always had a kind word of encouragement; J. D. Larson, a "roaming oddball," who had the foresight to document East Village before it all changed; Jim Jacobsen, who wrote *Lee Township against the World*, which provided the basis for my research; Jim Boyt, for his patience and easy way of storytelling; John Burgeson, for recognizing the importance of east Des Moines history and keeping it safe for others to enjoy; City of Des Moines staff, particularly Mary Neiderbach and Kathy Cahoun, who allowed me to spend days sifting through a pile of disorganized negatives in the staff kitchenette (from which many treasures came); the staff of the Des Moines Public Library, who accommodated my every request; Kirk Blunck, for opening his renovation files to me; Kent Carlson, who helped me understand the value of the buildings that have been lost in Des Moines; my Ya-Ya sisters, who kept me laughing; my pets Lucy, Doolittle Lynn, and George, who sacrificed hours of playtime and attention during the writing of this book; and finally, my sister Susan, for being awesome in general and who allowed me access to the Brooks Borg Skiles Architecture Engineering LLP archives, which provided great insight on the development of the Gateway East Urban Design plan. Lastly, I wish to thank all those who donate their photographs and ephemera to history institutions so that others may learn from them.

Unless otherwise noted, the photographs included in this work came from various sources and are abbreviated as follows: Capitol Hill Lutheran Church (CHLC); City of Des Moines (CDM); Des Moines Public Library Iowa Collection (DMPL); Des Moines Business Record (DMBR); Iowa State Bank (ISB); J. D. Larson (JDL); Jim Boyt (JB); Library of Congress, Farm Security Administration, Office of War Information Collection (LOC FSA/OWI); Library of Congress Historic American Building Survey (HABS); Matt Niebuhr (MN); and State Historical Society of Iowa (SHSI).

INTRODUCTION

Just after about 1900, there were two distinct downtown areas of Des Moines, with the Des Moines River serving as an unintentional boundary. The east side was at a disadvantage early on, with its land lower and less usable than the high ground to the west, where tall buildings could create a towering skyline. But the east side had successfully secured the state capitol, completed in 1886, and its residents were looking forward to the growth and prosperity a building of its stature was sure to bring.

Even so, those expectations were never fully realized. Large insurance companies preferred the west side, and residential growth grew faster heading west than east. As such, the two sides became seemingly independent of each other. The area also had a high immigrant population, particularly Scandinavians, who were able to form their own pocket community in which they could observe their traditions freely.

Horace E. Teachout was a civic leader for the east side and built the first skyscraper in the neighborhood in 1911. "We must look after our interests, because unless we do, nobody else will," reported the *Plain Talk* newspaper. Teachout was instrumental in beginning the East Side Commercial Club, which unified business owners and strengthened them as one voice.

City leaders recognized the need for aesthetic improvements along the Des Moines River and began the City Beautiful Movement. Changes unfolded gradually between 1900 and 1937, as the city built up its new municipal center on the east side, cleaned up the area along the river, and established parks and a citywide boulevard system. Well-worn billboards were cleaned up but not altogether abolished until some time later. All these outdoor improvements allowed east side residents to enjoy and be proud of their own neighborhoods.

In 1957, the city of Des Moines and the state of Iowa began plans for a metro freeway to tie into the 41,000-mile system officially known as the Dwight D. Eisenhower National System of Interstate and Defense Highways. That year, the Des Moines City Council voted 5-0 in support of the freeway plan. Vast areas of land on both the east and the west sides of downtown were purchased and cleared for this major undertaking, which began in 1958.

It was at this time that enclosed shopping malls began to make their mark on society. This was no more apparent in the Midwest than when the Southdale Center in Edina, Minnesota, opened in 1956, the first fully enclosed mall with a two-level design. It had central air-conditioning and heating, a comfortable common area, and competitive department stores as anchors. Nine years later, there were 7,600 shopping centers in the United States. Suburban development in Des Moines and population growth after World War II created the need for more housing and more convenient retail shopping. Many of the strip malls of the 1950s and 1960s served these new housing developments and directly competed with the mom-and-pop establishments.

The scope of downtown living and conducting business in Des Moines was shifting even farther westward. By 1971, the city had cleared obvious areas along East Grand Avenue east of Fourth Street, the block north of the federal courthouse, and the east end of Walnut Street between

Fifth and Sixth Streets. The riverfront area north of Des Moines Street was also completely cleared and being redeveloped. On the east side alone, 105 buildings were demolished between 1948 and 1989, 41 of them between 1980 and 1989.

By the 1990s, what became known as East Village was run down. The buildings that remained were ignored, showing obvious disrepair or patching attempts, like outdated siding and false facades. The after-hours bar scene intensified and crime increased. On weekends, the streets emptied as downtown workers went to their western suburban homes.

Architect Kirk Blunck, an early east side supporter with strong historic preservation ideals, purchased several structures, including the Teachout and Hohberger buildings, and began restoring them in the late 1990s. His efforts began a chain reaction that made neighboring building owners begin to clean up their own properties. The real coup came once these renovations were completed in 2000. West side suburban businesses moved back downtown and chose East Village as home. Places like Kitchen Collage (an upscale culinary supply store) and Sticks Gallery (led by nationally known artist Sarah Grant) began to filter in.

It was also during this time of resurgence that a group of individuals came together to advocate saving what historic buildings remained. Threatened by the loss of two blocks of structures deemed important to the East Village historic character and sense of place, these individuals formed Historic East Village in 2002 (incorporated in 2003). The organization's goals were to reverse the trend of demolition by undertaking activities designed to preserve East Village as a healthy, vital center of commerce and social activity and to promote preservation, rehabilitation, and reuse of the commercial, civic, residential, and religious buildings in this traditional business district.

With assistance and cooperation from the City of Des Moines, East Village brought itself back into focus, with a clear identity and reinvention of itself as a hip, urban place to shop and live. Innovative development such as the East Village Square artist live-work lofts drove the sense of uniqueness. Des Moines was ready to embrace the diversity upon which it had been built, and this was apparent particularly in the East Village, as it became home to gay bars and organizations. There is also a high African American population residing in low-income housing just to the north and a center of Latino business just to the east.

The golden dome of the state capitol once again became a symbolic backdrop to the neighborhood oriented around it. The urban revitalization, where old buildings abut new and where longtime east side residents live alongside young professionals, continued in 2008. The river that once divided the east and the west is being redeveloped as a center of recreation in the metro and brings with it a renewed sense of pride for East Village, the little neighborhood in the shadow of the capitol.

One

EAST VERSUS WEST

The Des Moines River flows through the city of Des Moines with little interference. It was this river, however, that flowed its way right through the heart of a community in the late 19th century. Those on the east side of the river were jealous that the west side was recruiting large employers in the insurance and finance industries. The west side held a grudge against the east side for getting the state capitol and the bulk of the railroad access. While industry was building on the east side, its residents were forming their own solidarity. A vibrant immigrant community of Scandinavians, Jews, and African Americans formed businesses and found it easy to purchase homes. They could carry on their traditions and speak their native language in familiar surroundings. Surprisingly, it was the east side that stepped forward to unite the downtown, and that started a movement to work together for the good of the whole. Slowly, both sides came to recognize the benefit of uniformity, with or without the river running between them.

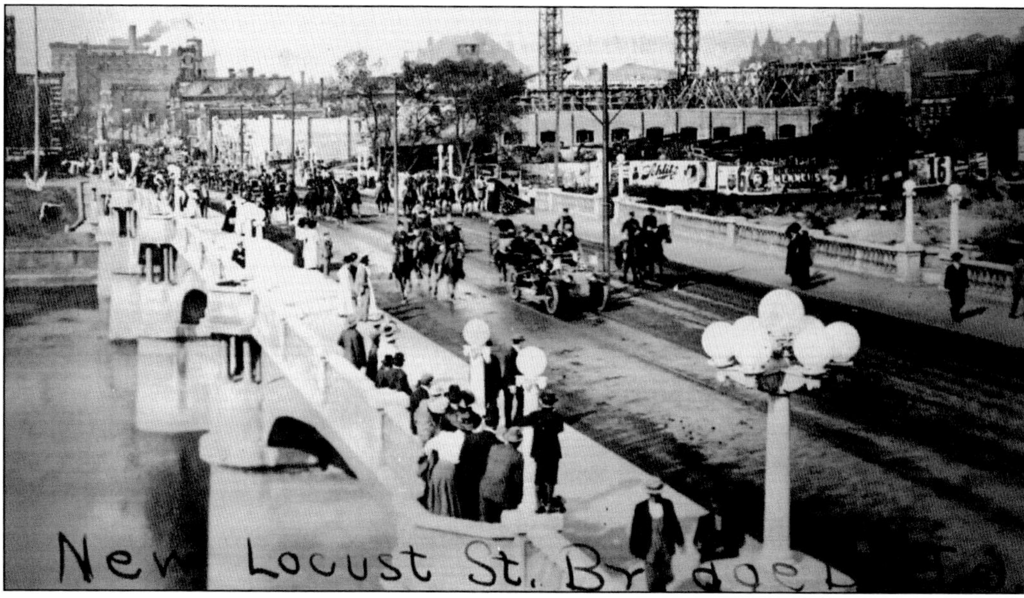

Pres. William Howard Taft made a visit to Des Moines after being elected in 1909. This view is of Taft's motorcade as it crossed the new Locust Street bridge and headed toward the state capitol. In the background, the Coliseum is under construction. Taft was in town to staunchly defend his tariff views. (SHSI.)

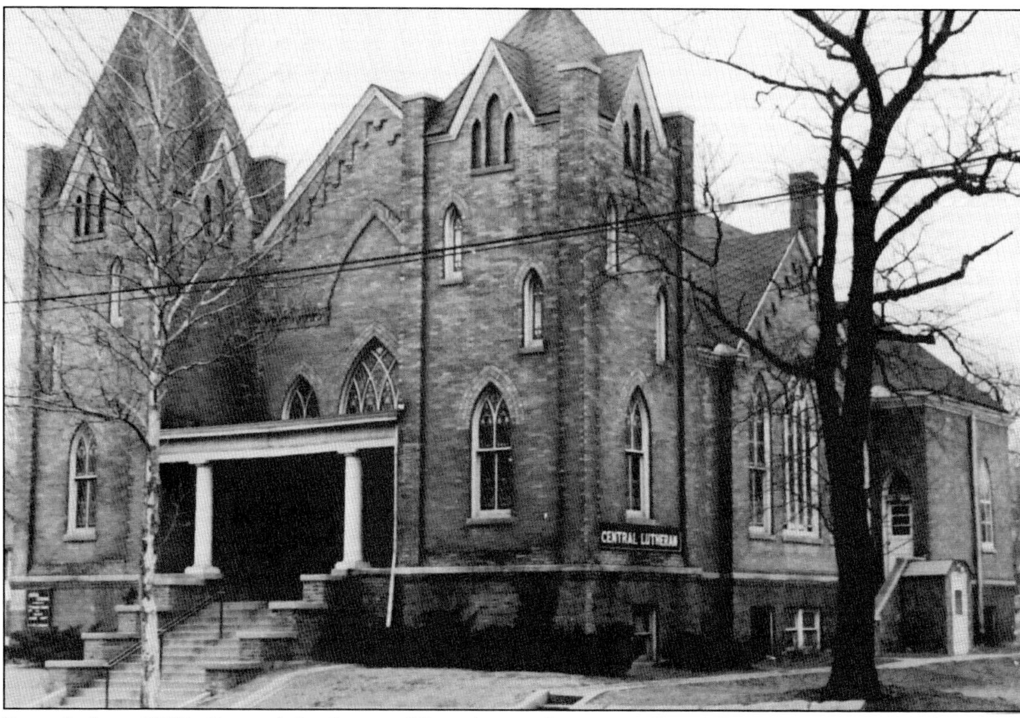

Founded in 1877, Central Lutheran Church was home to Des Moines's Norwegian-language Lutherans. Located at the corner of East Ninth and Des Moines Streets, the church grew with the city, reaching a membership of 1,200 by the 1970s. The original church shown here was built in 1908. (CLHC.)

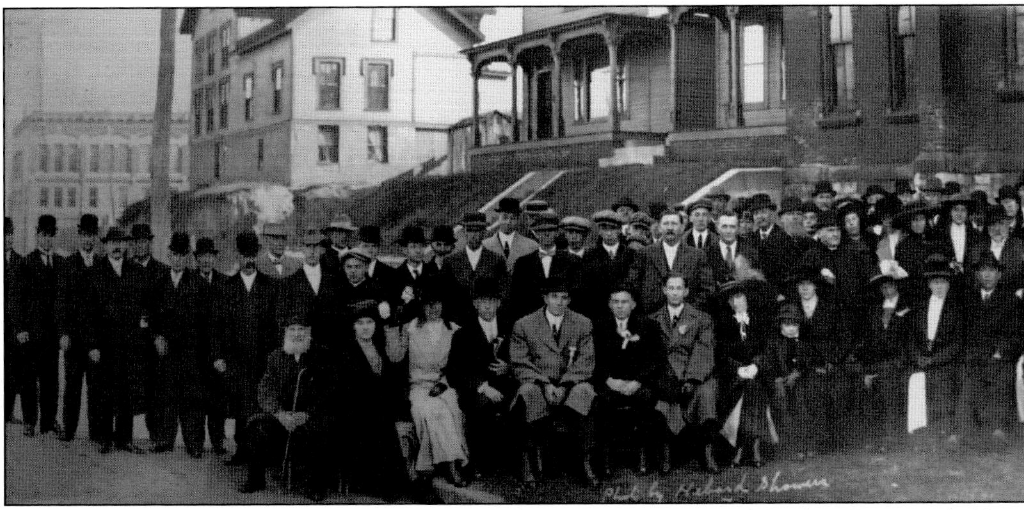

Members of the first-annual convention of the Augustana Synod Luther League, held on November 16–17, 1912, pose for this photograph outside the First Swedish Lutheran Church at East Fifth and Des Moines Streets. In 1907, the Augustana Evangelical Lutheran Church, formed to serve Swedish immigrants, recommended local congregations organize Luther Leagues. The first was held in Des Moines and served as a testament to the tight-knit Swedish community. (CHLC.)

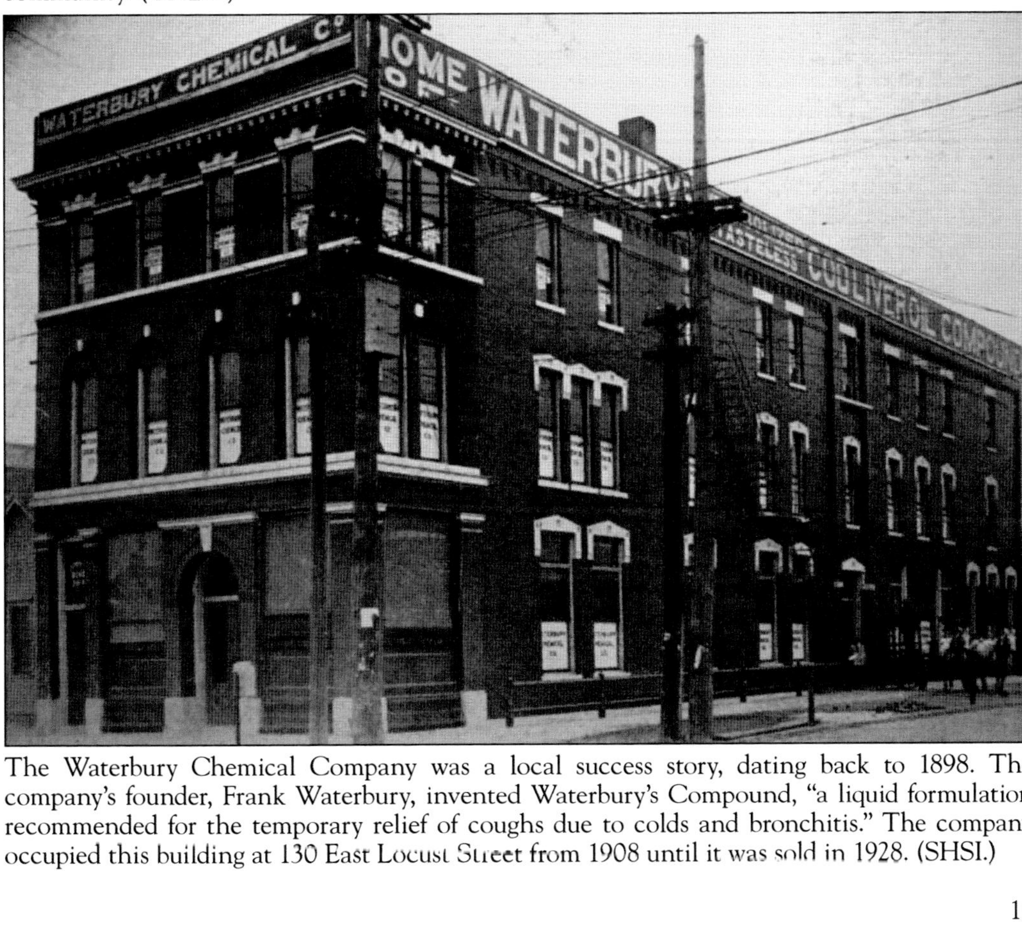

The Waterbury Chemical Company was a local success story, dating back to 1898. The company's founder, Frank Waterbury, invented Waterbury's Compound, "a liquid formulation recommended for the temporary relief of coughs due to colds and bronchitis." The company occupied this building at 130 East Locust Street from 1908 until it was sold in 1928. (SHSI.)

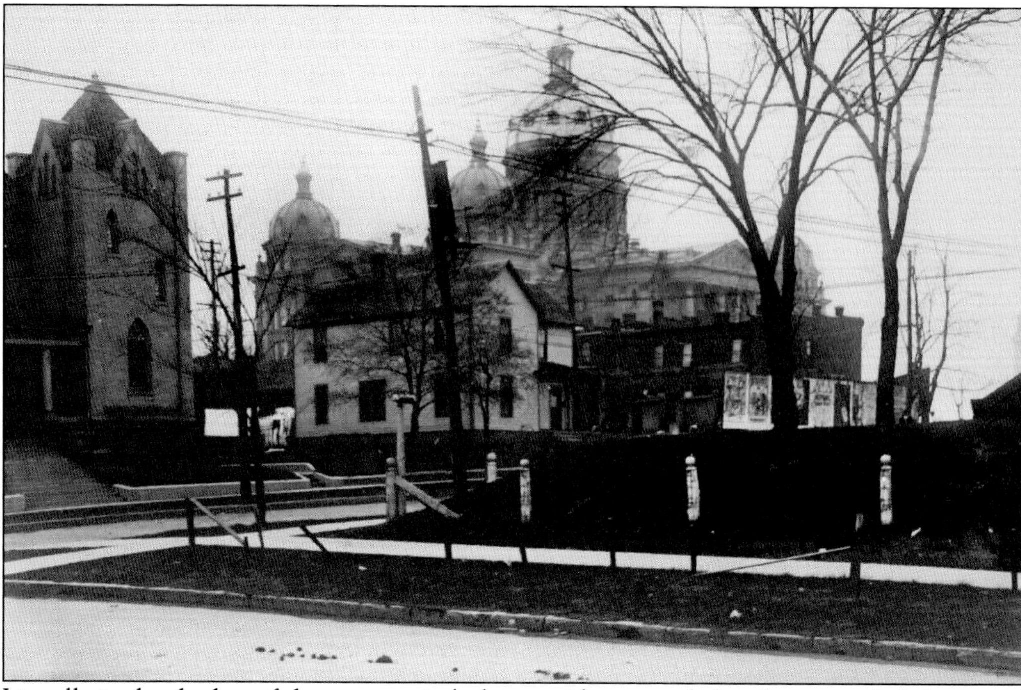

Literally in the shadow of the state capitol, these residences and church surrounded the capitol building at East Ninth and Des Moines Streets around 1912. The church is the Central Lutheran Church, formerly the Danish Lutheran Church, and was torn down in 1956. The other houses were cleared to make room for state office buildings along Grand Avenue between 1962 and 1970. (SHSI.)

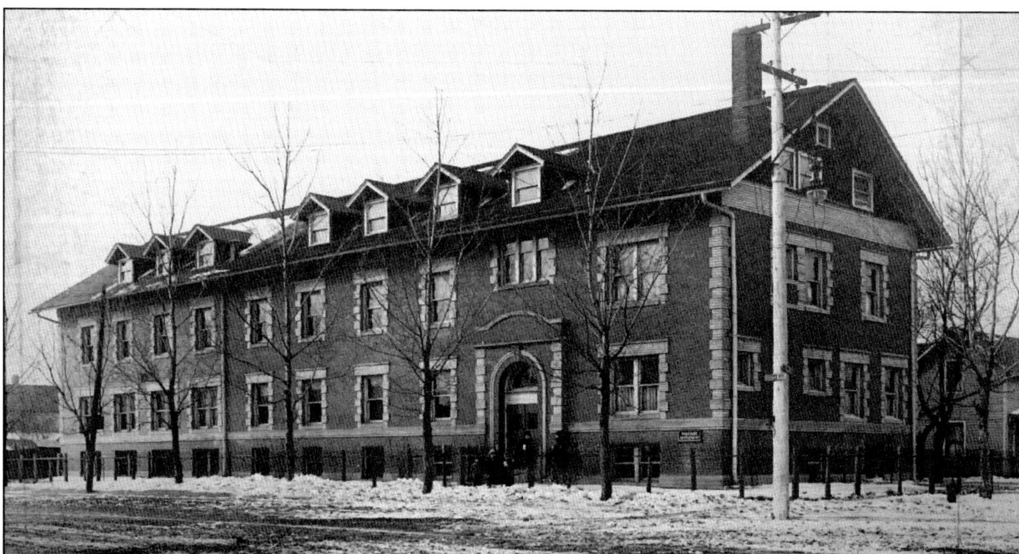

The Roadside Settlement House at 620 Scott Avenue was built in 1906 for the Union of King's Daughters organization. It served as an early community house to immigrant and poor residents of the "southeast bottoms," an area just south of East Village. The house was close to the business center, adjoining a district of railroad employees homes, and it was not far away from a region called "below the dead line." (SHSI.)

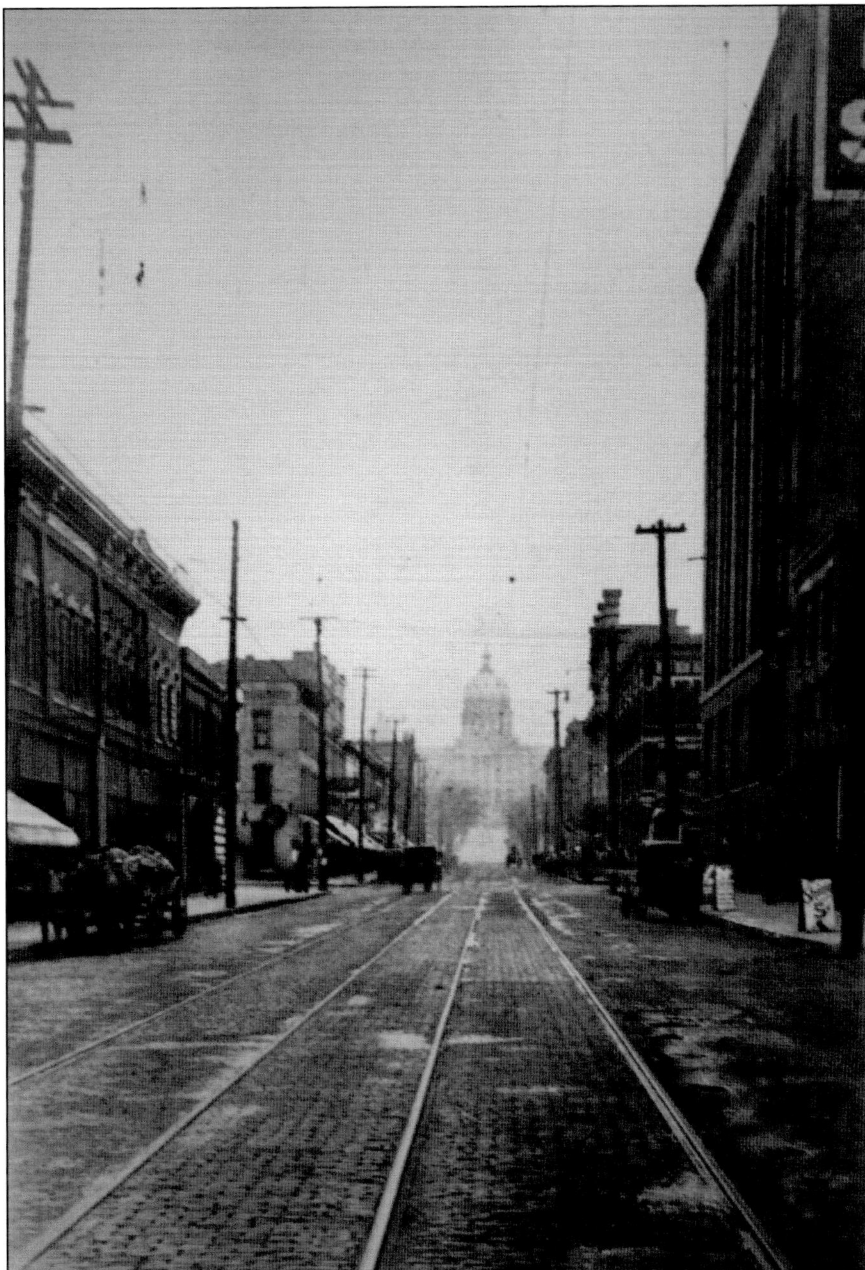

The Teachout building has yet to go up in this 1910 image of East Locust Street. Although Horace E. Teachout owned the property as of 1894, he did not build his skyscraper until 1911 and 1912. Capital City State Bank has already been built and is seen at right. The sign on the sidewalk at right says, "Shine 5 cents." Also visible is the very ornate top to the Lewis Opera House in the middle right. The photograph also indicates it was taken prior to the 1904 fire that nearly destroyed the northern dome of the state capitol, just barely visible here. The fire began on January 4 and was still smoldering 11 days later, with nearly half a million dollars in damage before it was all over. Residents thought their prized state capitol would be destroyed before it even turned 20 years old. (SHSI.)

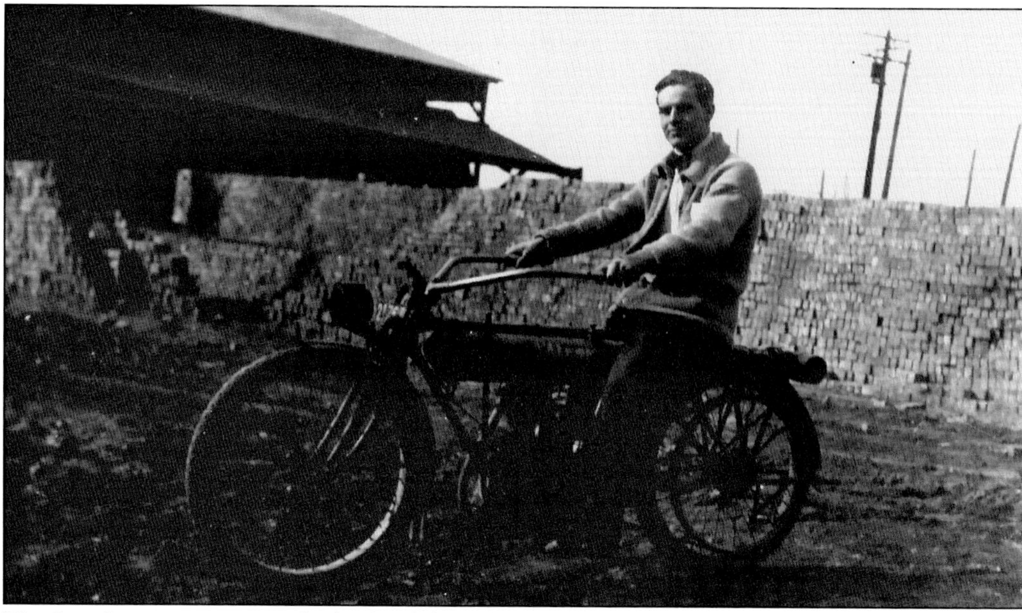

The handwritten note on the back of this photograph identifies the gentleman in the picture as "my father," by Mabel L. Needs, with an address on Southeast Sixth Street. He is sitting on a Yale motorbike around 1912. This early model produced five horsepower at the rear wheel, yet resembled a regular bicycle, complete with pedals. (DMPL.)

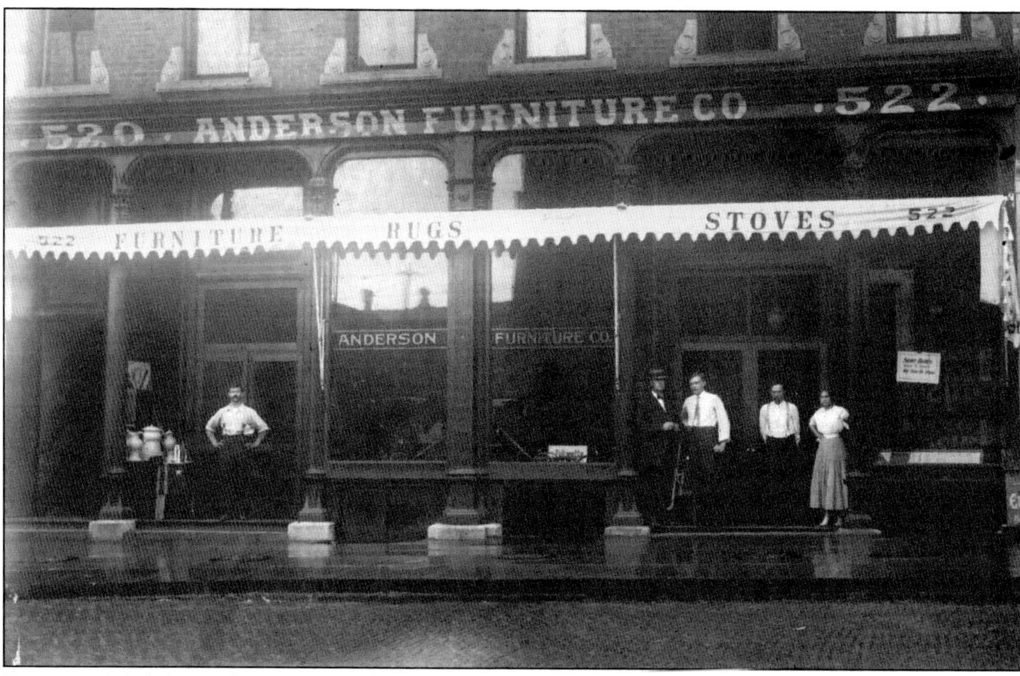

By 1911, Adolph Anderson had split with his partner, Alexander Elliot, and moved into a new location at 520–522 East Grand Avenue, where he remained for more than 40 years. Baby buggies and chamber pots are clearly visible, as is a sign that reads, "Skirt Boxes made to order—any size, any style." (JB.)

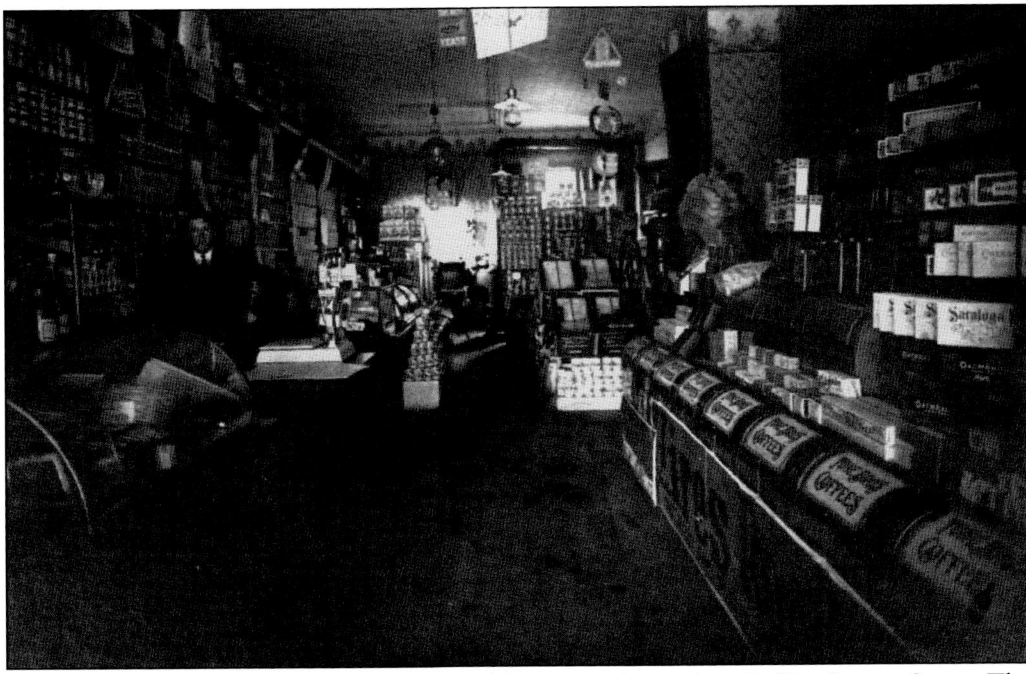

Carl Stenstrom and Company Groceries and Meats was located at 414 East Locust Street. This image shows what a typical dry goods and grocery store looked like shortly after 1900. In his shop, he offers Tone Brothers Coffee, Hires Root Beer, and oatmeal. Note how narrow the store is—the early buildings on the east side were narrow, rarely more than 20 feet wide. (SHSI.)

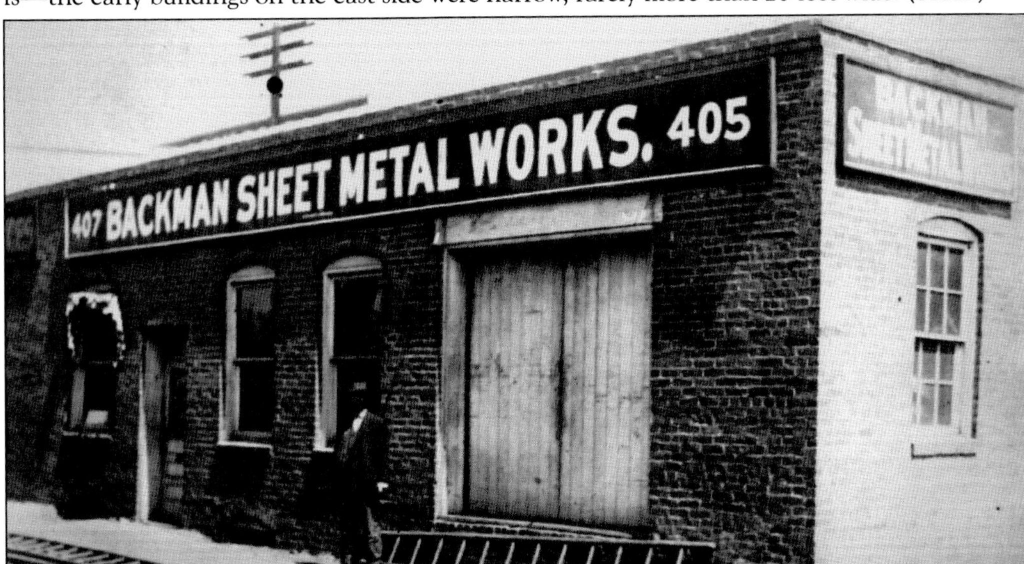

J. A. Backman stands in front of his business at 405–407 East Second Street. A Swedish immigrant, Backman started the business in 1897 and ran it for 40 years. The introduction of air-conditioning in 1937 also produced a need for sheet metal work, and the ducts for Des Moines's Equitable building were created by the Backman company. (SHSI.)

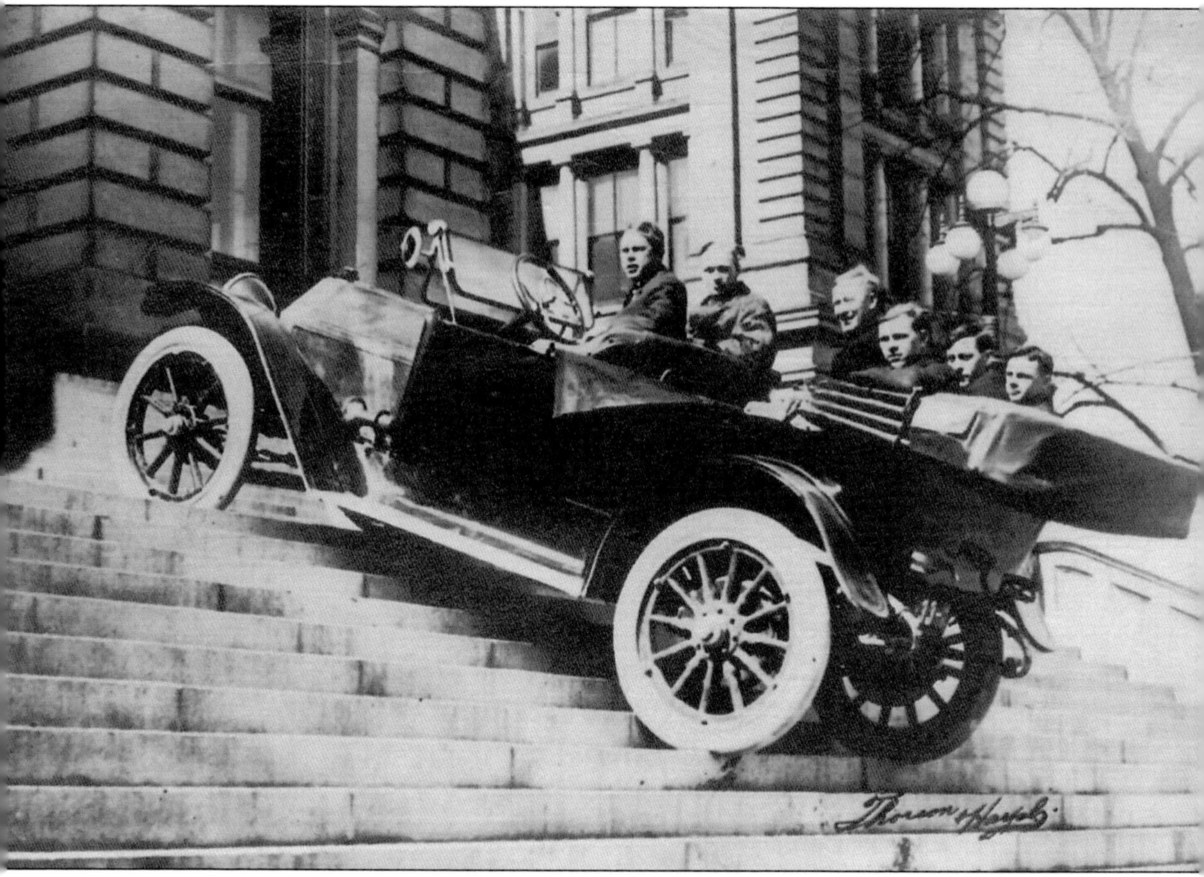

It was either a challenge, a publicity stunt, or both for cars to attempt to climb the steps of the state capitol. The Deusenbergs did it with four people in their Mason car, and now the Spaulding Manufacturing Company wanted to do it fully loaded with people—and on both the east and the west steps. Identified are E. H. Spaulding, driver; Hal Wells, who established a record for driving from "river to river" across the state on dirt roads in October 1913; C. B. Kurtz, a Spaulding Manufacturing Company employee; Fred Claiborne, part owner of the Claiborne Reno Paint Company; and George L. Towne, a Des Moines realtor. The Spaulding earned even more recognition a year later when San Diego businessmen chose it as their vehicle of choice for a cross-country trip, aiming to map out a route to be used for travelers to the Panama-California Exposition held in 1915. (Stewart Library.)

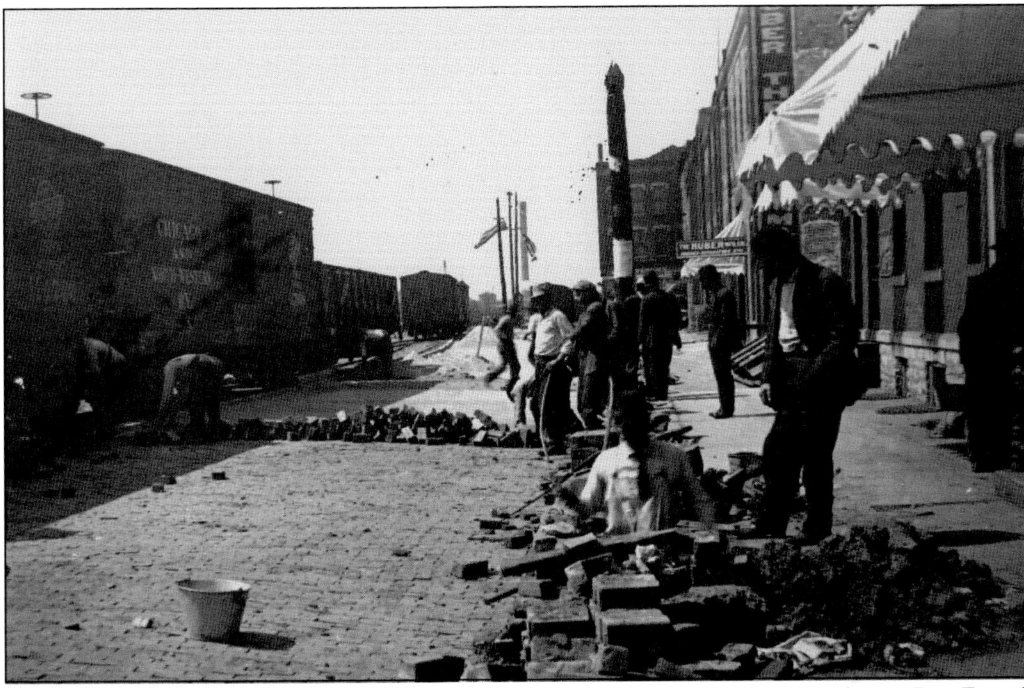

A street crew lays bricks along the Chicago and North Western Railway tracks on East Fourth Street between East Walnut and East Locust Streets around 1910. This view is looking north from East Walnut Street, and Huber Manufacturing Company of Ohio can be seen above the awning. Aside from its invention and manufacturing of various farm machinery, Huber is most noted for developing the first workable gasoline tractor. (SHSI.)

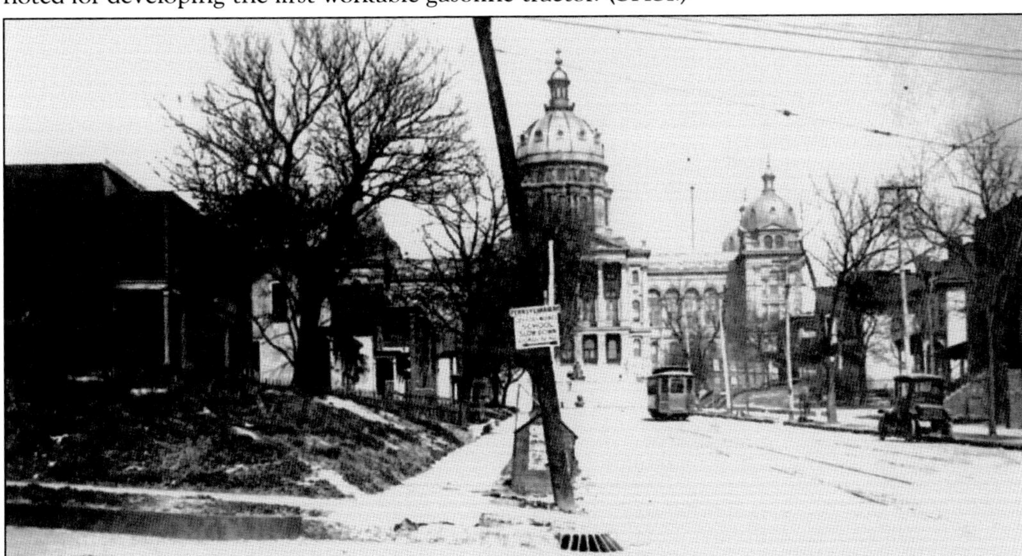

This is East Locust Street, where it junctions with Pennsylvania Avenue, about 1912. The sign reads, "City of Des Moines School, Slow Down to 10 miles per hour," alluding to the Bryant School one block north. The car parked on the street is an Anderson electric car, noted for getting 80 miles per charge and a top speed of 20 miles per hour, more than adequate for driving within city limits. (SHSI.)

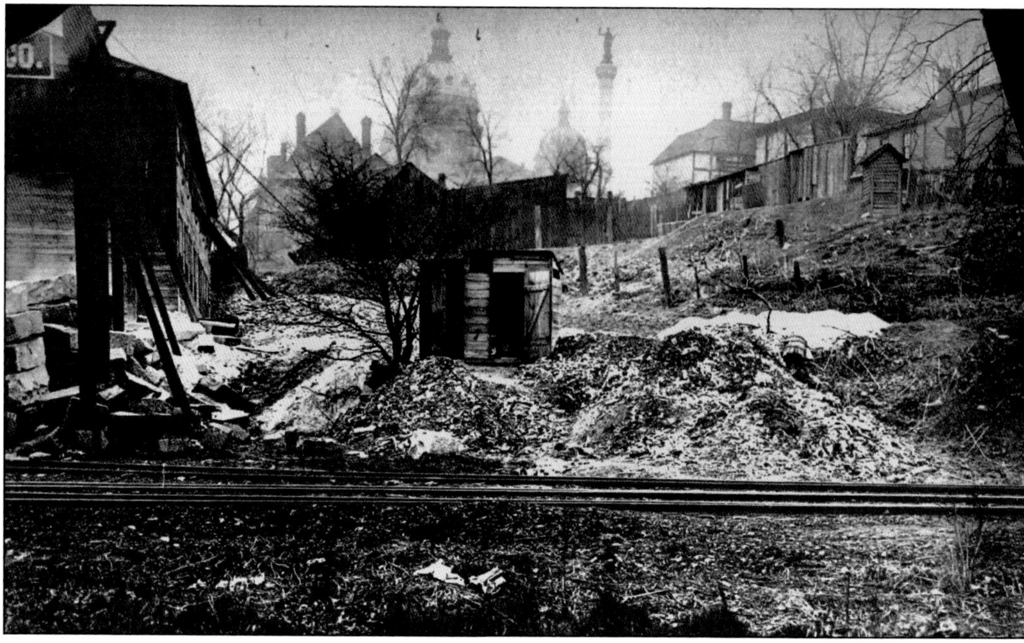

A lone outhouse sits in what could be called a slum neighborhood to the south of the state capitol in this 1908 photograph. The Iowa Soldiers' and Sailors' Monument is visible in the middle background; the chimneys to the right of the monument belong to the Catholic Church of the Visitation. (SHSI.)

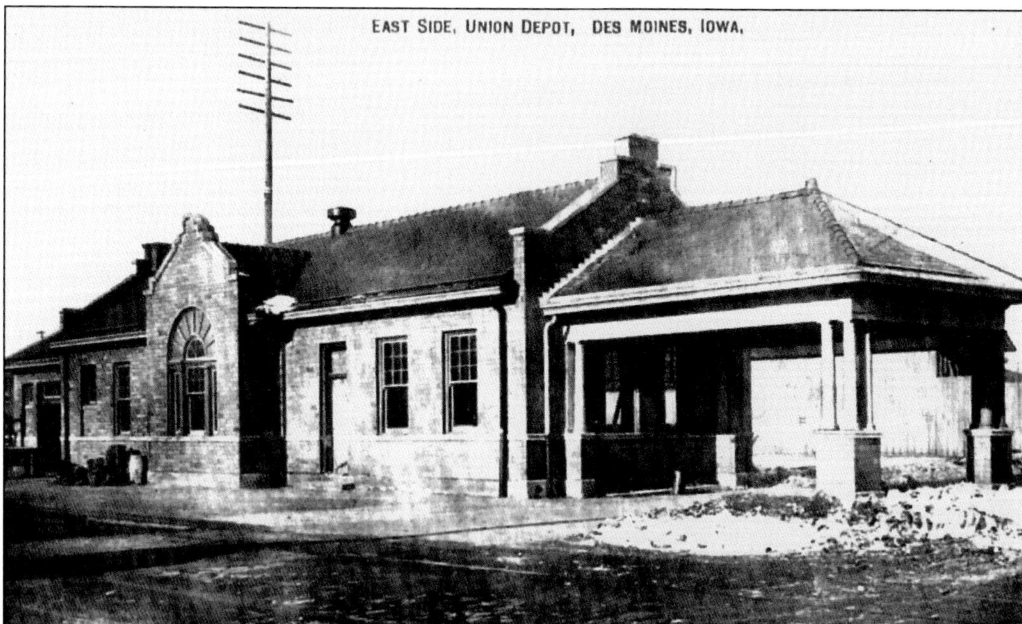

This postcard touts the Des Moines Union Railway depot at 120 East Fifth Street. Built in 1900, the depot came under scrutiny only four years later for not being big enough to accommodate the growing number of passengers. At the time, there were four railroads stopping at the "little station": the Wabash Railroad; the Chicago Great Western Railway; the Chicago, Burlington and Quincy Railroad; and the Des Moines, Iowa Falls, and Northern Railway. (Brad Snodgrass.)

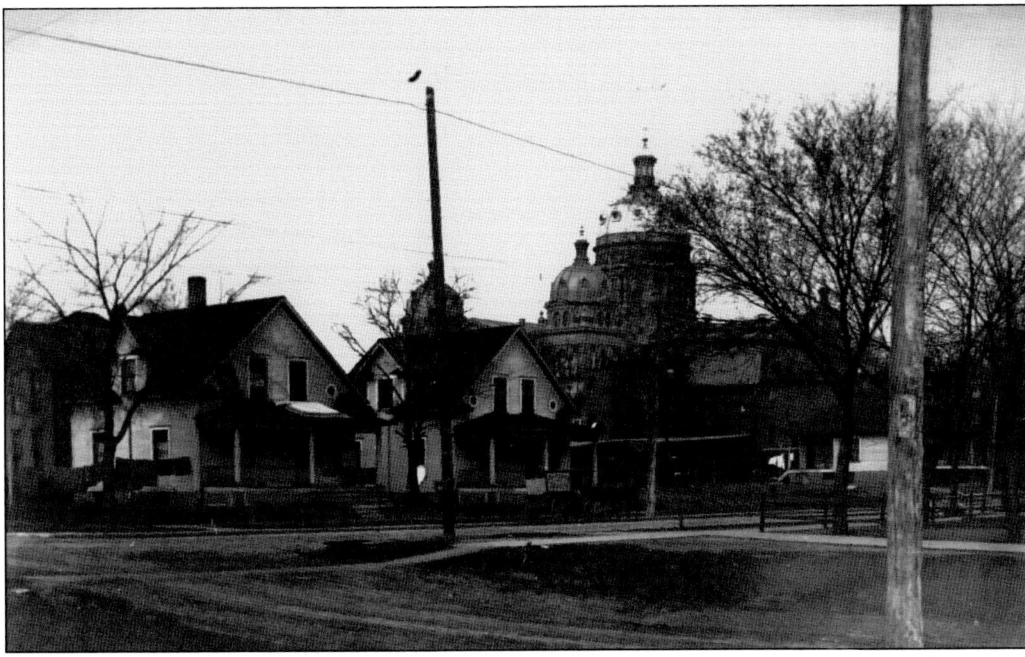

The homes were here first. This is a striking image of homes around the state capitol with the golden domes rising up behind them. Outbuildings indicate there were farm animals kept within city limits. The horse-drawn delivery wagon's sign says "Anderson's Dairy," an early east side business that later became Anderson-Erickson Dairy. (SHSI.)

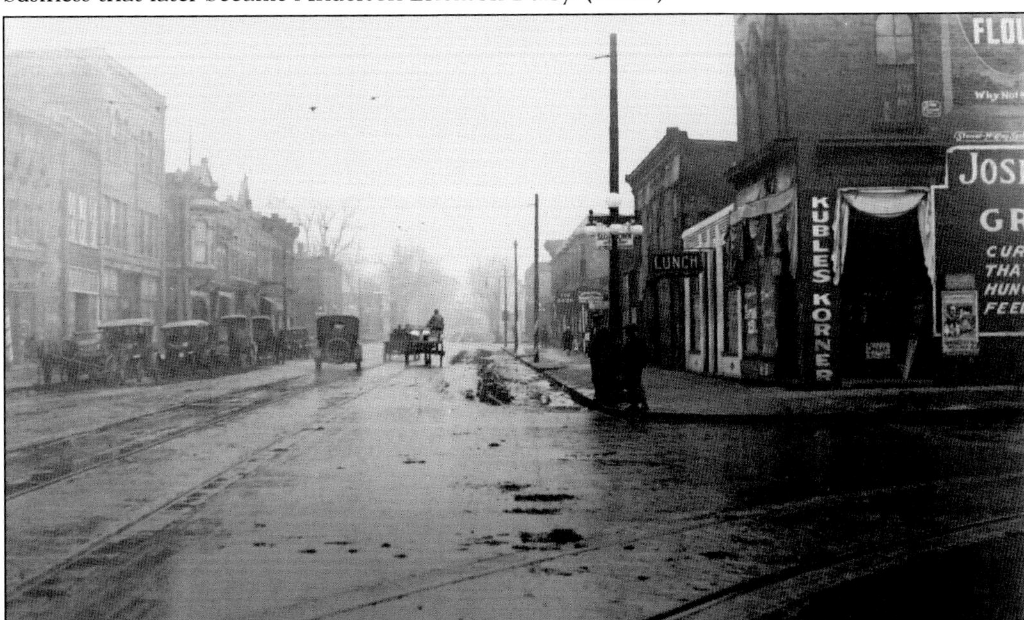

The corner of East Fifth Street and East Walnut Street was the site of an accident on July 20, 1915, when grocer J. C. Kuble was struck by a motor vehicle while unloading his goods. The driver of the car had never driven before and, in fact, had only ridden in a car a few times. The driver lost control and struck Kuble, who suffered numerous injuries as a result. (SHSI.)

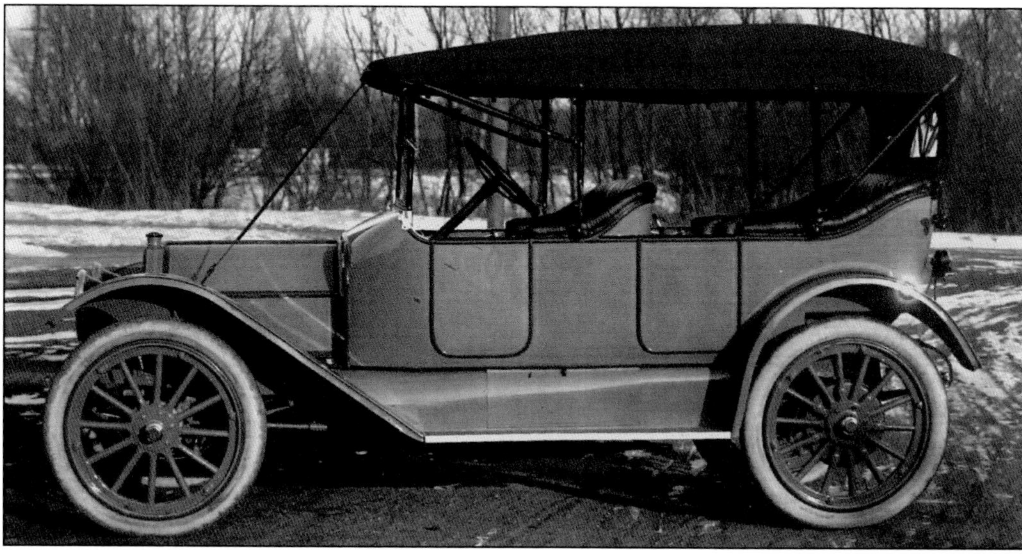

Brothers Fred and Augie Duesenberg started the Mason Automobile Company in 1907 at 300 Southeast Fifth Street. With a Duesenberg-designed, two-cylinder engine, the Mason could pump out 22 horses. The car was so good and sold so well that in 1910 the entire business was bought by washing machine tycoon Frank Maytag. Maytag Mason cars remained in production until 1916. (DMPL.)

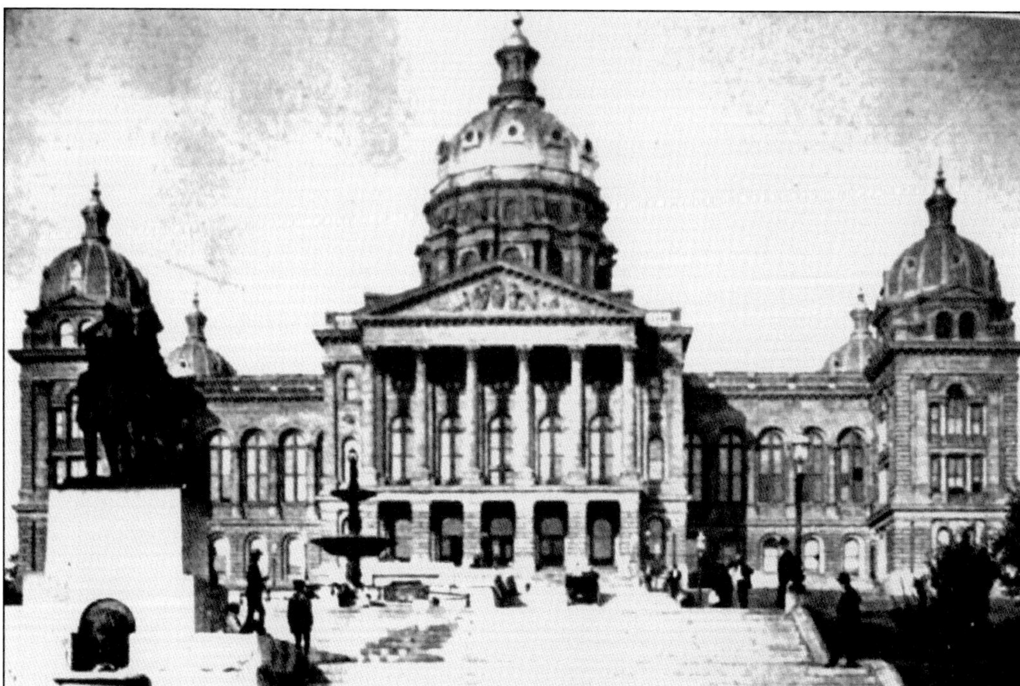

In 1909, the Mason Automobile Company made headlines in Des Moines by driving up the west steps of the state capitol. One advertisement of the 22-horsepower Mason says, "There are 47 steps on a 40 per cent grade. It is made strong and powerful for use on hilly country roads and meets every requirement." (SHSI.)

Two

THE CITY BEAUTIFUL

Thomas C. Hines described the City Beautiful Movement as an "ambitious effort . . . on the part of civic-minded Americans to achieve for their own raw cities something approaching a cultural parity with the distinguished urban centers of an older, grander European civilization." In Des Moines, the shift in attitude toward unifying the downtown brought on board these ideals as it looked to blend together the public buildings to be located along the riverfront. The area was known as the Civic Center and included the Des Moines Public Library (1900–1903), the U.S. Postal Service (1909–1910), the municipal building (1910–1911), the Coliseum (no longer standing), the Municipal Court and Public Safety Building (1918–1920), the federal courthouse (1927–1928), and the Armory and World War Memorial Building (1934–1935). Each building was designed to work as a planned unit with similar features in design, style, scale, use, and materials. With the river used now as a focal point rather than a barrier, the City Beautiful Movement fostered an undeniable sense of pride that all could share.

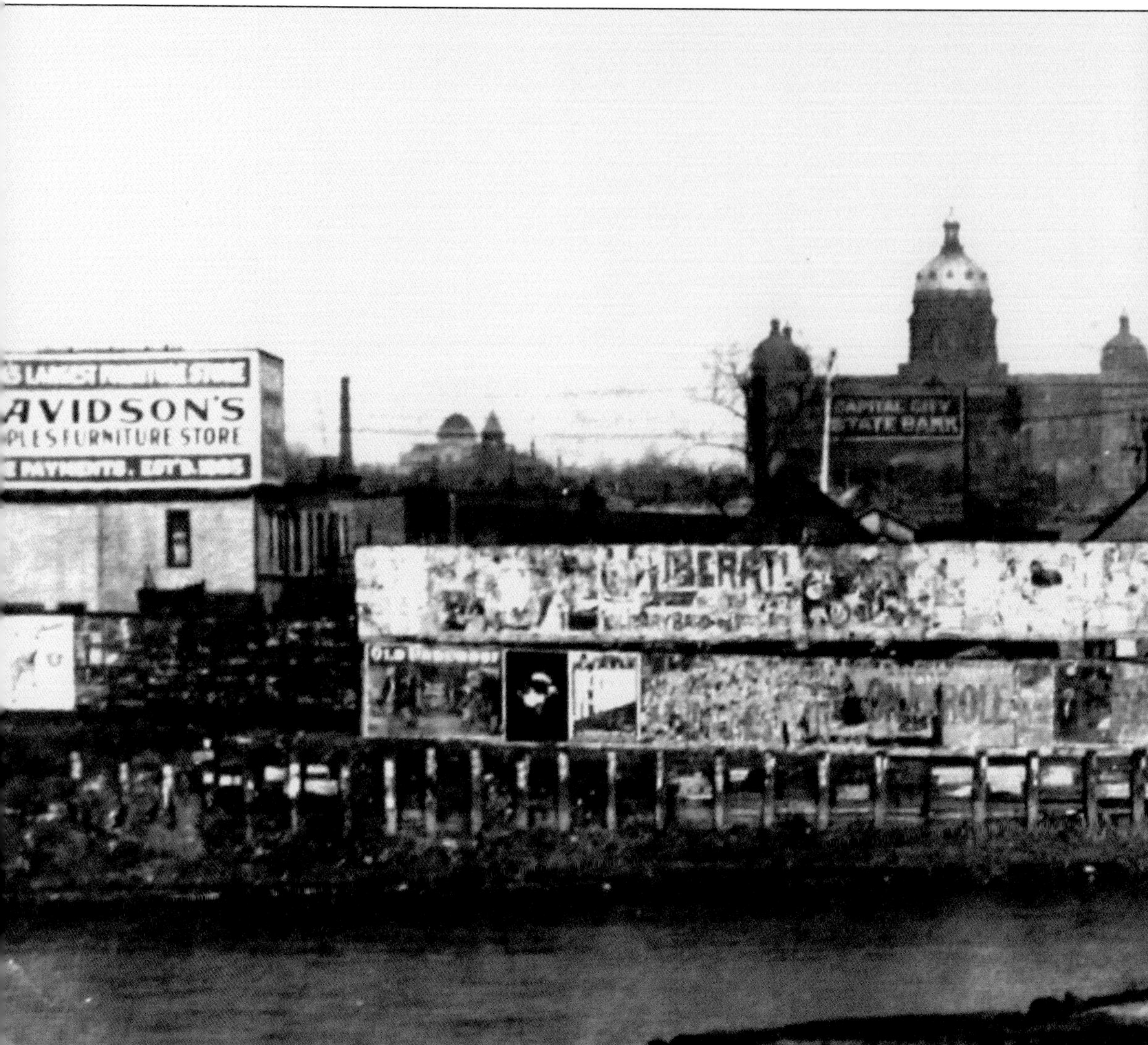

What is interesting about this photograph from 1909 is not only the run-down appearance of the east river bank, but also the island rising above the water. The photograph was taken just prior to the city's initiative to clean up the riverfront and rid the water of its islands, giving it a neater appearance. Residents of Des Moines utilized the river for swimming, with bathhouses and beaches north of the downtown. Through downtown, however, the river was prime property

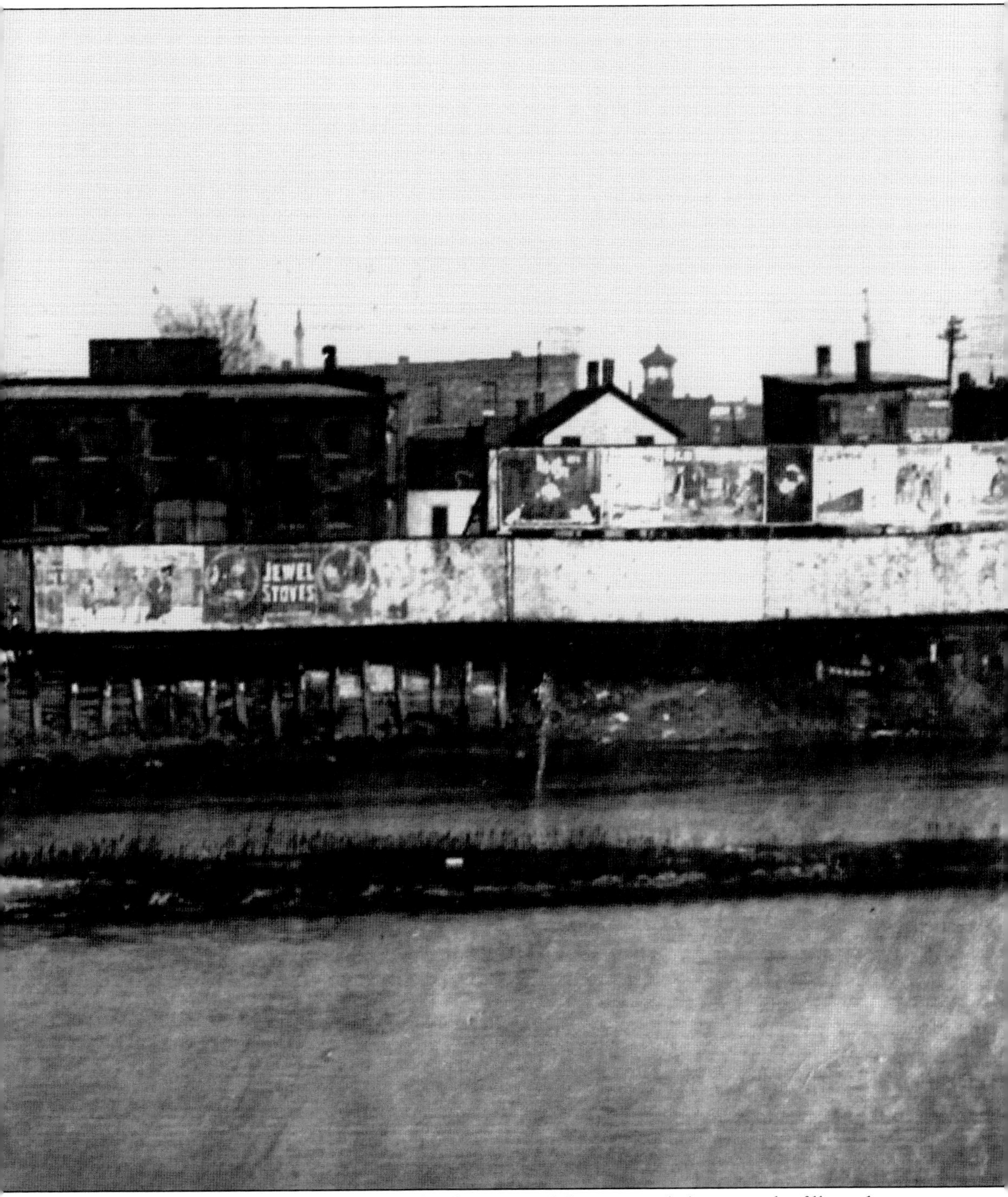

for advertising, and business owners took advantage of their east side locations by filling the east bank with their products, even though they let them deteriorate. The river through downtown never fully developed as a source of recreation; dams installed by the U.S. Army Corps of Engineers made boating impossible. (DMPL.)

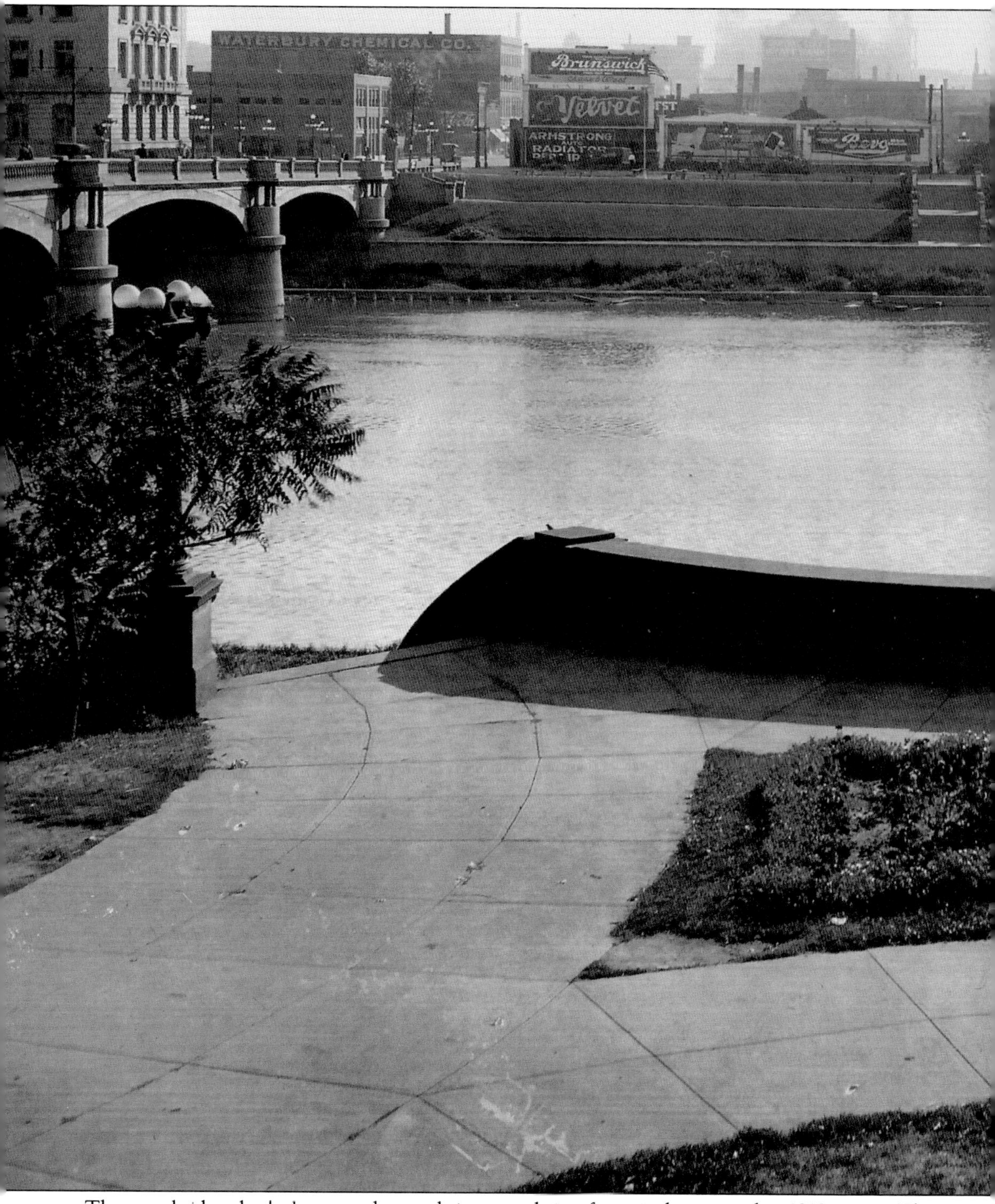

The new bridges look sharp, and a much improved riverfront is shown in this 1919 image. The banks included landscaped terraces and a nice flower bed. The billboards also have been cleaned up by this time, although they are not altogether gone. Benches and promenades lent themselves to use of the river as a backdrop to entertainment and recreation. Each of the four bridges across

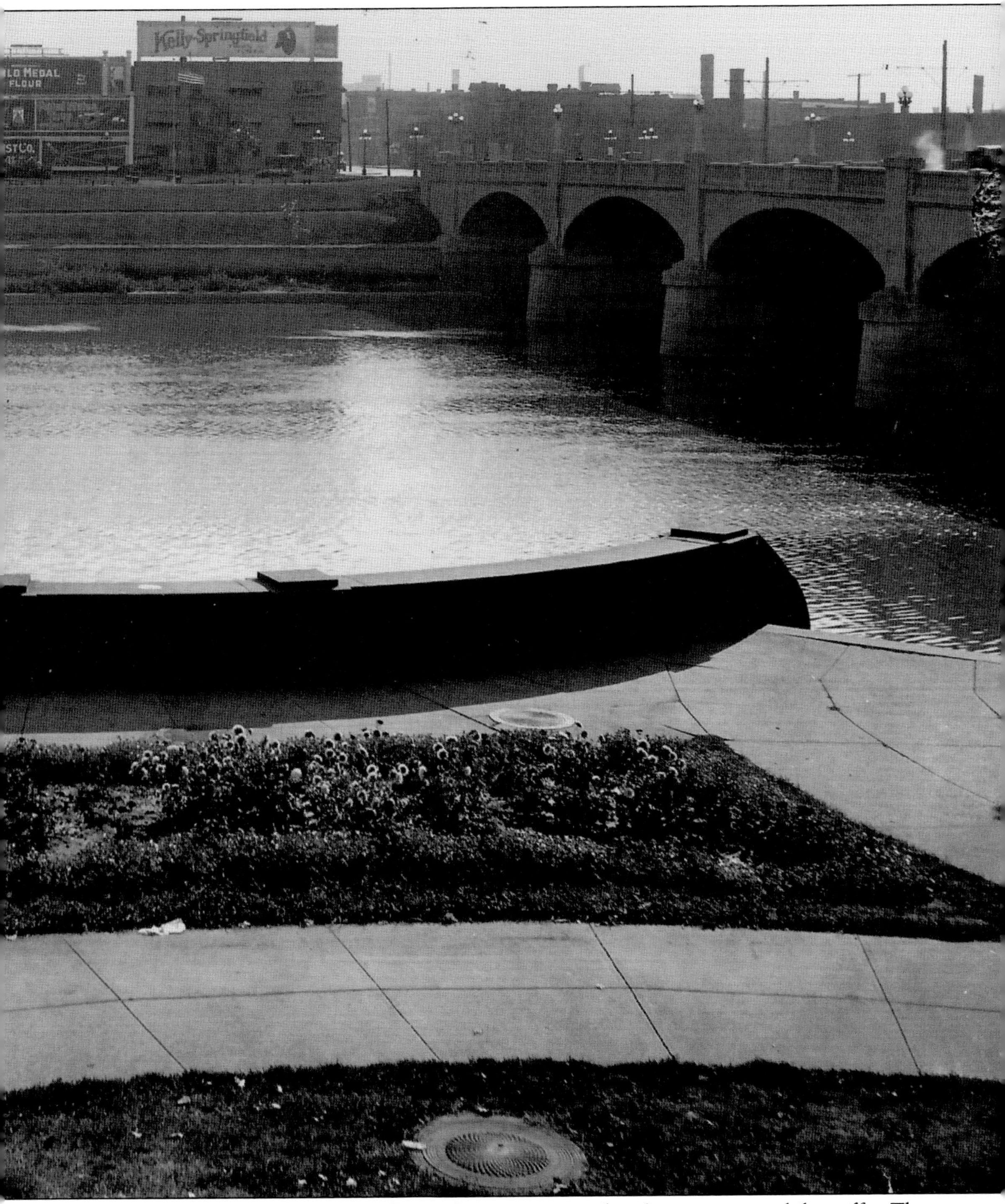

the river were redone and improved in order to accommodate heavier automobile traffic. The stairs on the terraces leading down into the water were likely a safety measure for quick access to someone in trouble. (DMPL.)

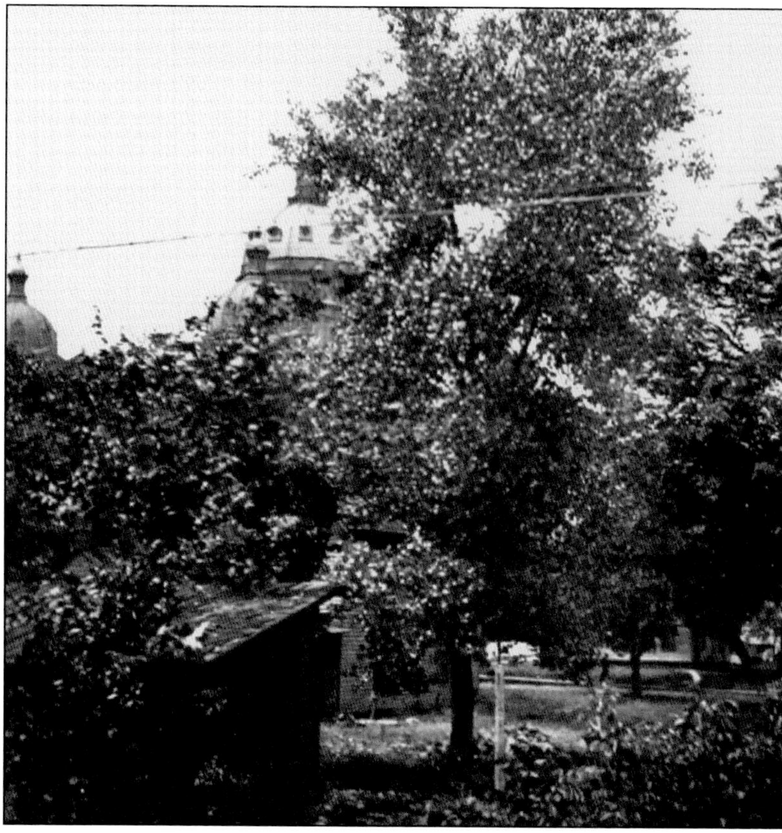

The golden domes of the state capitol can barely be seen beyond the overgrown trees in the yards of nearby neighbors. This image shows just how closely the capitol was to the residents who lived nearby. It is an obvious contrast between the splendor of the capitol building and the modest homes around it. (SHSI.)

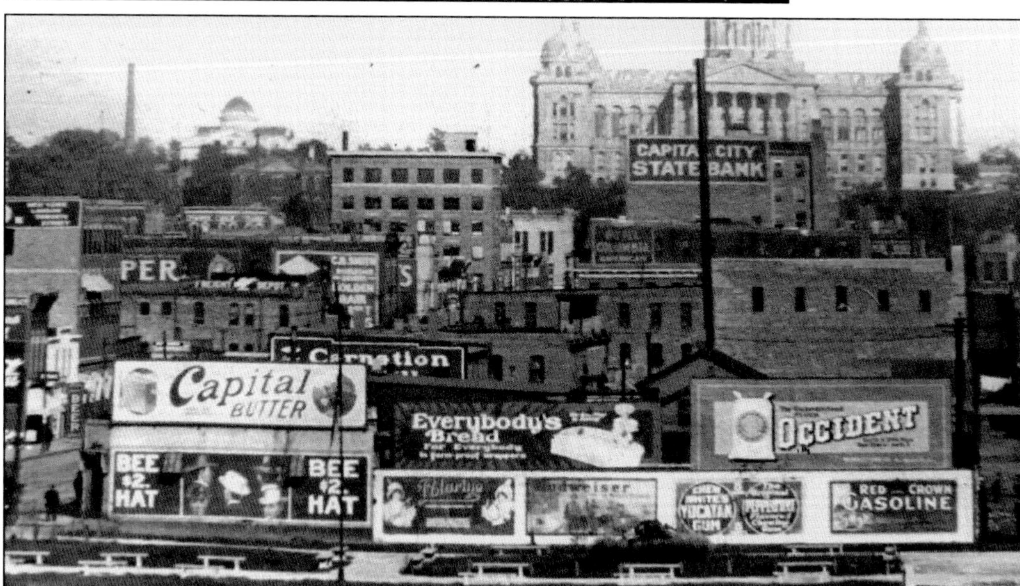

Billboard advertisements dot the east side of the river, nearly blocking the view to the state capitol in the background. Although this was after the riverfront beautification efforts of 1909, as noted by the benches and walkway in the foreground, the city had yet to crack down on the large amount of advertising blaring from the east. (SHSI.)

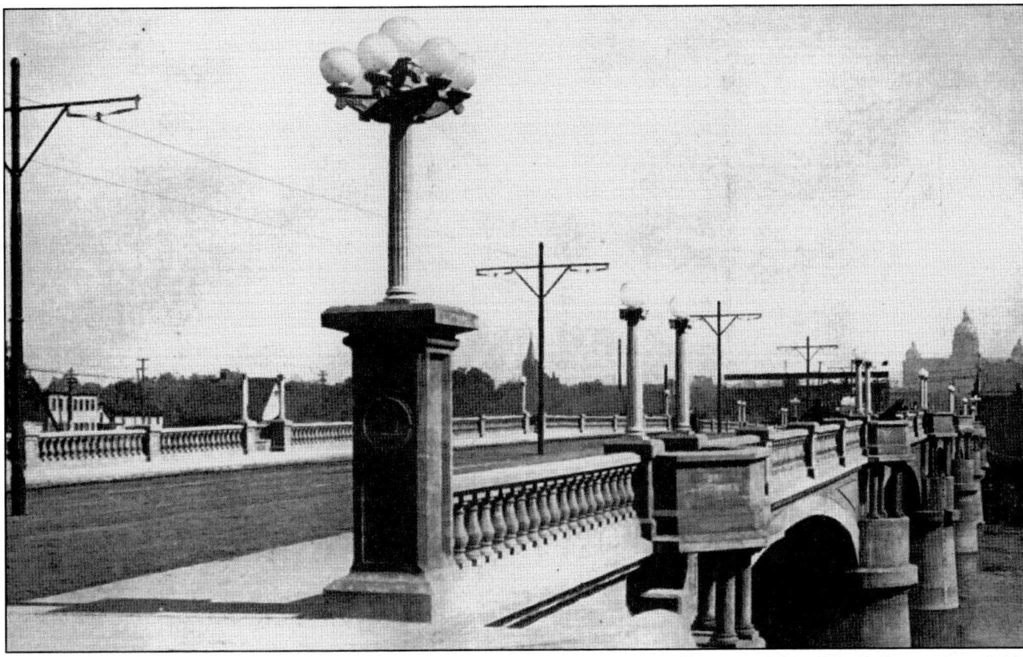

The new Locust Street bridge was completed and open to traffic in 1909. Work began in 1907 by the Marsh Bridge Company. Oddly, the old Locust Street bridge was never fully disassembled and hauled away and laid in the weeds along the riverbank for nearly two years. Finally, in 1911, city councilman John MacVicar announced the city would sell the remains of the old bridge to whoever wanted it. (SHSI.)

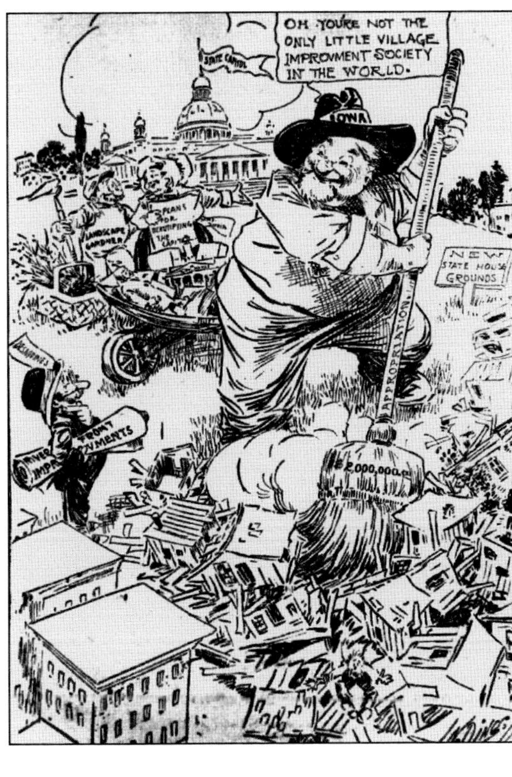

Des Moines Register and Leader editorial cartoonist Jay "Ding" Darling lampoons the capitol extension legislation with this artwork from April 1913. It reads, "Oh You're not the only little village improvement society in the world." Following the lead from the city, the State of Iowa spent $2 million to purchase 20 blocks surrounding the state capitol for targeted improvements. (SHSI.)

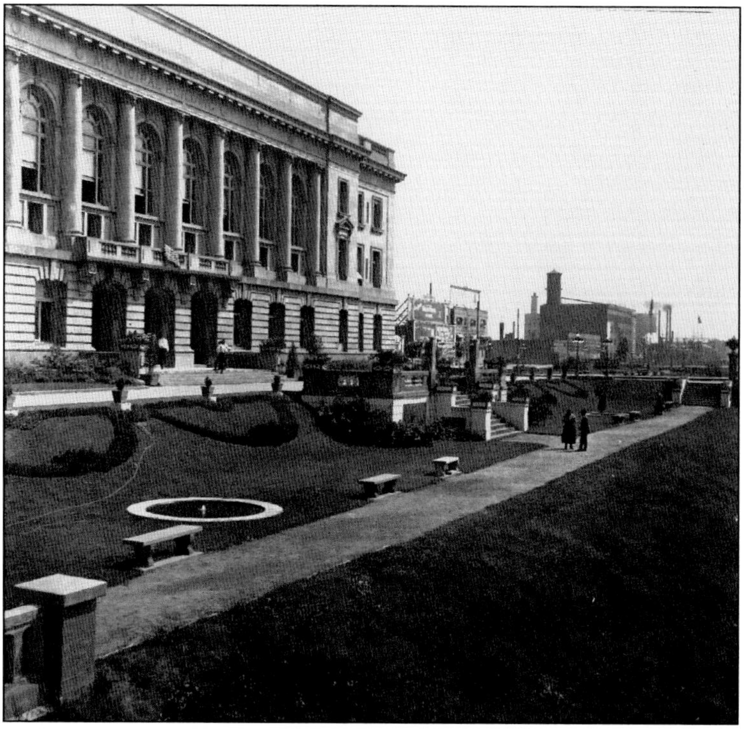

Just after city hall was built and open in 1911, the grounds around it became the focus of beautification efforts. Many improvements to the riverfront occurred at this time, during what was called the City Beautiful Movement (1900–1937). Both sides of the river were improved with the addition of parks, which complemented the new buildings. (DMPL.)

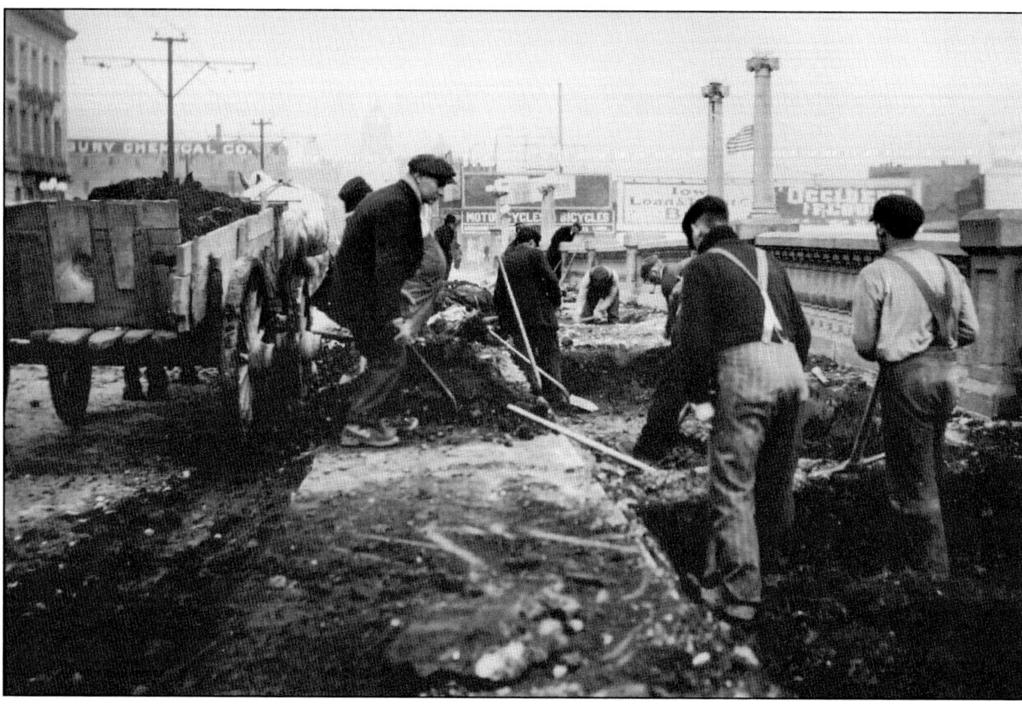

City crews excavate along the Locust Street bridge for the installation of water mains. The horse-drawn wagon on the left hauled the dirt away. Billboards for Iowa Loan and Trust Company Bank, Occident Flour, and motorcycles and bicycles can be seen beyond, as can the Waterbury Chemical Company building along East Locust Street. (SHSI.)

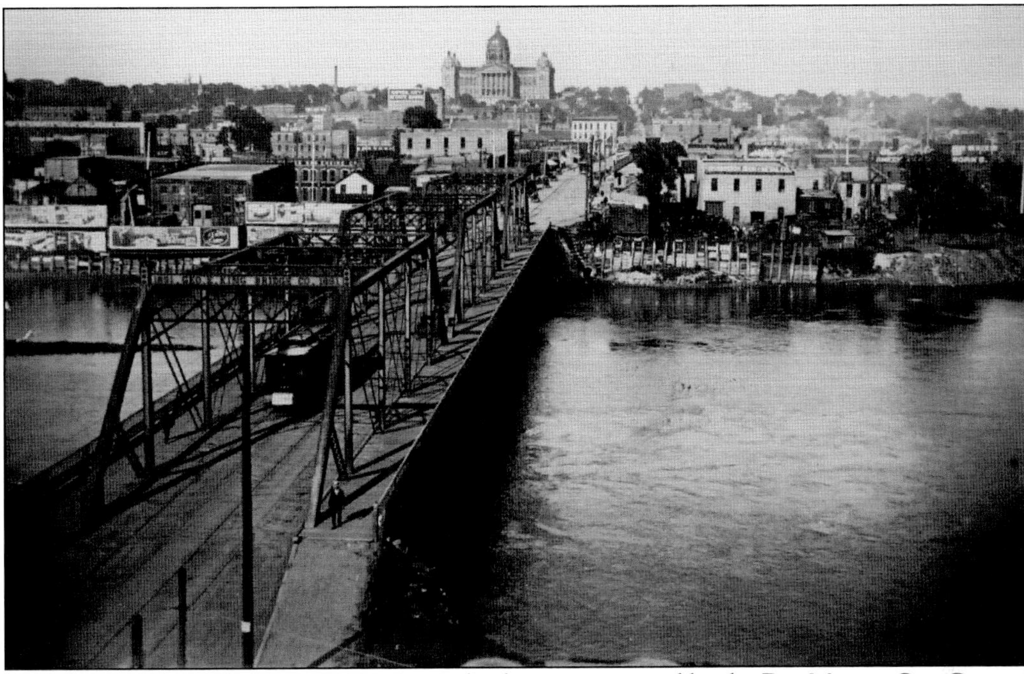

The decision to build a new Walnut Street bridge was approved by the Des Moines City Council in 1910, amid controversy. Locust Street had already been built up, and its bridge was replaced and made flood worthy, but it was not yet paid for. This photograph shows the old Walnut Street bridge and the dilapidated east bank, which was cleaned up with the new bridge. (SHSI.)

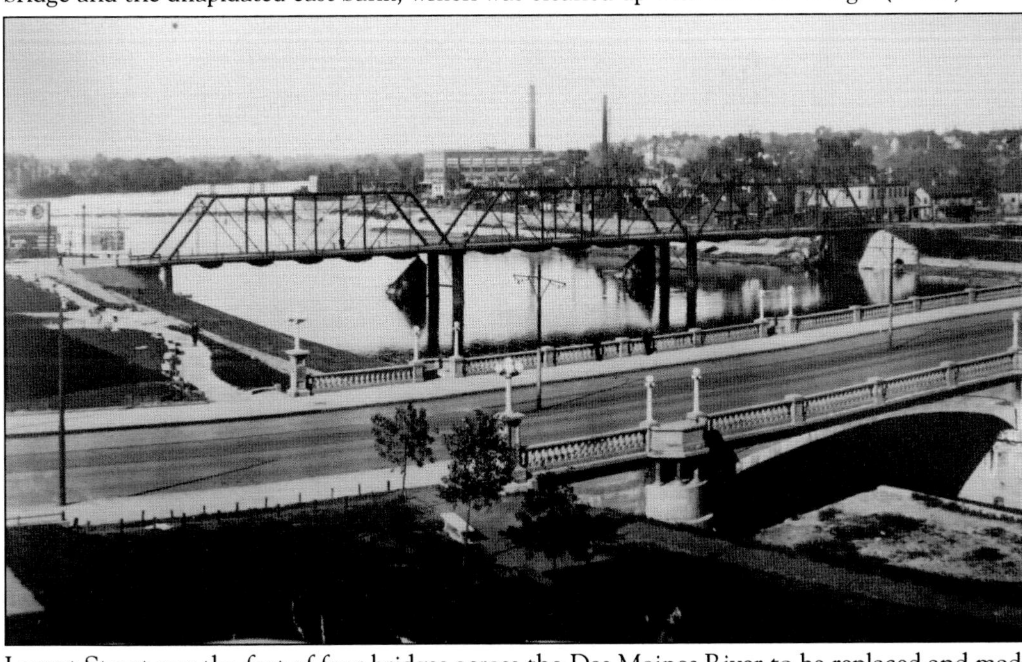

Locust Street was the first of four bridges across the Des Moines River to be replaced and made suitable for automobile traffic, most likely because it was the main thoroughfare straight to the state capitol. In this photograph from 1912, the Grand Avenue bridge to its north has yet to be replaced. (SHSI.)

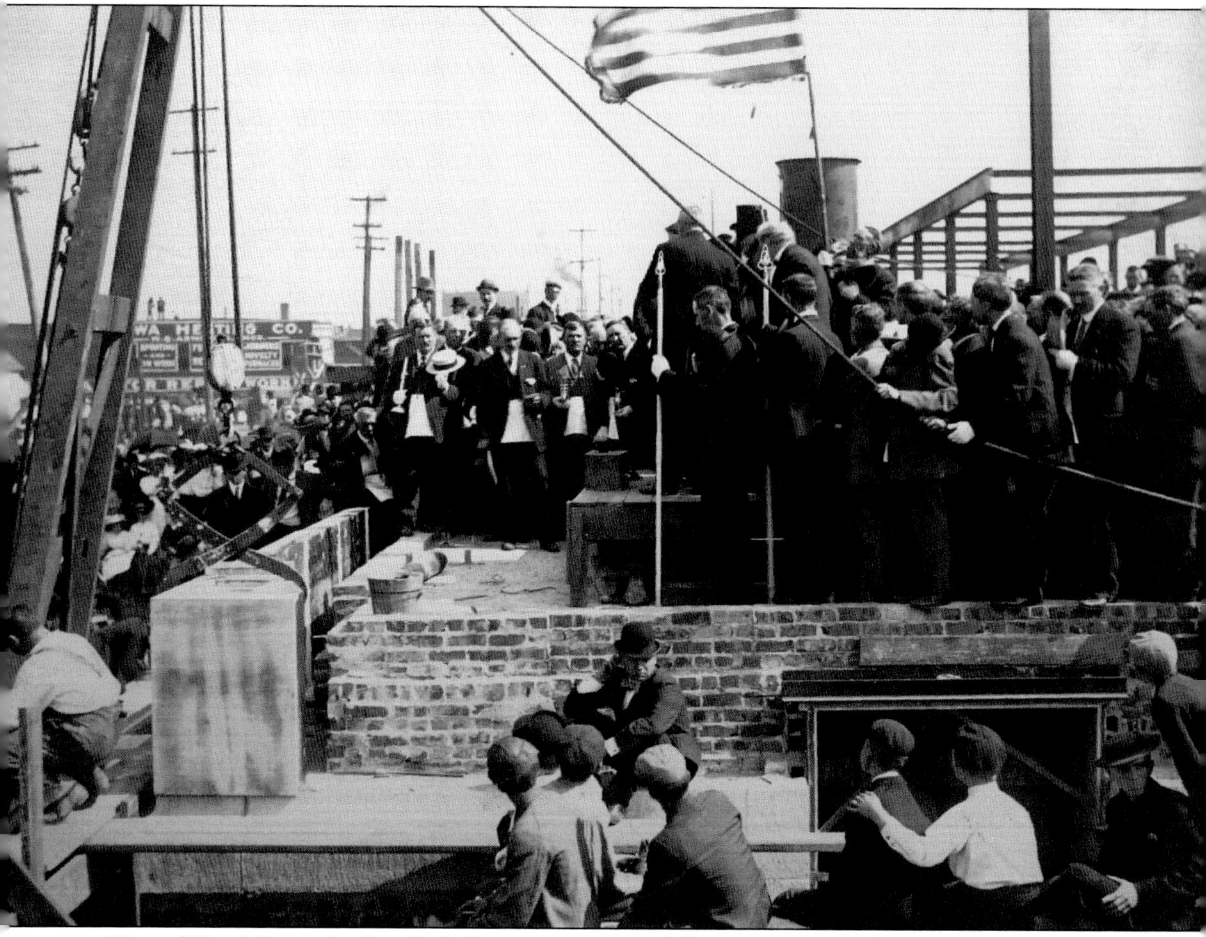

City of Des Moines leaders laid the cornerstone of the new municipal building with a grand celebration on June 14, 1910. It marked not only a new era of municipal government for which Des Moines could be proud but also the construction of a grand building that was reflective of its use. The *Des Moines Daily News* reported, "Des Moines is a growing and a prosperous city. It is time that a new city hall should be erected. But it is especially appropriate that we should have this celebration under the auspices of a city government which everywhere is attracting attention as being the best system which has yet been devised for economical and effective city management." (SHSI.)

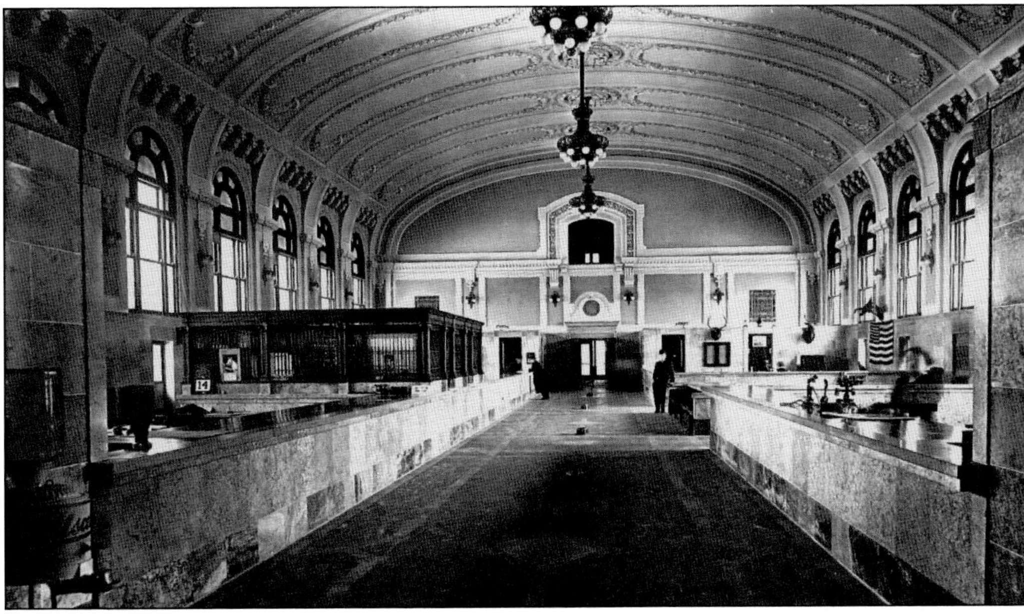

The June 12, 1910, *Des Moines Daily News* reported, "This new city hall of Des Moines is going to be a marvel. The interior will look a good deal like, and will be conducted with much the same system and courtesy to visitors, as a large department store." City hall was open for business in 1911. (SHSI.)

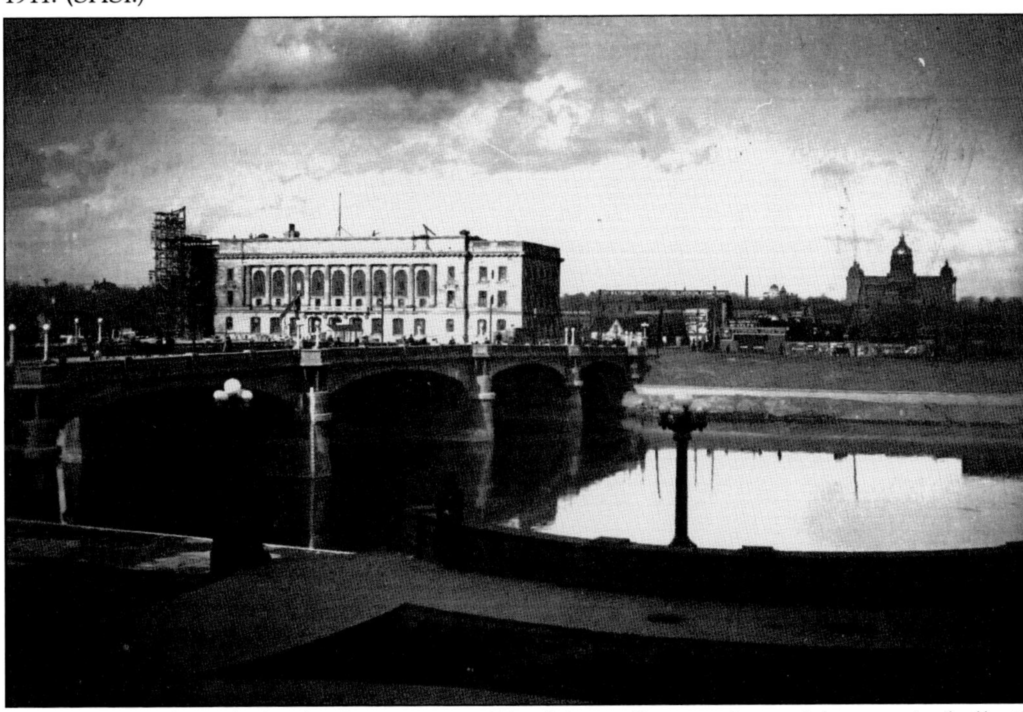

A woman sits along the bank of a rejuvenated Des Moines River in front of the new city hall still under construction in this photograph from 1911. The tidy riverbanks reflect what was dubbed the beautification movement, an effort that led to a citywide boulevard system, modern parks program, and aesthetic improvements around the state capitol. (SHSI.)

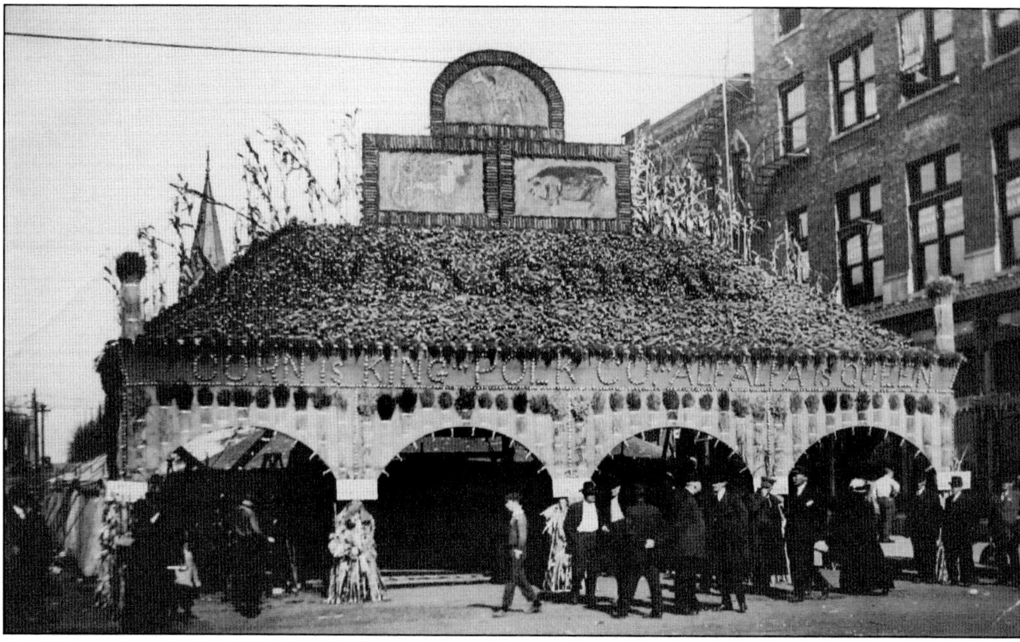

On November 4–7, 1915, East Village hosted the Polk County Corn Show. A massive tent was set up on East Fifth Street north of East Locust Street with an entrance pavilion proclaiming, "Corn is King—Alfalfa is Queen." The October 29, 1915, *Des Moines Capital* reported, "One of the striking features of the East Des Moines Corn Show . . . will be the picturesque front which encloses East Fifth street on Locust." (SHSI.)

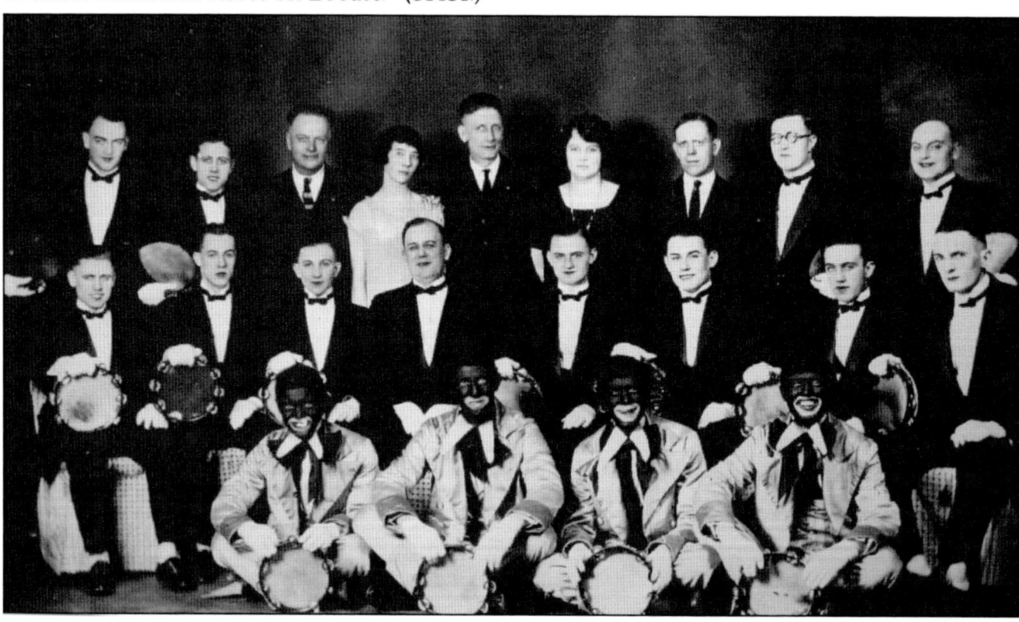

The notes on this photograph call this group the East Des Moines Minstrel Players. Minstrel shows were very popular beginning after the Civil War through the 1960s. They lampooned blacks with comic skits, variety acts, and dancing and music, as performed by white people in blackface. Most likely, this troupe appeared at the 1917 corn show and was heralded to rival the show itself in attracting crowds. (SHSI.)

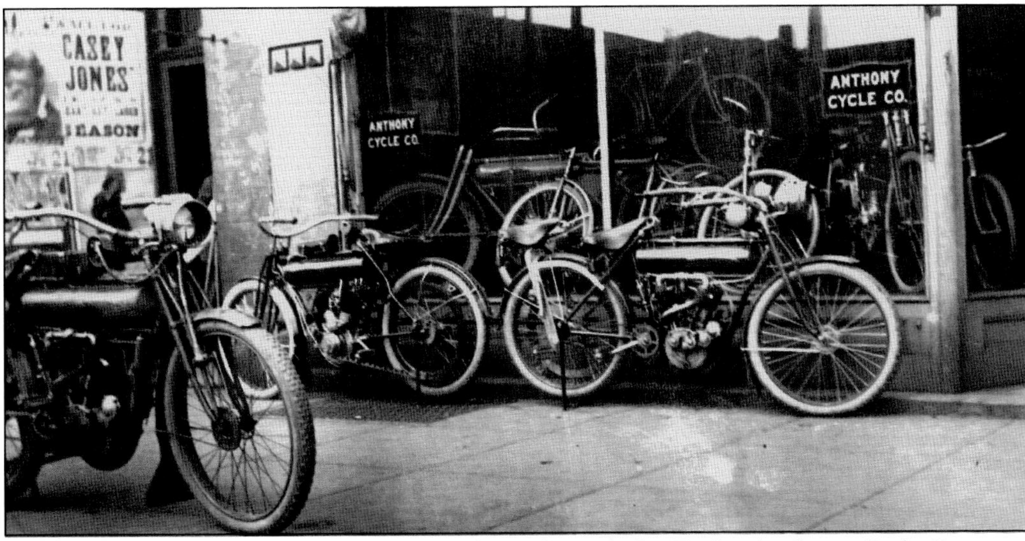

Warren Earle Tapley and Edwards P. Anthony formed the Tapley-Anthony Cycle Company located at 630 East Grand Avenue. Both were bicycle repairmen and competitive racers. In 1904, Tapley moved on, and Anthony renamed the business the Anthony Cycle Company. Although the company grew to include motorcycles and opened several locations around Des Moines, it was out of business by 1917. This photograph was taken about 1912. (DMPL.)

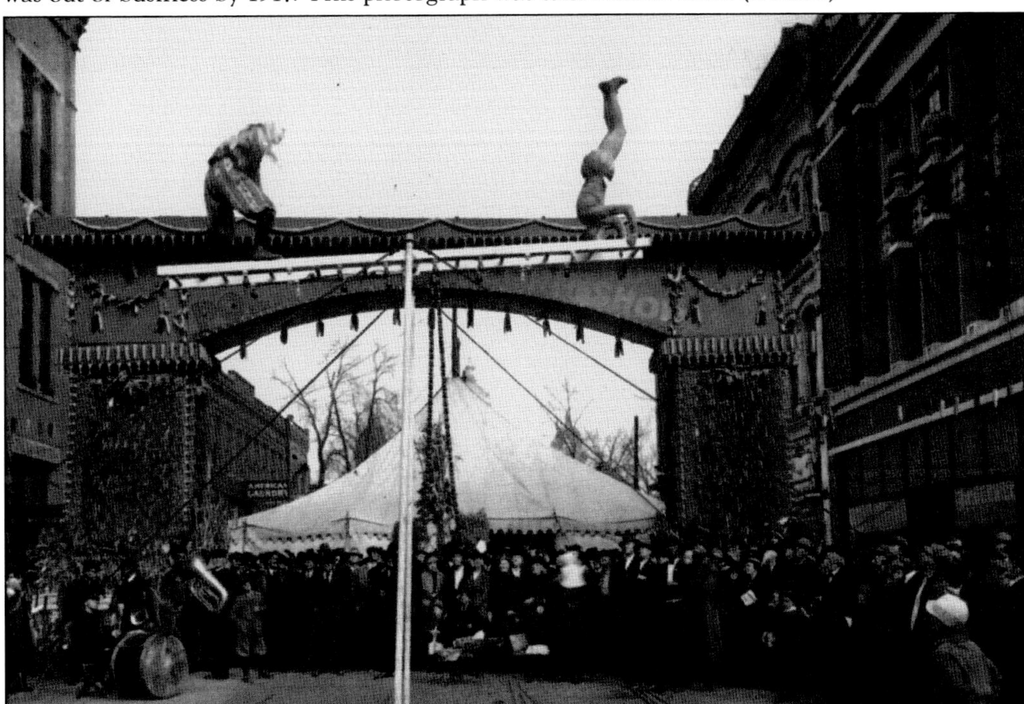

The annual Polk County Corn Show returned to the east side in November 1916. Clowns perform acrobatics on East Sixth Street during the event. The *Des Moines News* said, "In addition to a number of lectures from Ames and a free moving picture show, the program committee will spend $600 for musical, acrobatic and trained animal acts to entertain visitors at the corn show." (ISB.)

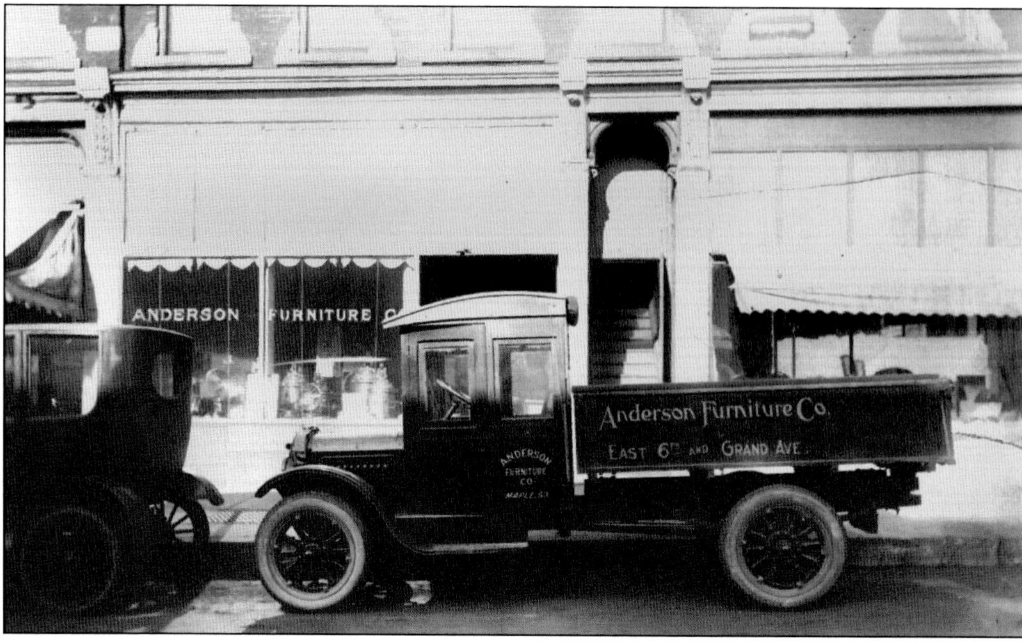

This 1917 image of the Anderson Furniture Company delivery wagon was taken outside the store at 520–522 East Grand Avenue a few years before the company expanded to occupy the entire building, or four storefronts, in 1921. Owner Adolph F. Anderson operated the family furniture store in this location until 1963. A Swedish immigrant, Anderson was active in the Scandinavian community and helped promote other immigrant-owned businesses in the neighborhood. (JB.)

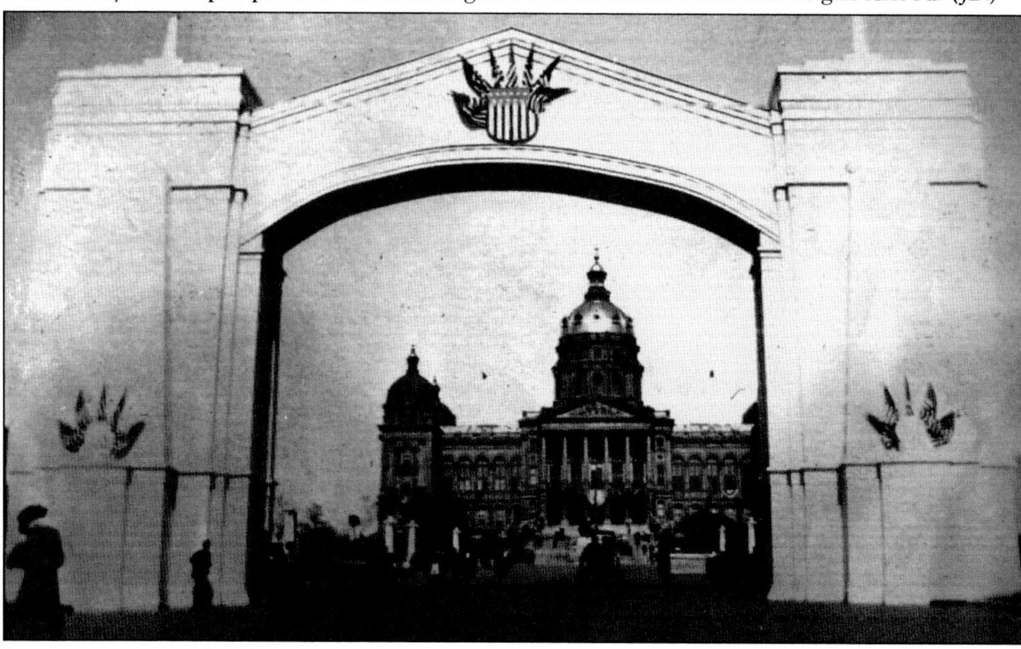

In 1918, a memorial arch was erected at the western base of the state capitol grounds to welcome the men returning home following World War I. It was not a permanent structure and was torn down shortly after the 168th Infantry of the 42nd Rainbow Division marched to the capitol grounds on May 15, 1919. (DMPL.)

Three

Big Business

In the middle of the 20th century, the east side included among its most prosperous businesses those that worked in lumber, machinery, or car sales. Gilcrest Lumber (East Second and East Walnut Streets), Queal Lumber (216–224 East Grand Avenue), and Jewett Lumber (615–617 East Walnut Street) were all born on the east side and maintained flourishing mills and shipping businesses. Globe Machinery patented a new hoist for car garages that became so successful it renamed itself Globe Hoist Company. By 1945, the company had its own complex of buildings located in the vicinity of East First Street and East Court Avenue. Cars became more popular as they became more affordable, and the east side had two large car sales businesses, O'Dea Chevrolet and Friedmans' Plymouth-Chrysler-Imperial. Midas, Firestone, and other car repair shops established businesses along East Locust Street, while gasoline stations sprang up on nearly every corner. Post–World War II Des Moines was experiencing a flourishing economy much like the rest of the nation. On the east side, that translated into businesses and operations that were more industrial, as shopping centers started to come in to the west.

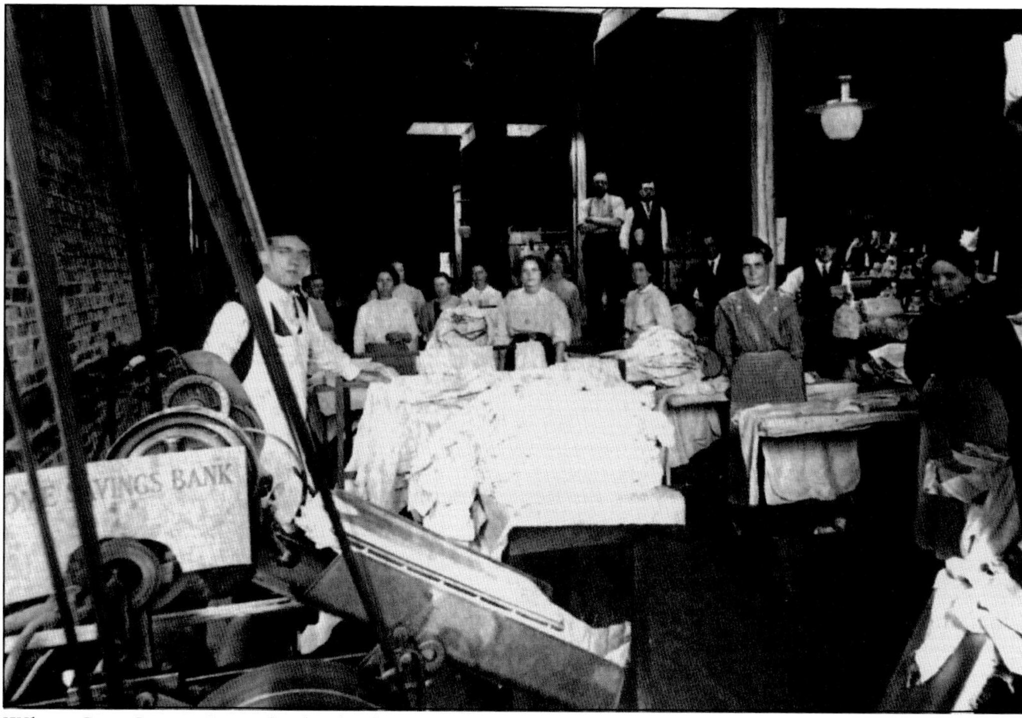

White Star Steam Laundry had a large operation located at 212–218 East Locust Street. It was one of two in the neighborhood. American Laundry, located at 616 East Locust Street, was the other. Like most of the laundries at the time, White Star built its business upon the increasing popularity of washable fabrics. This 1918 photograph shows the interior of the factory and its employees. (DMPL.)

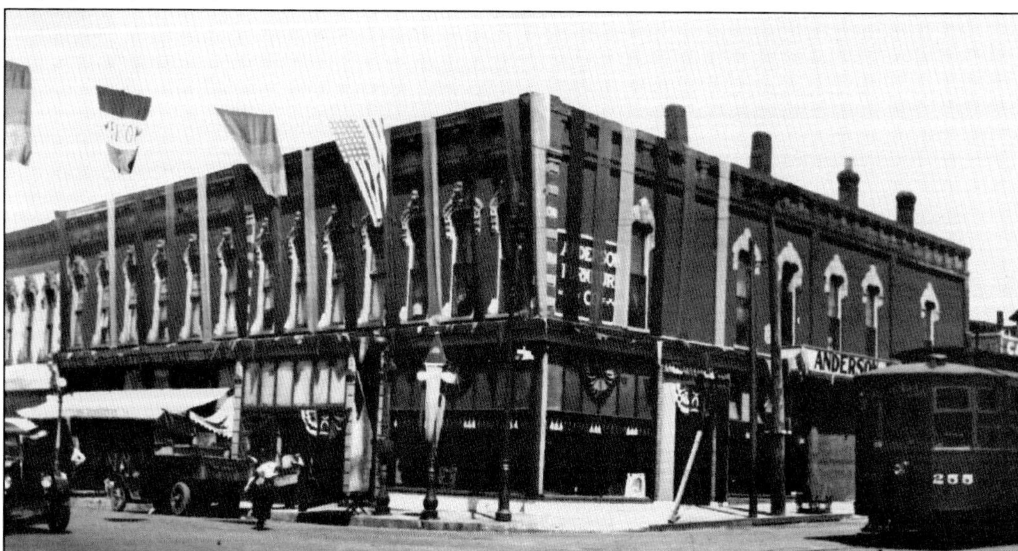

The Anderson Furniture Company sports decorations to welcome the Shriners Convention on June 4, 1921. Note the globe streetlights and the trolley at right, with a sign on the front that reads, "East 6 and 9." A woman is walking across the street with an armful of parcels, while a young boy appears to be loading a wicker bassinet into the delivery wagon. (JB.)

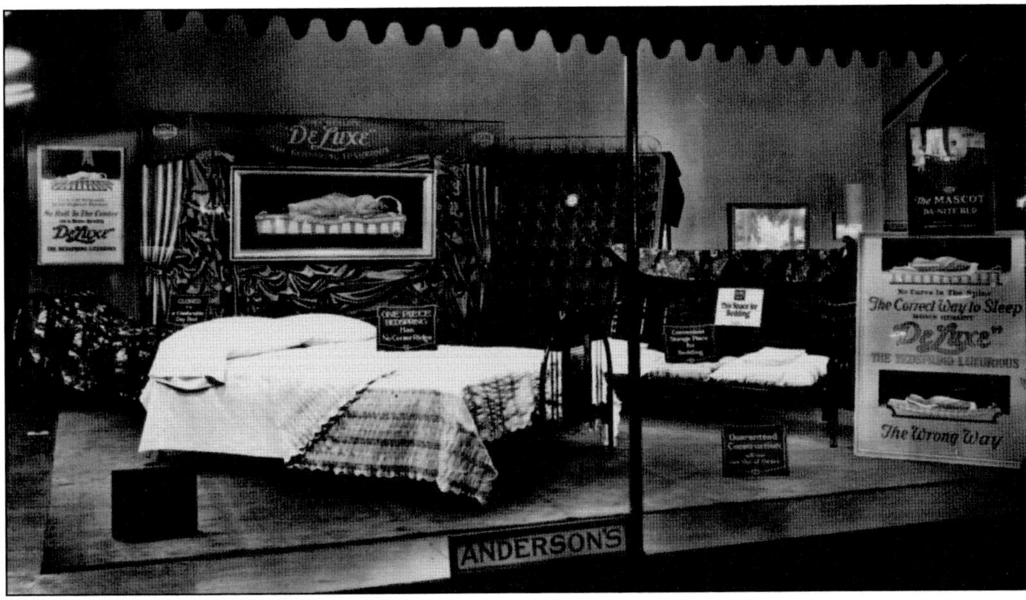

Here is a rare postcard advertising Anderson Furniture Company and "Home Quality 'DeLuxe'—The Bedspring Luxurious." The elaborate window highlights the correct sleeping position, the ever-important "No Roll to the Center" feature, and the correct way to sleep for better bone quality. Although Anderson was not known specifically for its beds, the postcard indicates the store carried the most modern of beds and mattresses. (JB.)

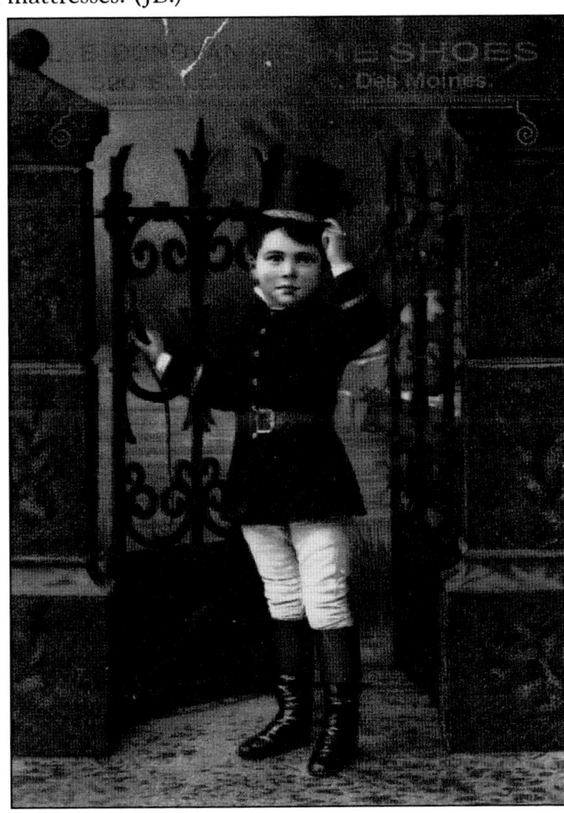

This beautiful postcard advertises L. E. Donovan Fine Shoes, which was located at 520 East Locust Street. The store opened it doors in 1877 and often had large advertisements in the newspaper. There were actually two locations, with the other being right next door at 518 East Locust Street. The stores were operated by brothers. (DMPL.)

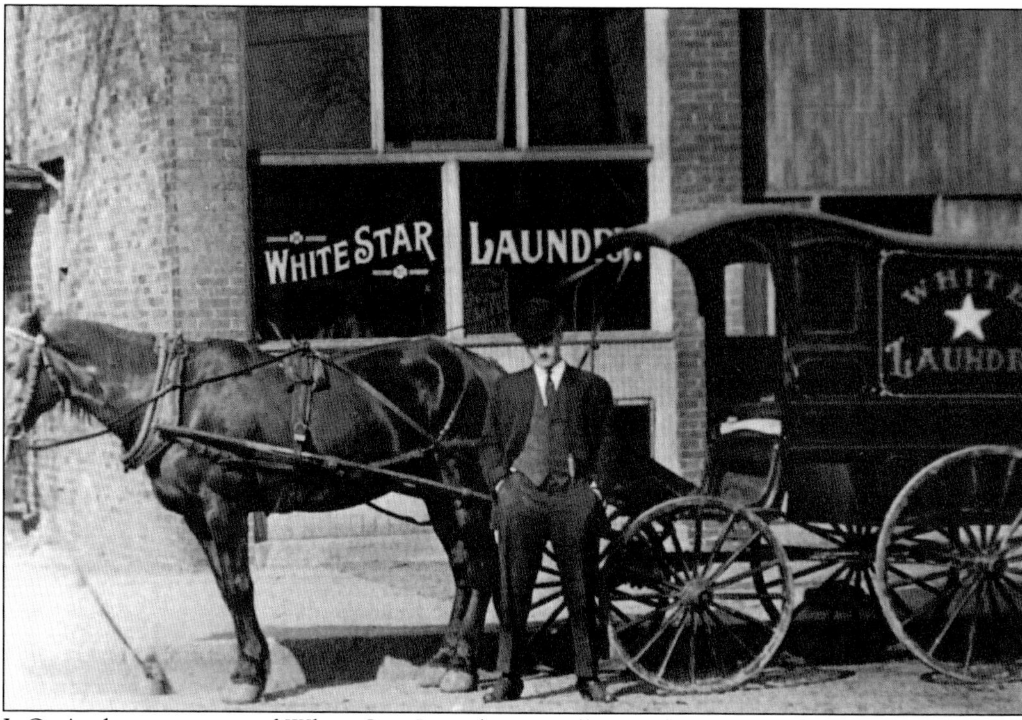

J. O. Anderson, owner of White Star Laundry, proudly stands outside his business at 212 East Grand Avenue about 1920. Advertisements for the business at the time stated, "The White Star Laundry will please you because you will get good work plus the White Star management's personal attention. Send us your shirt and collar bundle this week and see how well it will please." (DMPL.)

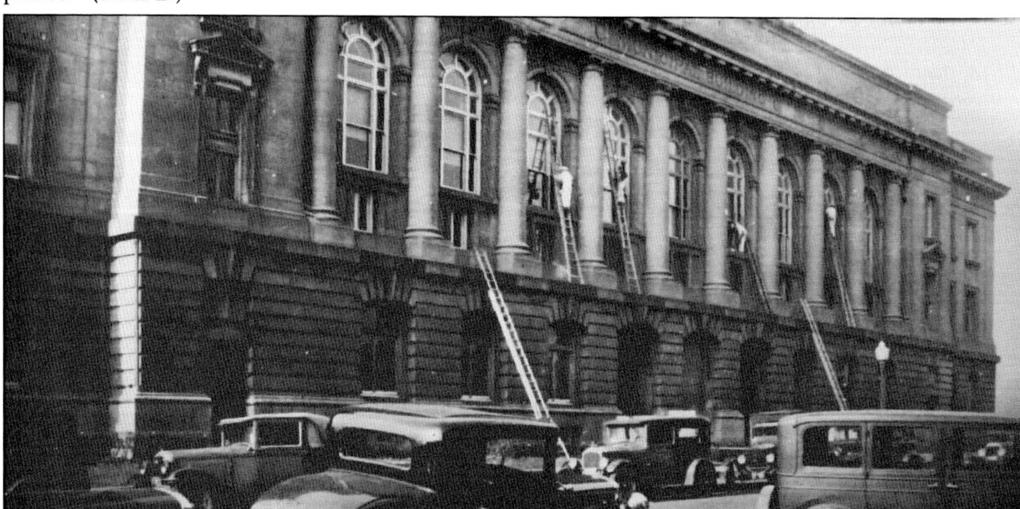

Federal Emergency Relief Administration (FERA) workers paint city hall on December 6, 1933. FERA (1933–1935) preceded the Works Progress Administration (WPA), which was not created until 1935 under Pres. Franklin D. Roosevelt. WPA administered $5 billion for public works, with the goal to employ as many people as possible on projects that would provide long-term benefit to local communities. (SHSI.)

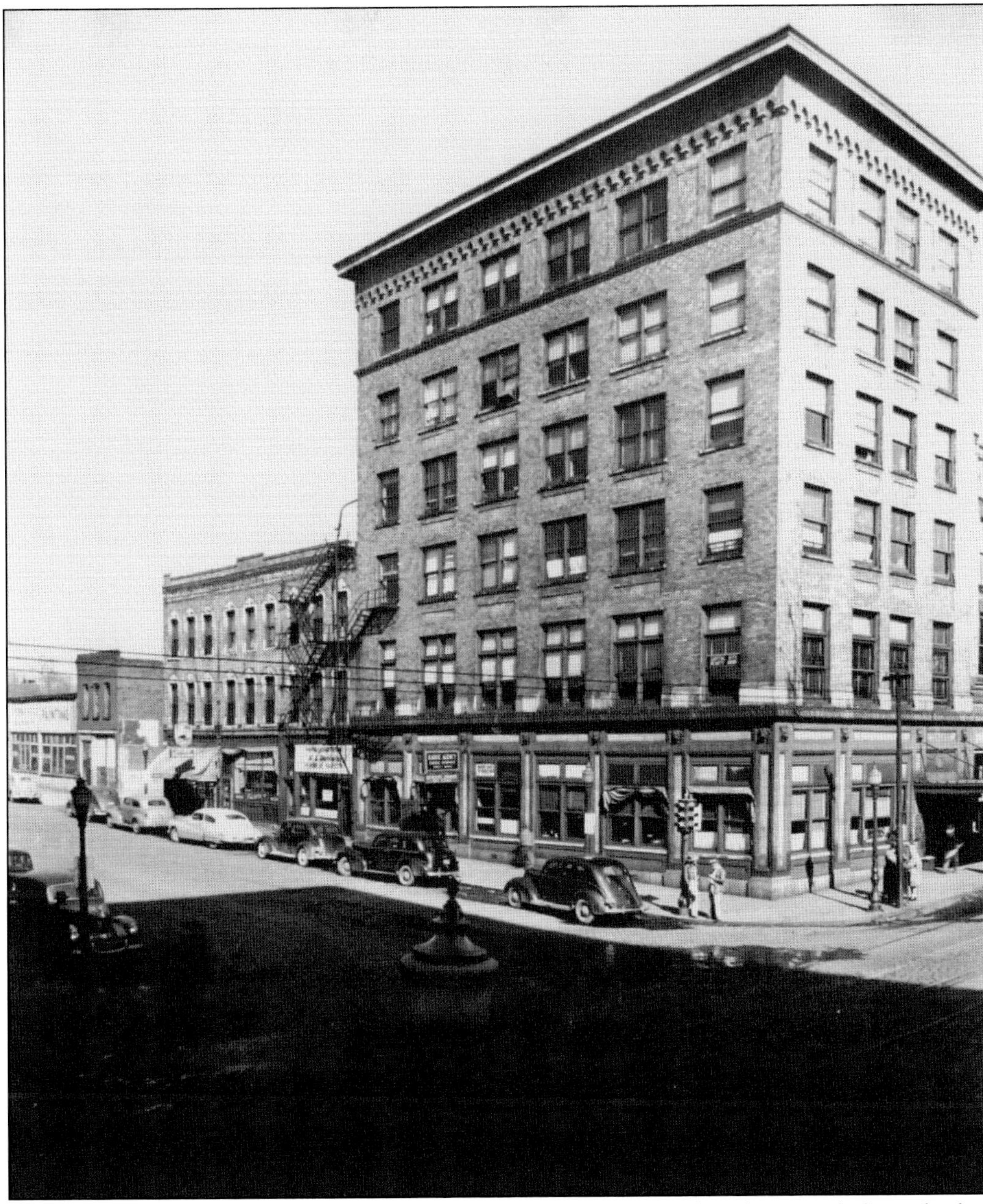

The streets bustle with people around the Teachout building in this photograph from the late 1930s. The fire escape is prevalent on its west side, probably because Teachout is surrounded on the back two sides by other buildings. None of the other buildings behind the Teachout remain, although the nearest one was rebuilt. Note the decorative streetlamps and the cobblestone streets with streetcar tracks still intact. Streetcar service did not end in Des Moines for good until 1951, as curb liners became a more attractive option for getting around the metro area. Insurance agents, professional offices, and the Capital City Beauty Shop were among the businesses occupying the Teachout building at this time. The 1958 City Directory shows a bowling alley on the third floor of the building as well. The businesses closer to East Grand Avenue were more hardware and service oriented, later becoming automobile garages. (SHSI.)

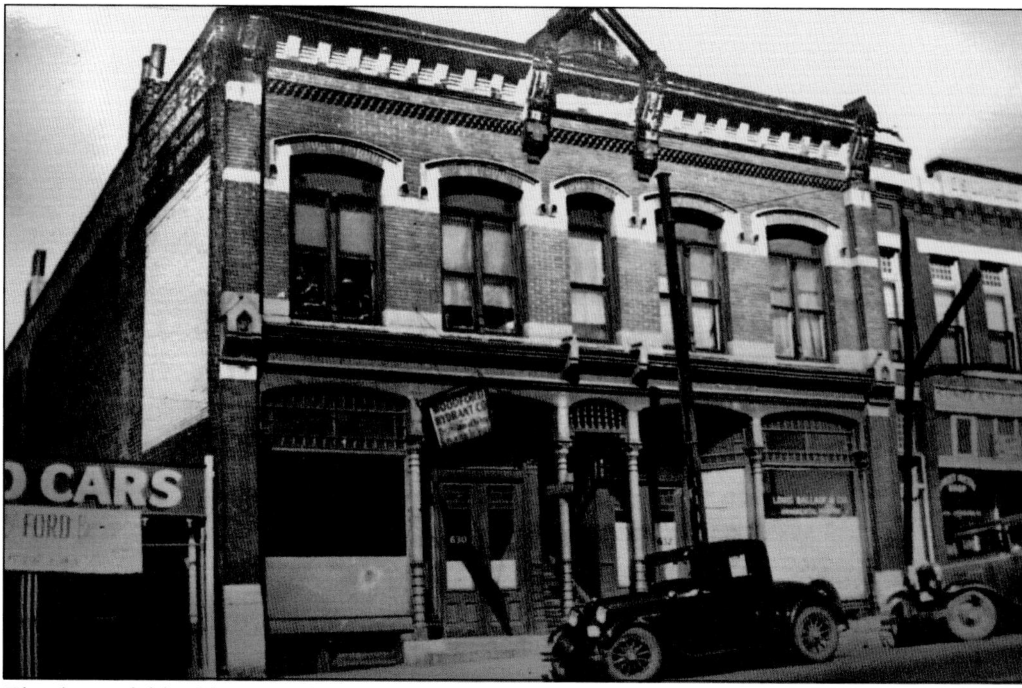

This beautiful building stood at 630–632 East Grand Avenue when this photograph was taken in 1936. Later it was stripped of all its architectural decorations and then torn down in the late 1960s. Oddly enough, the front left cornerstone still remains, preserved out in front of the Iowa Genealogical Society Library at 628 East Grand Avenue. (SHSI.)

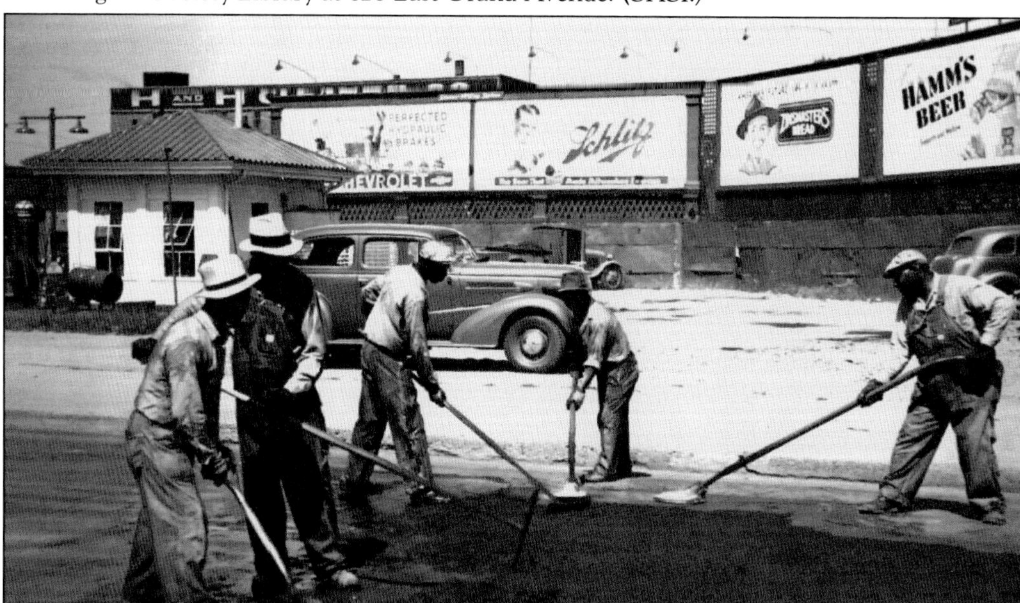

City workers in July 1937 found laying new asphalt at East First Street and East Locust Street a "hot job" during what the newspapers said was a heat wave. Note the small gasoline station at left with its tall pumps out front. The billboards facing the riverfront advertised Chevrolet, Schlitz, Zinsmasters Bread, and Hamm's beer. (SHSI.)

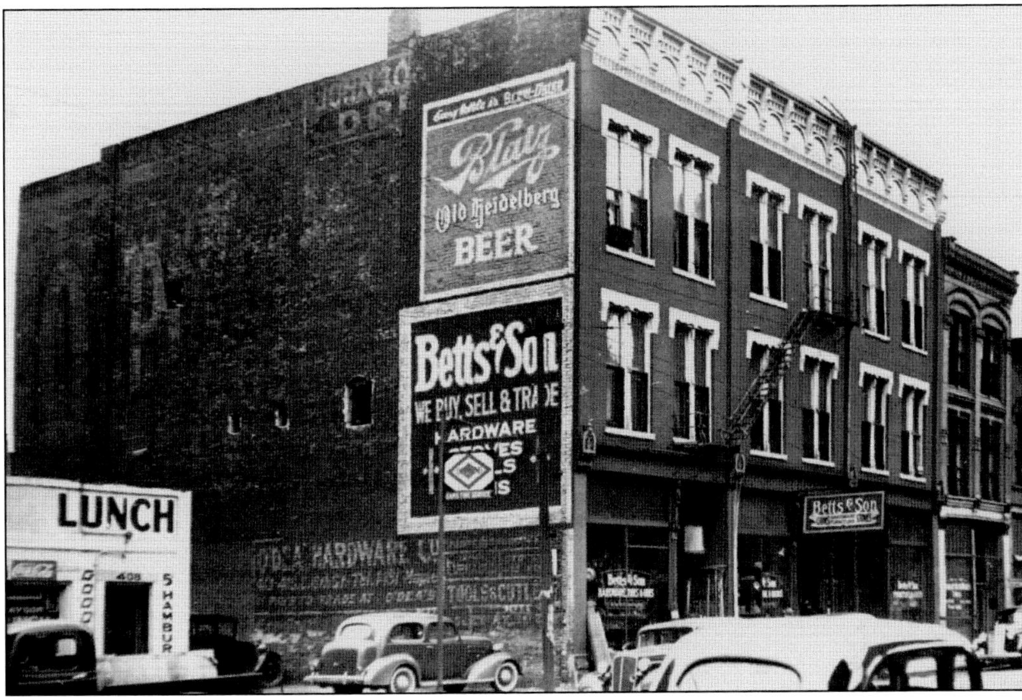

The original Betts and Sons Hardware Store, located at 412 East Locust Street, is seen in this photograph dated May 25, 1937. Interestingly, below the Betts and Sons painted sign on the side of the building appears an advertisement for the O'Dea Hardware Company, a competitor at 413–415 East Sixth Street. The upper two floors of this building were eventually removed, and the family shop moved out of East Village in 2004. Known as the Stubbs Block, this row of buildings was erected in 1884. (SHSI.)

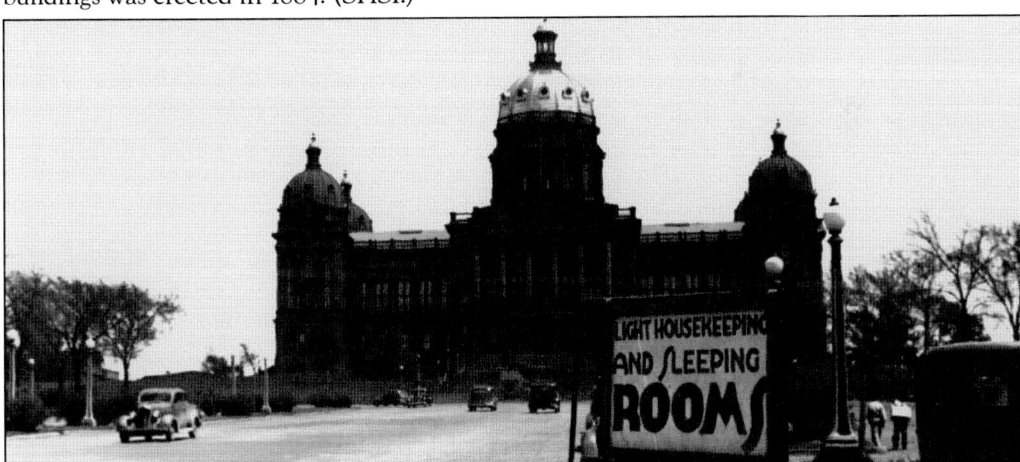

With the legislature in session during the months of January through April, many senators and representatives from around the state require accommodation throughout week and then travel home on weekends. How convenient it must have been to have sleeping rooms (with light housekeeping) within a stone's throw of the golden domes. The picture was taken by John Vachon, who was employed as a photographer with the Farm Security Administration in the 1940s. (LOC FSA/OWI.)

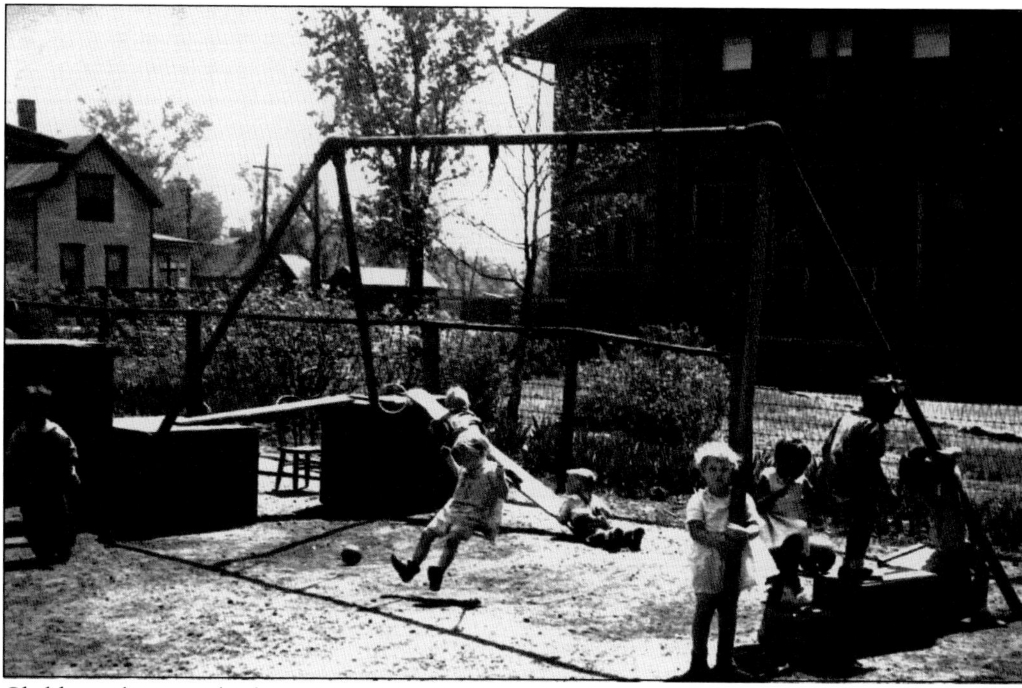

Children play outside the Roadside Settlement House at 620 Scott Avenue in the 1930s. The settlement supervised a public playground for the city and was instrumental in securing the ruling that allowed the public use of school playgrounds in cases where private agencies agreed to provide supervision. (SHSI.)

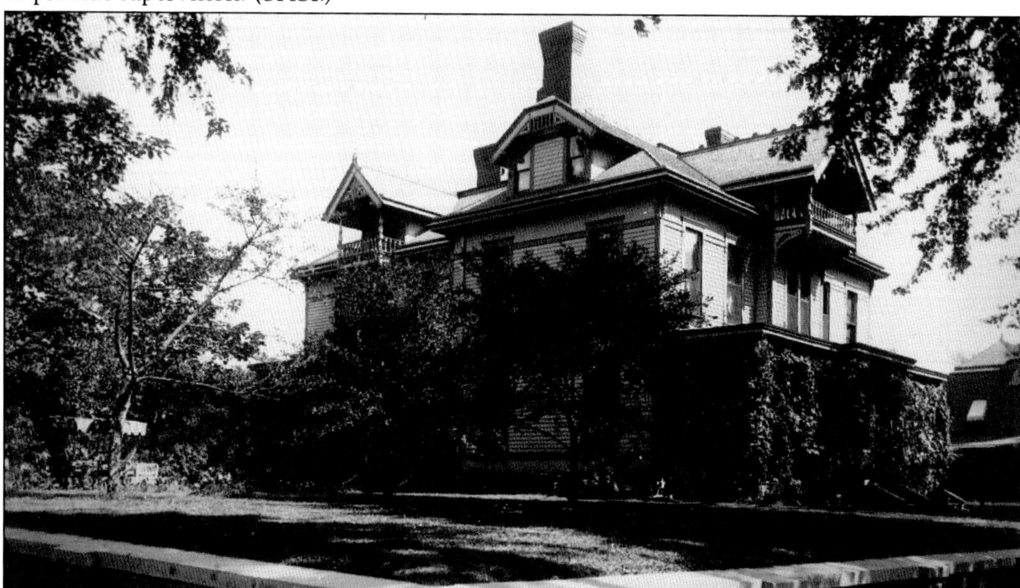

Cherry Place, so named for its cherry trees, was the home of Isaac Brandt, a pioneer east side merchant. Brandt, a friend of abolitionist John Brown, whom he hosted several times, may have housed escaped slaves on the Underground Railroad at his home at East Twelfth Street and East Grand Avenue. It was demolished in 1970 as part of a capitol expansion plan that was never fully realized, and it is now a parking lot. (SHSI.)

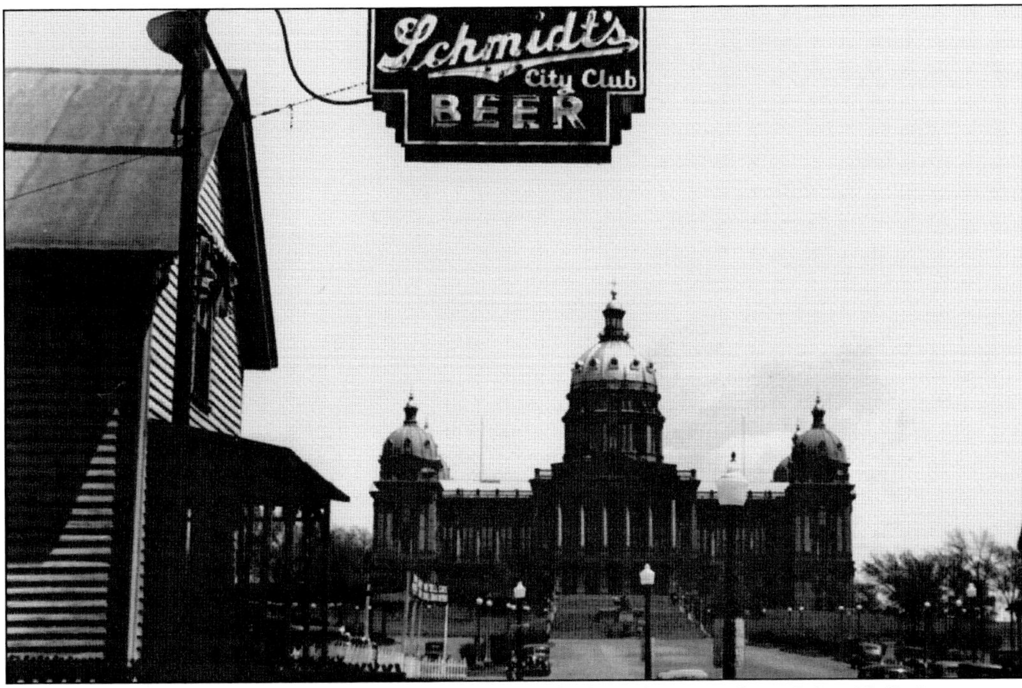

Photographer and Midwesterner John Vachon took this photograph in May 1940. It seems to poke fun at a tavern situated within steps of the state capitol. Much of Vachon's work in Des Moines during this time centers on the state capitol, often using it as a backdrop against an ordinary American pastime. (LOC FSA/OWI.)

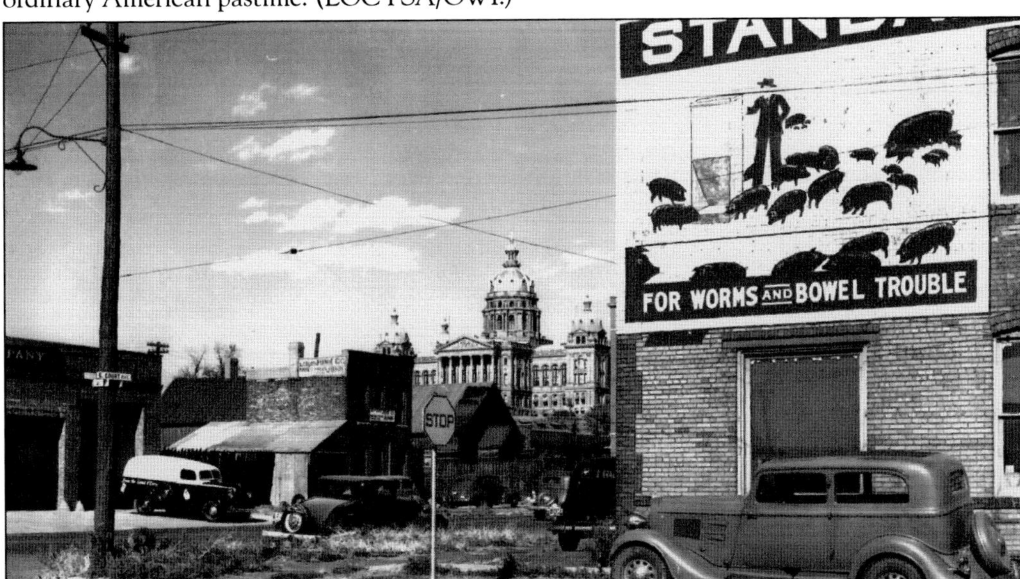

Farm Security Administration photographer Arthur Rothstein captured this picture in September 1939. "For Worms and Bowel Trouble," stated an advertisement for Standard Stuck Powders of Des Moines, located at East Sixth Street and East Court Avenue. The business and advertisement promote feed for hogs. Across the street are the Rath's Black Hawk Bacon Company garages. (LOC FSA/OWI.)

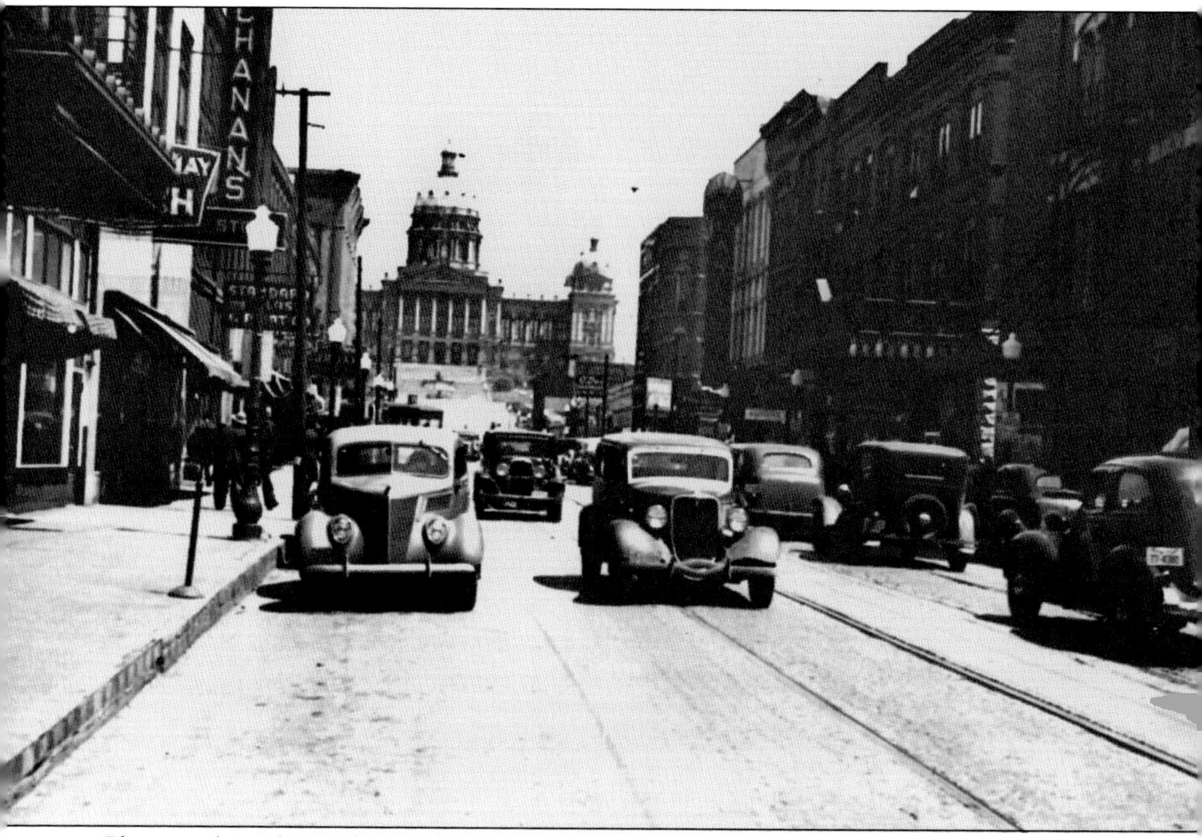

Photographer John Vachon took this photograph of cars moving along East Locust Street during a busy afternoon in May 1940. Vachon was standing in the 500 block looking west toward the state capitol. Visible are the following businesses: Buchanan's, Bolton and Hay restaurant, the Amuz-U Theater, Lozier the Florist, Standard Glass and Paint, and Garfield's Department Store. Although Vachon was based out of Omaha, Nebraska, he traveled throughout the Midwest on assignment for the Farm Security Administration. His curiosity about how things look outstripped his intellectual involvement in history and sociology. This photograph is an example of his images depicting the ebb and flow of life on disorderly city streets in anticipation of the postwar generation of street photographers. Critic Jonathan Green's description of fellow photographers Walker Evans's and Robert Frank's choices of subject matter as what was "considered beneath notice" applies to Vachon as well, with "images of the roadside, automobiles, gasoline stations, American flags in out-of-the-way places, barbershops, bums, billboards, luncheonettes, political posters, public monuments, and cemeteries." (LOC FSA/OWI.)

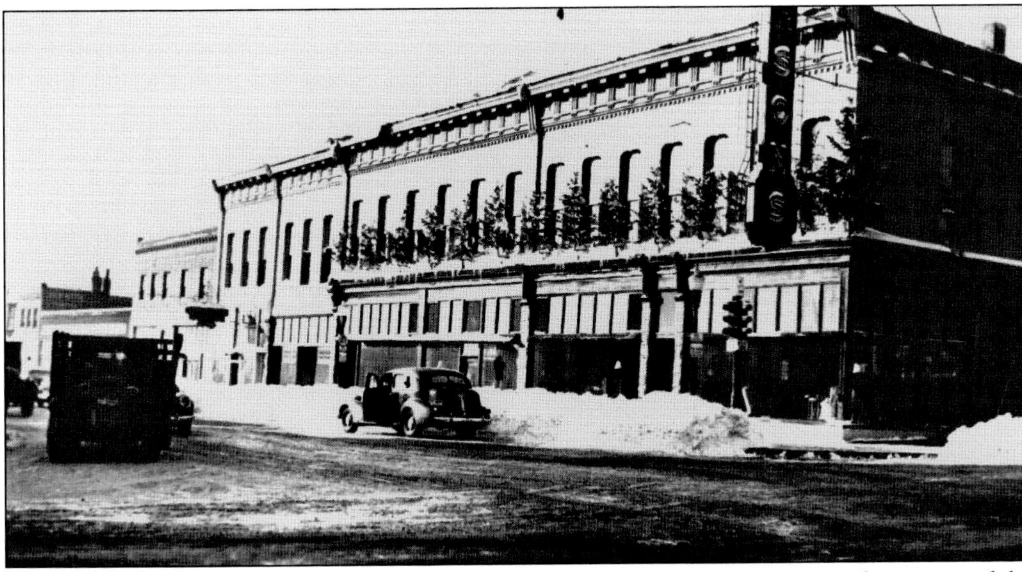

Anderson's Furniture is still going strong in 1942 with two large neon signs on the corner of the building at East Sixth Street and East Grand Avenue. This photograph shows how the building was decorated for Christmas and also how the facade had been changed from years before; the original exterior had been covered leaving the windows without their ornate Victorian-style caps. (JB.)

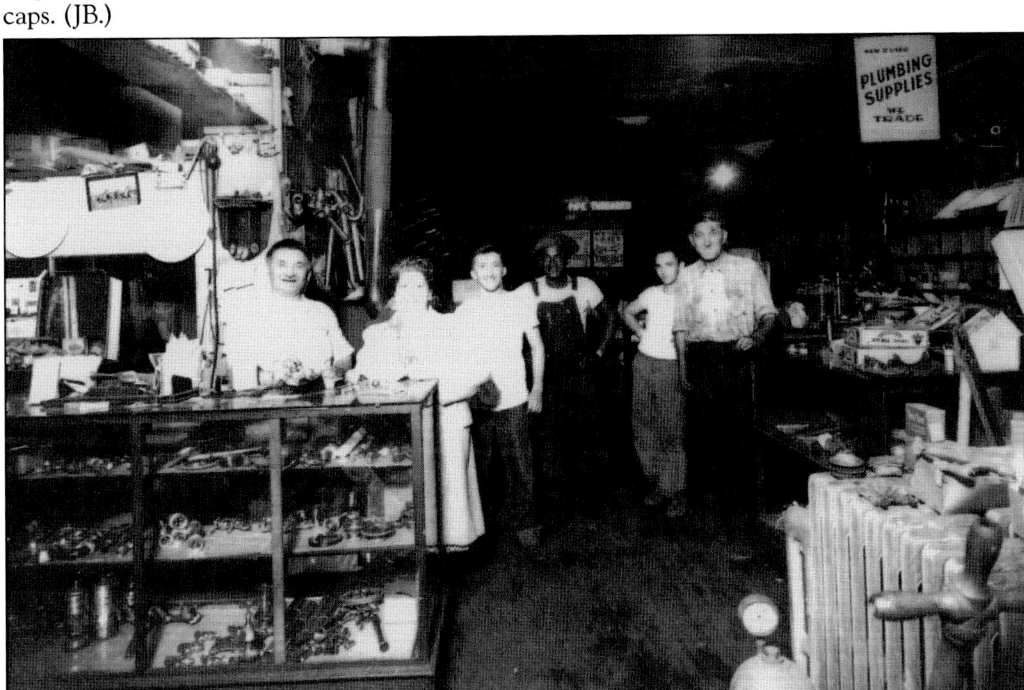

Harlan Lekowsky, former owner of American Plumbing, stands third from left in this 1946 photograph. His parents, who owned the store at that time, stand to his right. The interior of the shop at 504 East Grand Avenue remains much as it did at this time; even the cases and many of the signs remain. Lekowsky sold the business to his son but retains ownership of the building. (Harlan Lekowsky.)

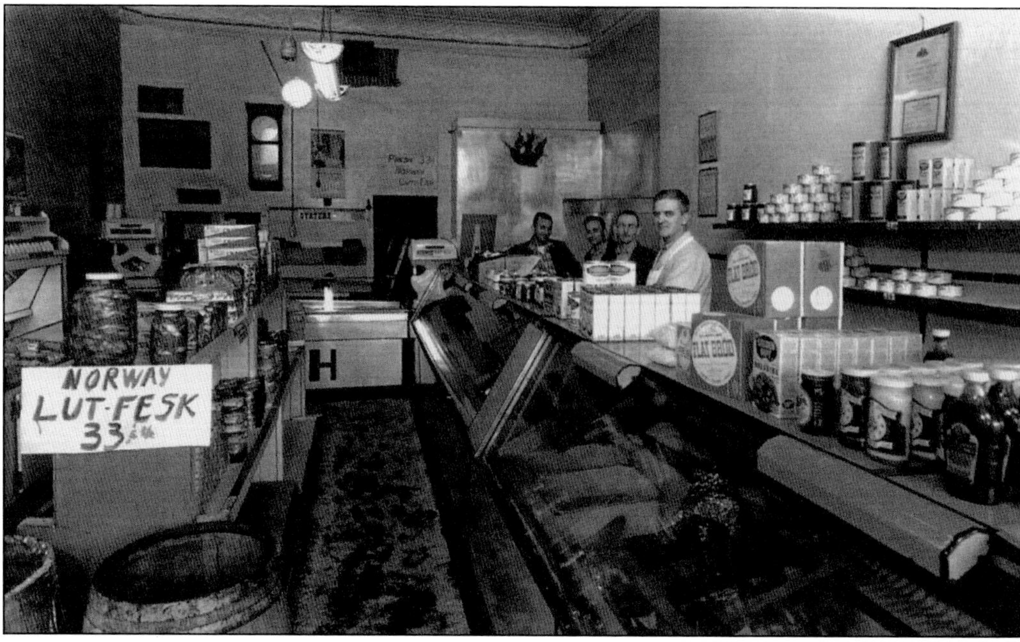

Art Veach worked alongside his sons at his East Side Fish Market, which he owned at 604 East Grand Avenue. Veach began the business in 1937, offering Scandinavian specialties and fresh fish, as seen here in 1945. Later his sons took over the business, rebuilding it into a fresh fish restaurant. The business remained in this location (although the building was torn down and replaced in 1980) until 1990. (FEH Associates/Denny Sharp.)

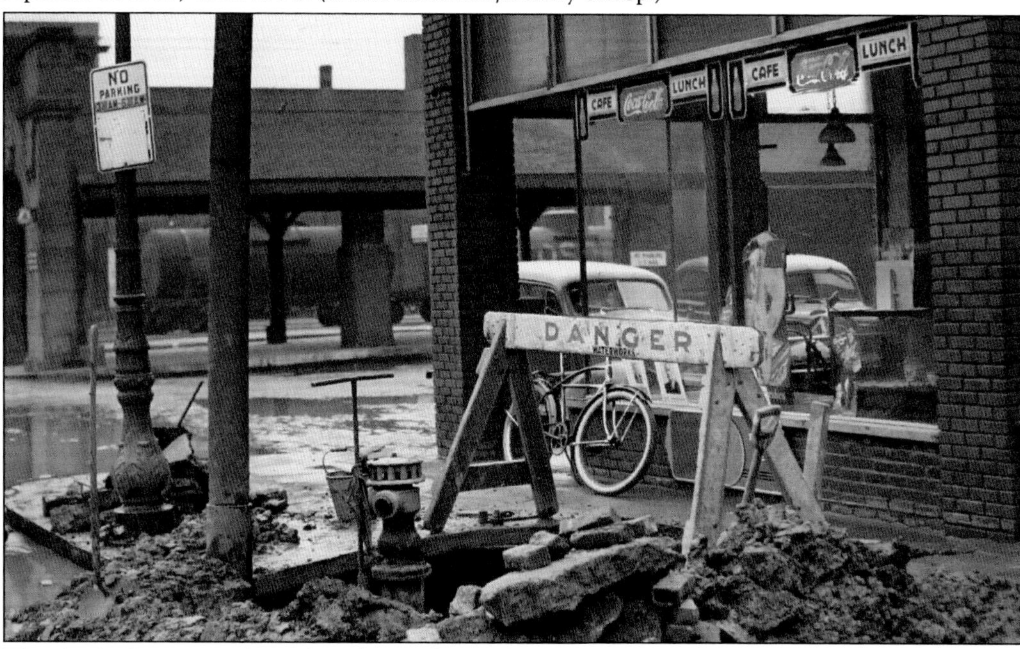

The fire hydrant was the culprit here when it broke on an early morning in May 1940. Water from the hydrant forced the sidewalk up outside the Northwestern Buffet at 313 East Locust Street. This view is to the east. See the passenger depot for the Chicago and North Western Railway depot in the background. (SHSI.)

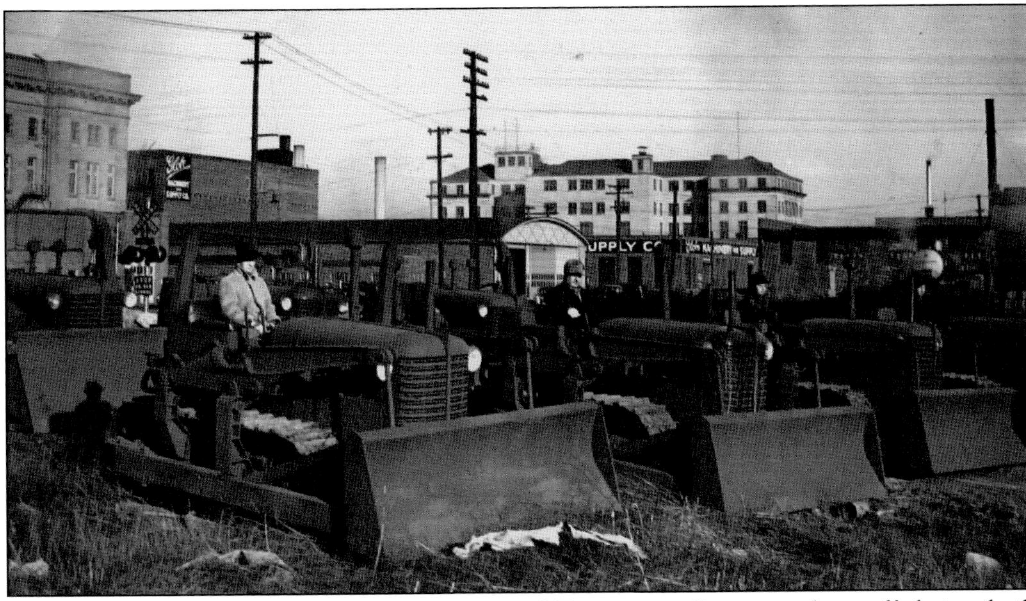

Workers from the Dukehart-Hughes Tractor and Equipment Company show off their rebuilt earthmovers in March 1946. The equipment was to be used by the U.S. Army Corps of Engineers. Globe Machinery and Supply can be seen in the background; the Municipal Auto Testing and Inspections building is in the center background. (SHSI.)

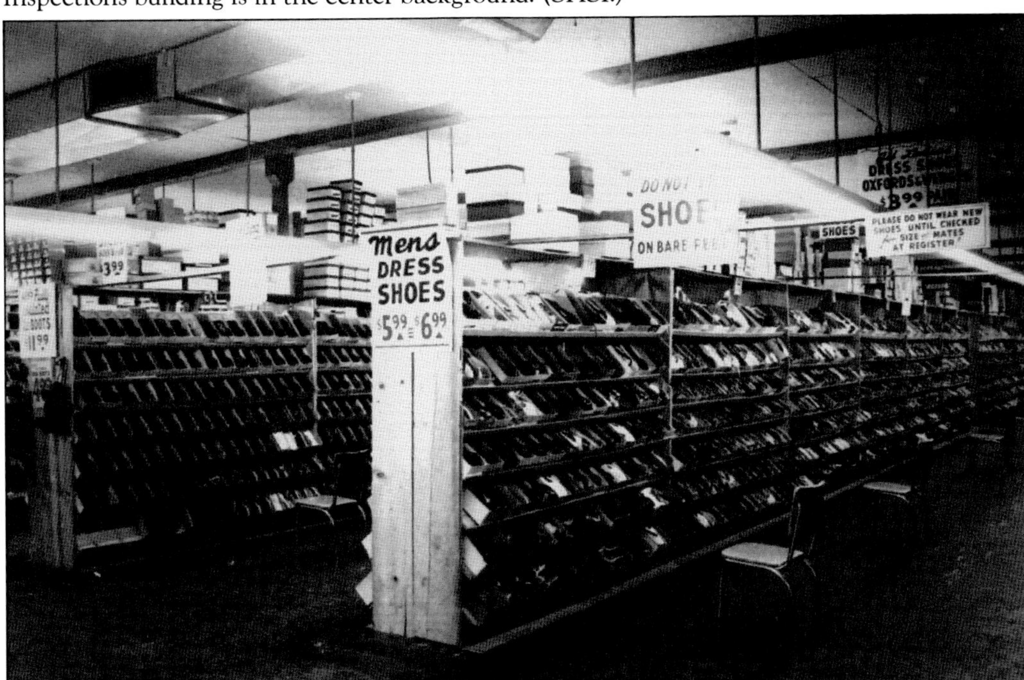

This photograph shows the interior of the Hill Brothers Self-Service Shoe Store at 523 East Grand Avenue. Women of the era who were accustomed to be waited on and fitted for shoes were now guided by rules evidenced in the signs hanging above, including, "Do not try shoes on bare feet," and "Please do not wear new shoes until checked for size and mates at register!" (SHSI.)

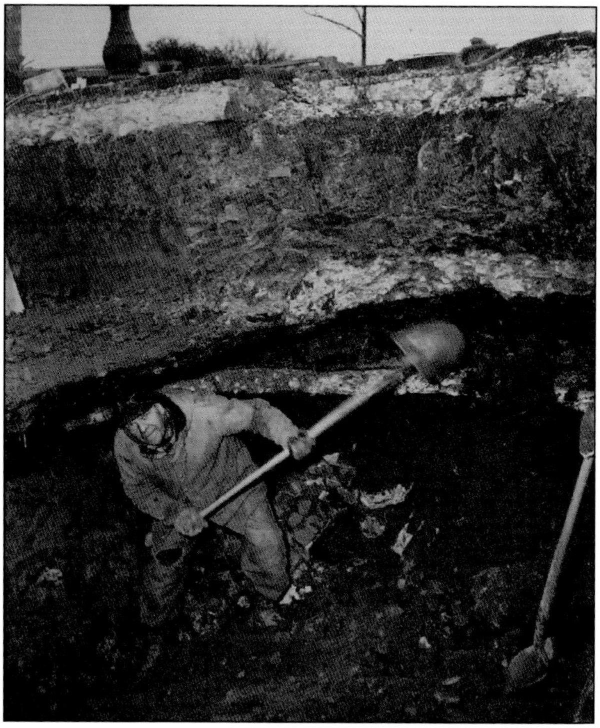

Repairs to a storm sewer in 1949 at East First Street and East Locust Street unearthed street matter five feet below, or what remained after the city raised the level of Locust Street as a preventive measure following the 1903 flood. The original street can be seen just beyond the head of the shovel. (SHSI.)

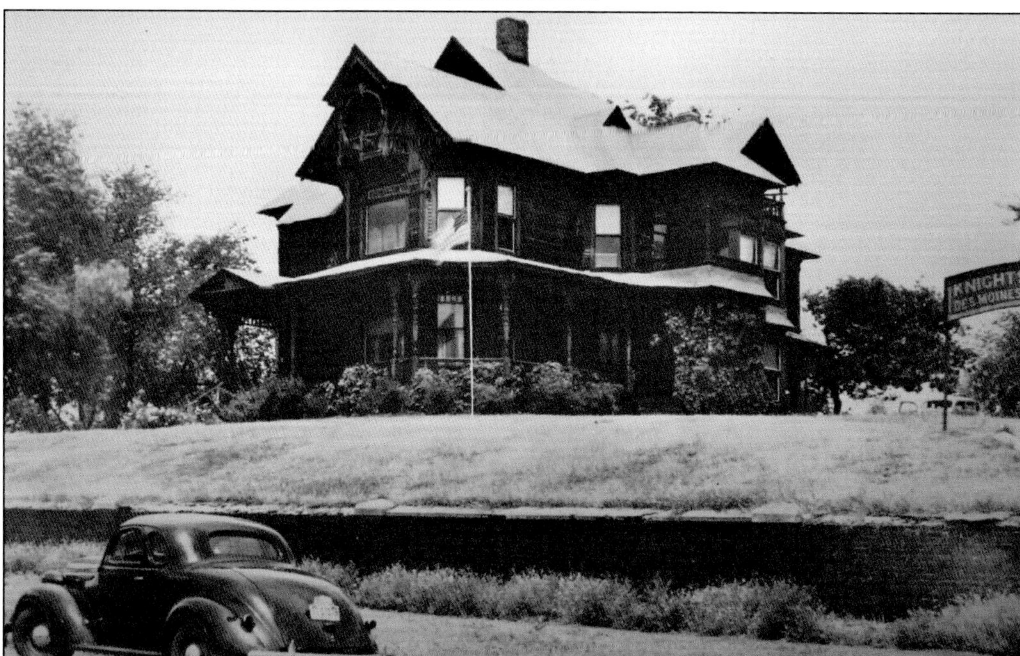

One-time residence of the Gilcrest family, this home was located on Des Moines Street between East Fifth and East Sixth Streets. Brothers J. K. and W. H. Gilcrest established a planning and turning mill. With several properties on the east side, Gilcrest's lumber business became a large part of the neighborhood industry. In 1985, Gilcrest Lumber merged with another longtime East Village lumber company, Jewett Lumber. (SHSI.)

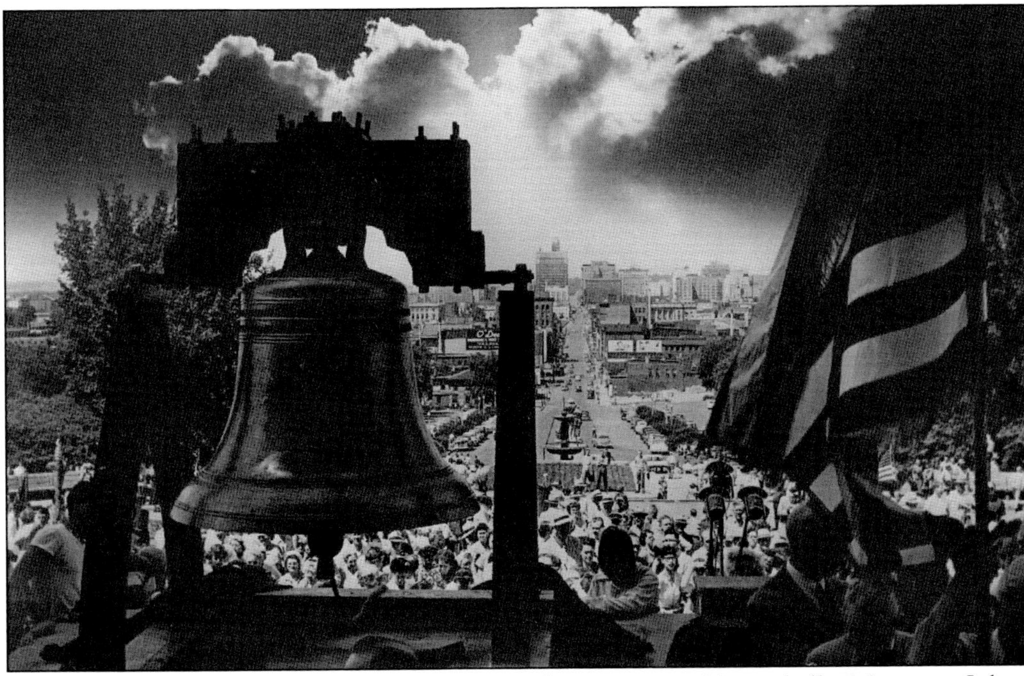

The U.S. Department of the Treasury presented a miniature liberty bell to Iowa on July 4, 1950, to thank the state for its efforts of the previous 10 years in war bond drives. Gov. William Beardsley appropriately dedicated this symbol of independence on Independence Day. The bell, cast in Annery-le-Vieux, France, weighs 2,000 pounds. (SHSI.)

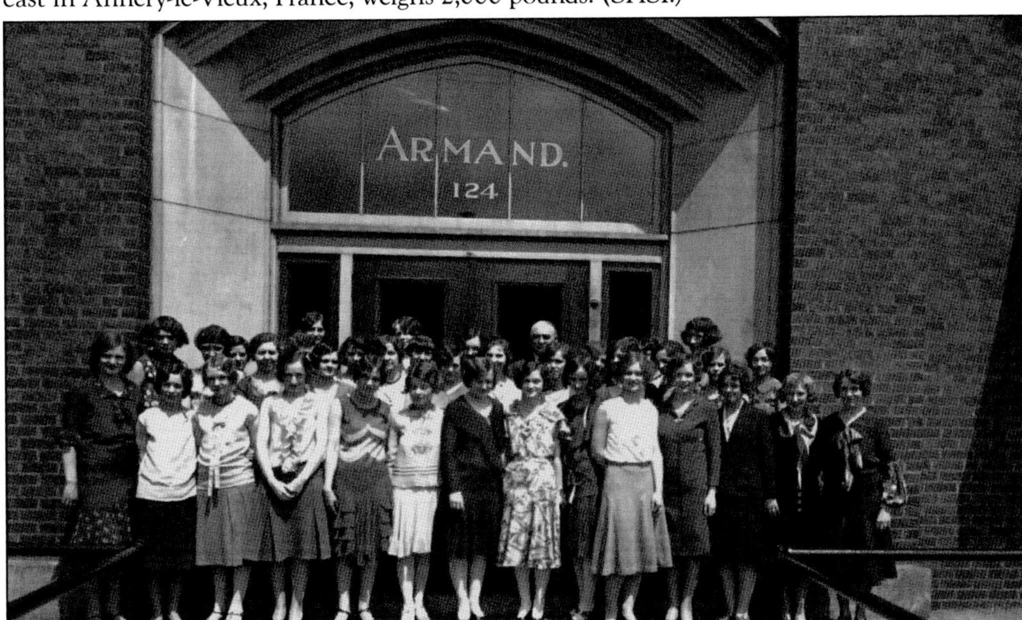

As a pioneer in the women's cosmetic industry, Carl Weeks built a fortune on the success of his company, Armand Cosmetics. The factory was located at 120–124 Des Moines Street. Weeks can be seen at the very back among his employees—all women. This photograph was taken in 1927. (Salisbury House and Gardens.)

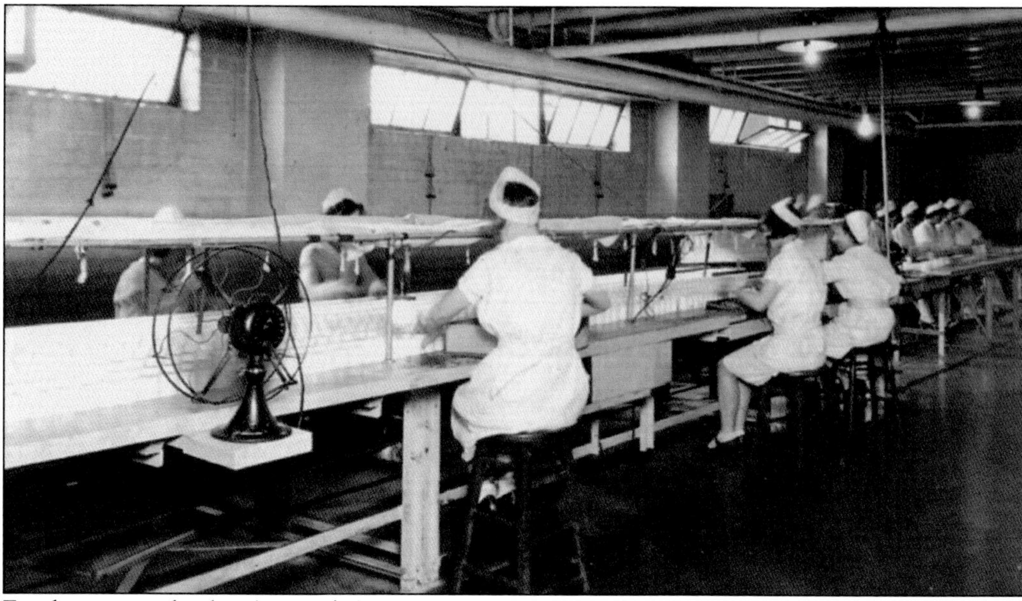

Employees inside the Armand Cosmetics company work to create cosmetics using only the finest imported ingredients, Italian talcs and colors, and French absolute perfume oils. By 1927, Armand was number one in the United States in face powder sales. Additionally, Armand is credited as the first manufacturer to recognize allergens in cosmetics, eliminate them, and to advertise in the *Journal of the American Medical Association*. (Salisbury House and Gardens.)

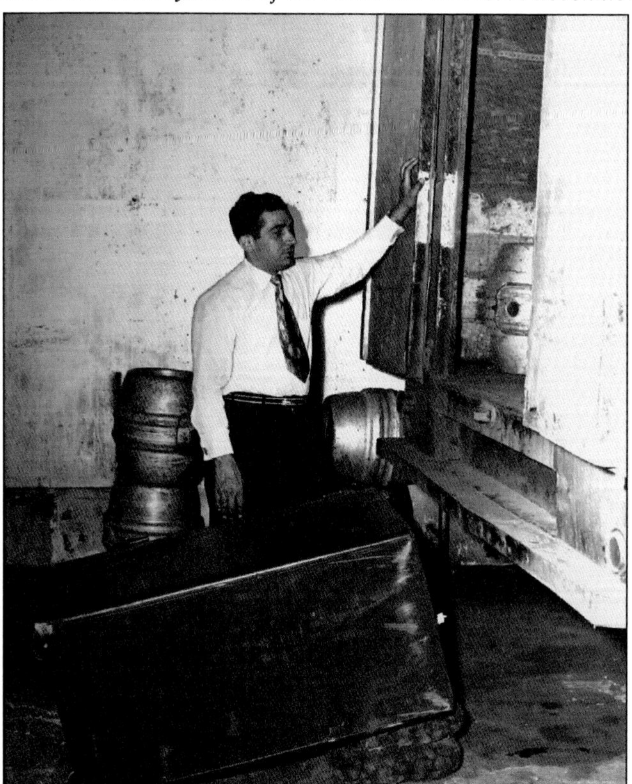

John Cimino, owner of Hamm's Des Moines Company at 613 East Grand Avenue, shows how burglars attempted to unload and haul away a 1,000-pound safe. They apparently became discouraged by the weight of the safe; it did not make it into the company truck they were also planning to steal in order to haul it away. (SHSI.)

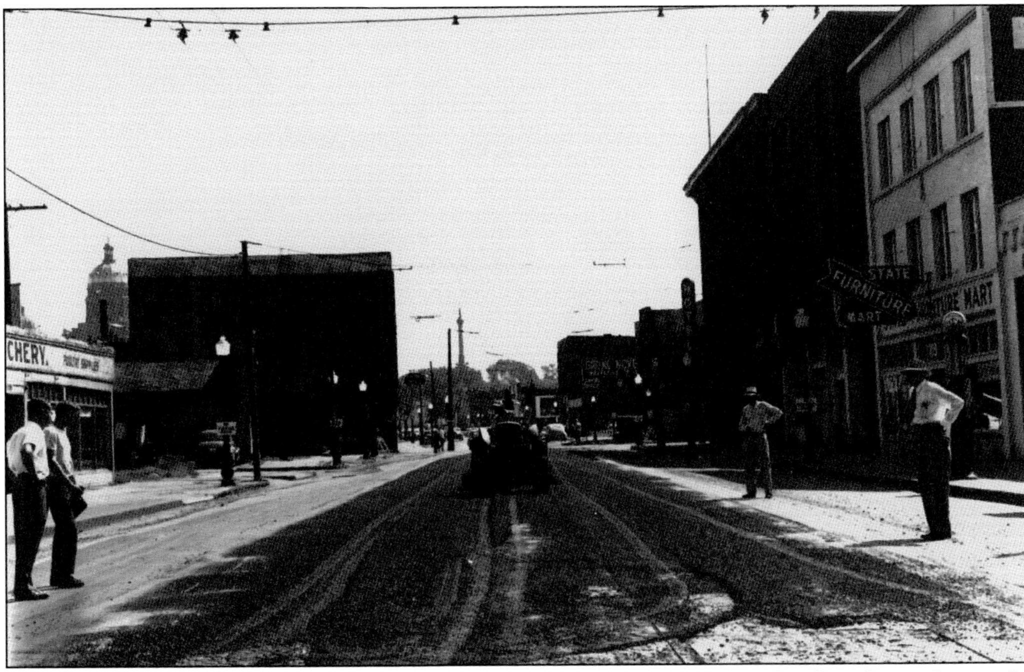

East Walnut Street gets graded and ready for paving as men watch. On the right is the Northwestern Hotel and State Furniture Mart. Both buildings remain today, although little else in this picture does. Note the streetcar tracks down the middle—these were paved over rather than removed, as was common practice. (Barbara Henning.)

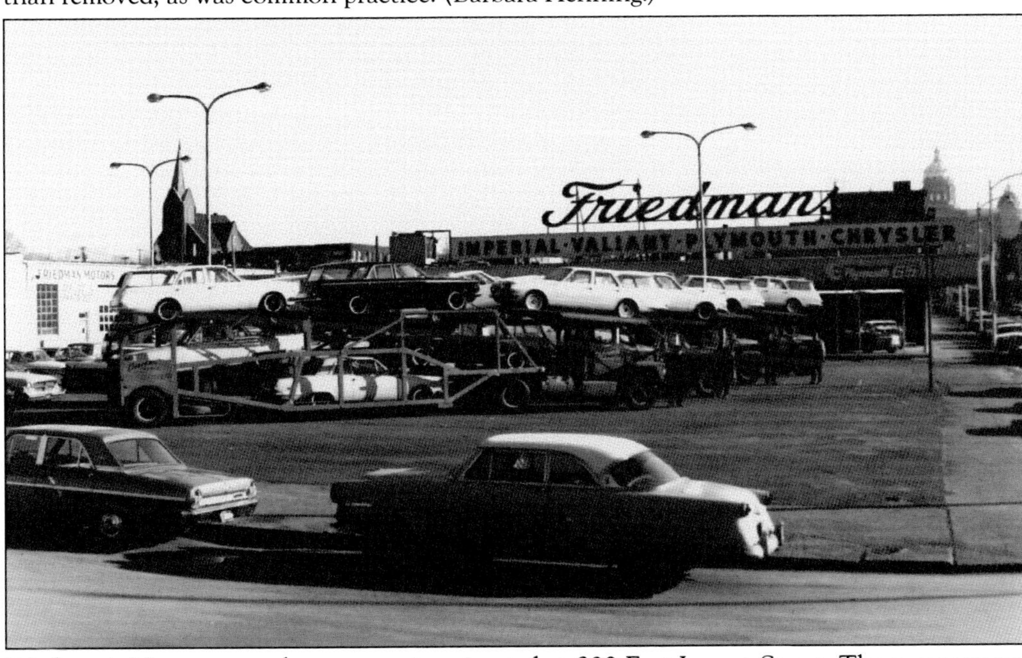

Friedman's Motors was a huge operation situated at 300 East Locust Street. The company was founded in 1919. It sold Imperial, Chrysler, Plymouth, and Valiant cars, although later it added Toyota and Honda to its list. The automobile industry, from manufacturing and gasoline stations to car dealers, was prevalent on the east side through mid-century. (SHSI.)

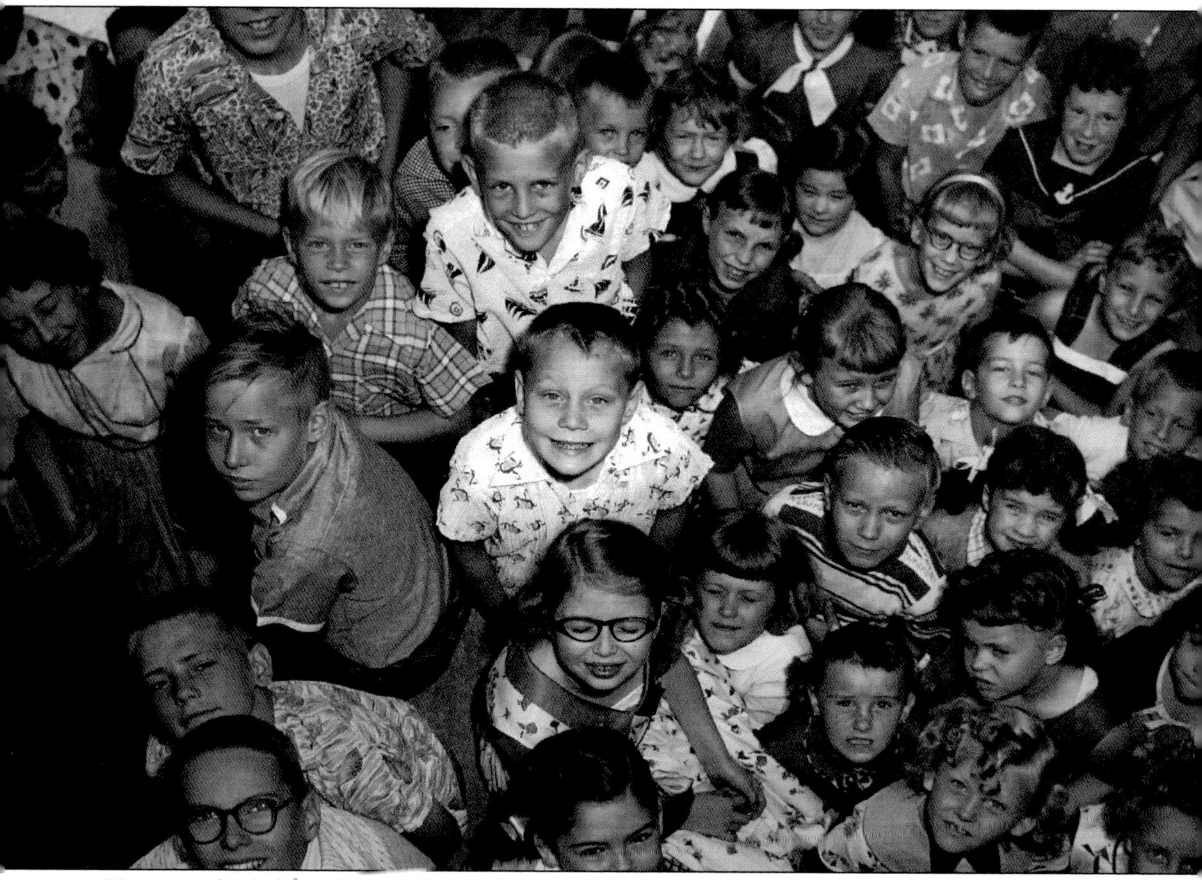

Here are the bright, shining faces of Sunday school children in attendance at First Lutheran Church about 1952. The 133-year-old church had been established to serve Swedish-speaking families in Des Moines. After World War II, Latvian language services were added. In 1959, the church purchased land to its immediate east and constructed an education building extension and choir room. In the 1960s, however, the membership began a slow decline, as people moved out to the suburbs and established churches closer to their homes. In 2002, First Lutheran Church joined with Central Lutheran Church to form Capitol Hill Lutheran Church, located at East Fifth and Des Moines Streets. In 2000, the congregation began welcoming Sudanese refugees to worship, with services in Nuer and also in Vietnamese. Like many churches, Capitol Hill Lutheran offers learning activities for its youth members that incorporate bible stories, arts and crafts, social skills, mentoring, and meals. (CLHC.)

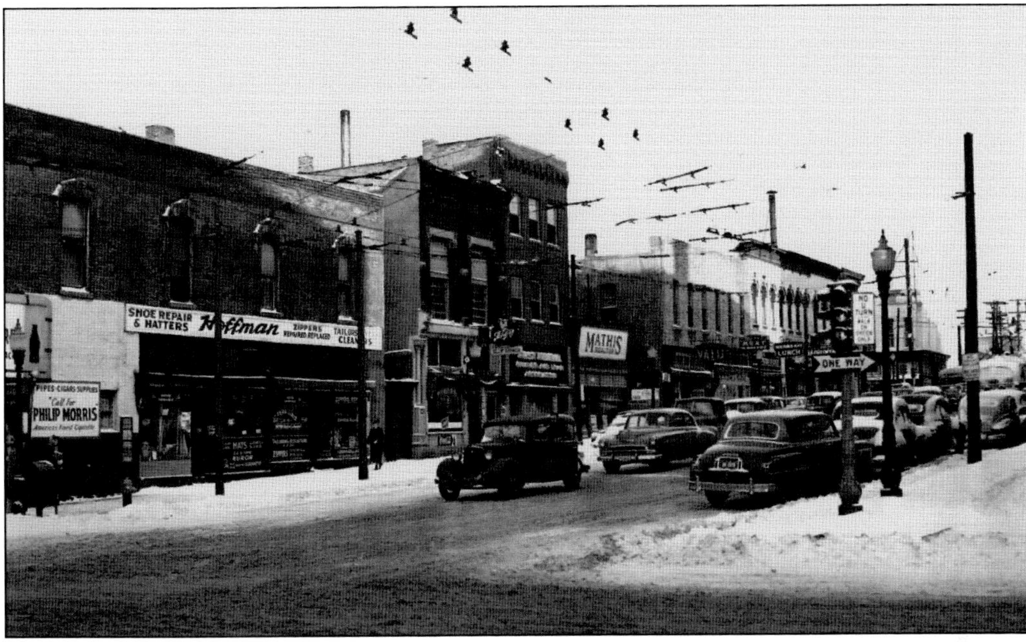

This photograph shows the west side of East Sixth Street in February 1953, looking north toward East Grand Avenue. The cold temperatures must have been the cause for the gentleman in the foreground to push his car down the street. Businesses along here included the Bolton and Hay restaurant, Hoffman Shoe Repair, and Hatters and Mathis Realtor. (SHSI.)

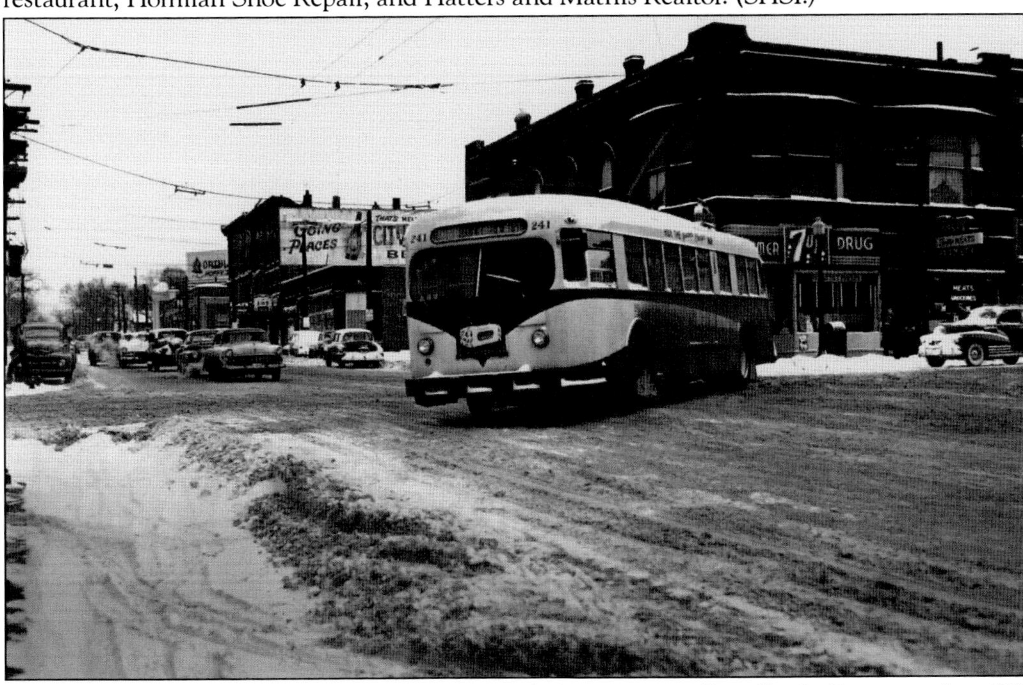

A curb liner turns the corner from East Grand Avenue onto East Sixth Street in this 1953 photograph. Hammer Pharmacy is on the right, and the Northland Dairy building can be seen in the distance up East Sixth Street. Hast's Quality Meats Market occupied the east side of the Hammer double storefront at this time. (SHSI.)

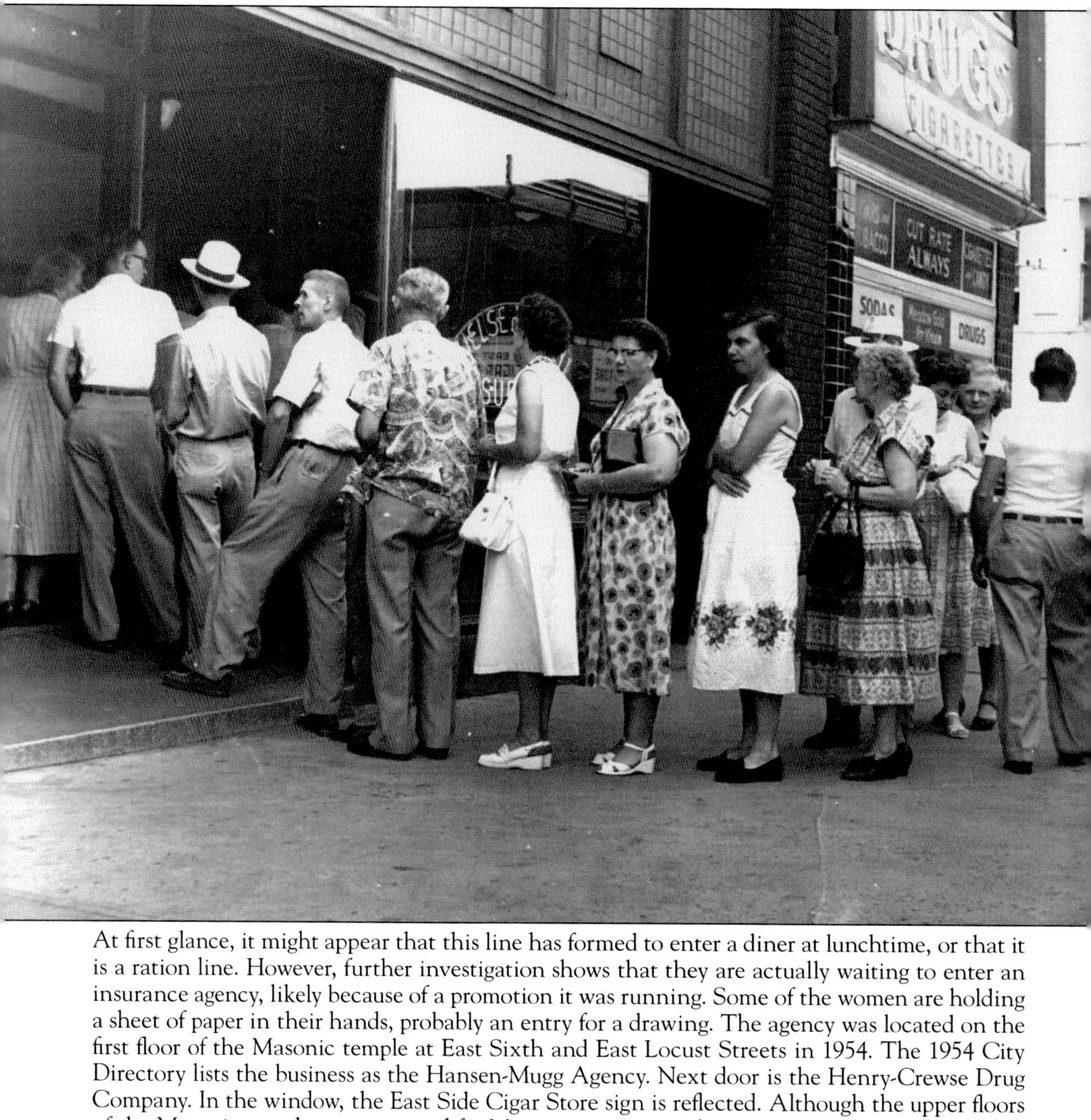

At first glance, it might appear that this line has formed to enter a diner at lunchtime, or that it is a ration line. However, further investigation shows that they are actually waiting to enter an insurance agency, likely because of a promotion it was running. Some of the women are holding a sheet of paper in their hands, probably an entry for a drawing. The agency was located on the first floor of the Masonic temple at East Sixth and East Locust Streets in 1954. The 1954 City Directory lists the business as the Hansen-Mugg Agency. Next door is the Henry-Crewse Drug Company. In the window, the East Side Cigar Store sign is reflected. Although the upper floors of the Masonic temple were reserved for Mason organizational meetings and activities, the first floor never had trouble being rented to an unaffiliated business. (ISB.)

Four

Out with the Old

The east side had to do something. After the freeway was built in the late 1950s and early 1960s, people could more easily travel throughout the metro area to buy what they needed. They were no longer tied to frequenting businesses within a stone's throw of their front doors. The competition was out there, and it just got more intense. Loyalties waned. Everyone wanted something new, including new houses, new clothes, and new cars. As established as it was, the east side turned its back on its history and began to actively demolish buildings, neglect them until they fell under their own weight, or reface them with new exteriors. Chain stores started popping up, and the mom-and-pop stores could not compete. The focus was on the suburbs, where there was room to build the American dream. Save for the state capitol, which brought legislators and lobbyists four months out of the year, and a year-round trickle of tourists, the east side had closed up its retail operation, electing instead for more commercialized businesses. Diners and pubs remained, but it was getting dangerous to frequent them. In the 1970s and 1980s, the newspaper reports coming from the east side were nearly all about crime. The state capitol itself had the reputation of being an unsafe area after dark until well into the 1990s. It was the east side business leaders who again banded together to bring back some semblance of a neighborhood and thus begin the long, slow process of rebuilding.

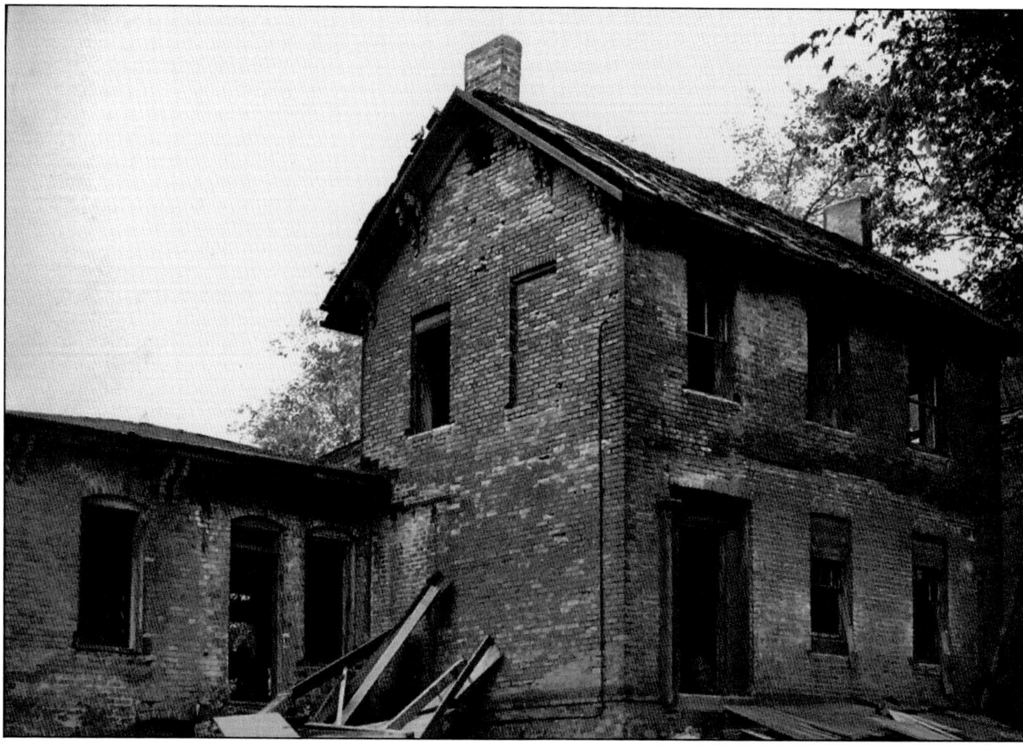

In May 1945, the city council voted to tear down this building, as it was "dangerous for children who play in it." The house was located at 614 East Sixth Street. On this site now is a low-income apartment complex. The details of the Victorian-era architectural style are apparent under the roofline. Inside the front door is what appears to be a beer keg. (SHSI.)

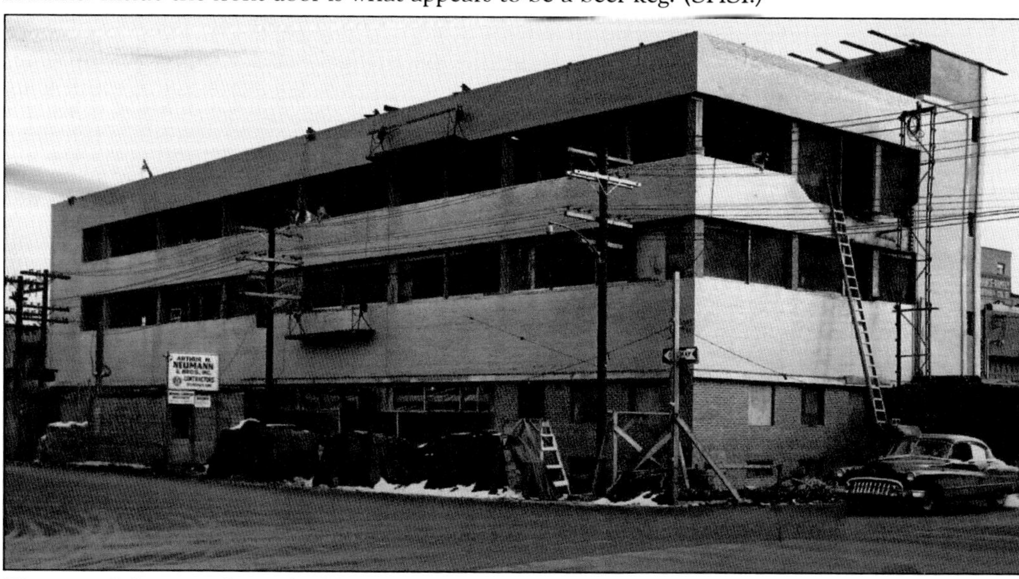

The new Salvation Army building at East Second Street and East Court Avenue was nearing completion at the time of this photograph in February 1956. At a cost of $500,000, the building replaced one that was burned in a 1954 fire. Among its features was a men's dormitory, a recreation room, a chapel, and a visiting physician's office. (SHSI.)

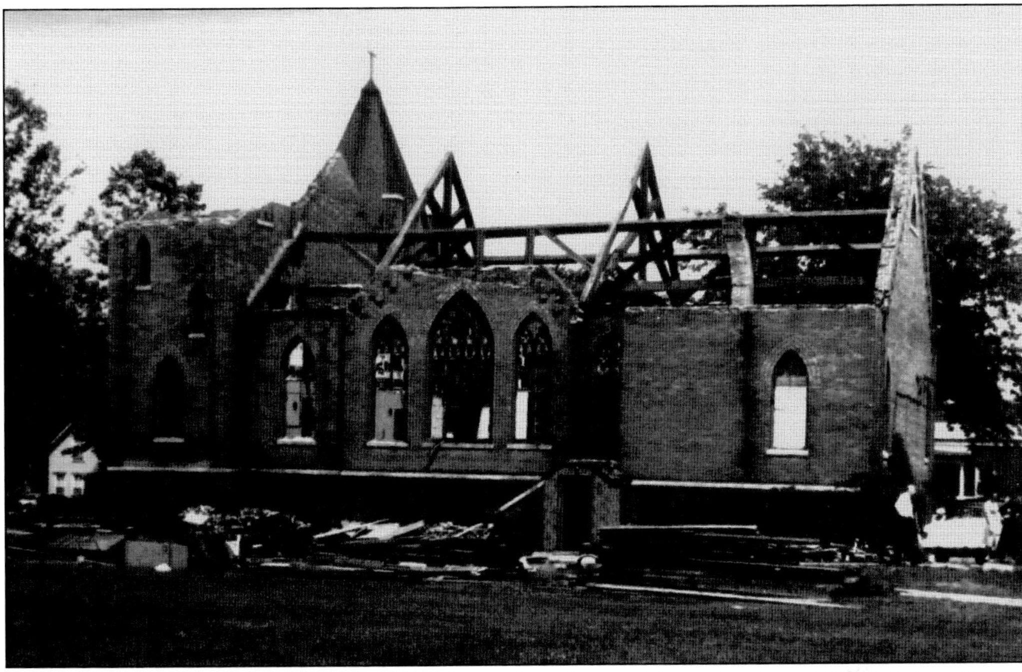

In 1959, the former Central Lutheran Church building at East Ninth and Des Moines Streets was demolished, although it hardly needed it as it was crumbling to the frame. The congregation constructed a new building on this site and remained together until 2002, when it officially merged with the First Swedish Lutheran to form Capitol Hill Lutheran Church. (CLHC.)

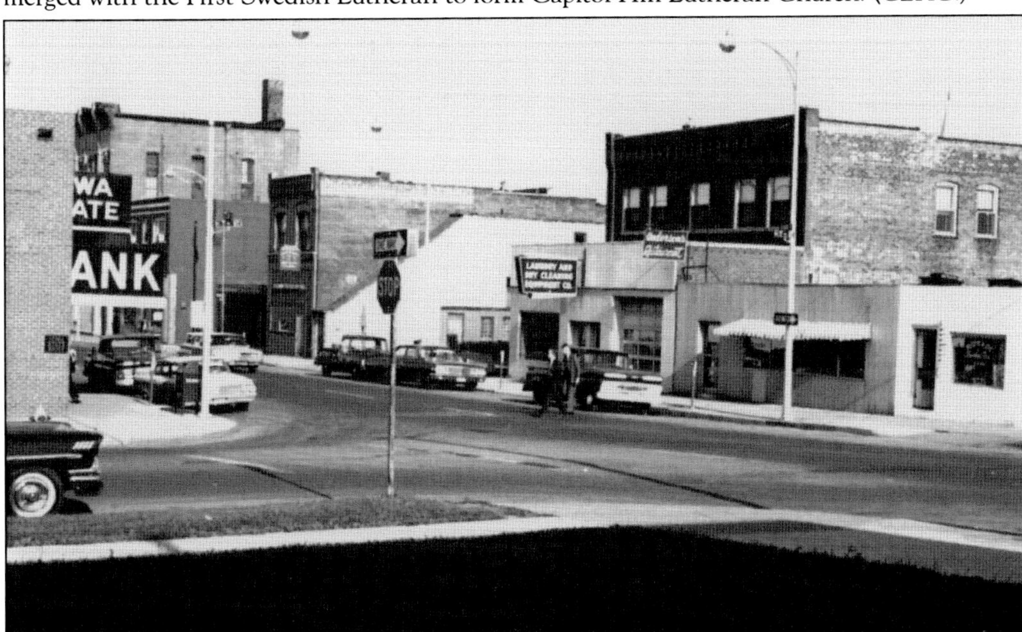

This image shows the north side of East Locust Street from East Seventh Street around 1954. American Laundry was a large employer that occupied the building seen in the middle of the block. All these buildings were demolished in the late 1980s to erect the State Historical Building. Iowa State Bank, on the left, is still there. (ISB.)

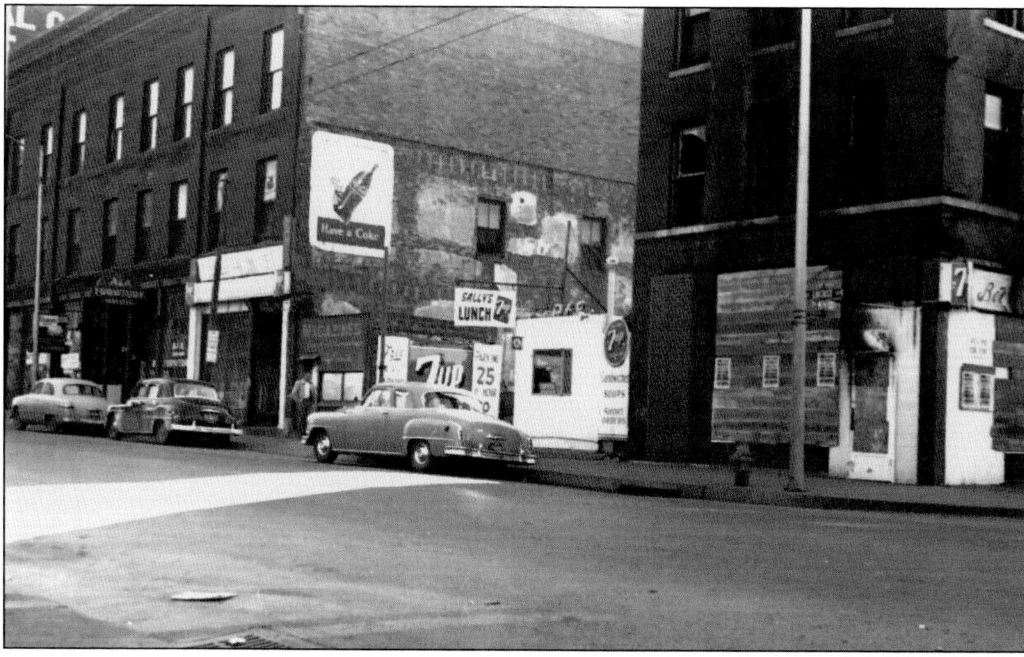

Betty Lou Gosek owned Betty's Place in the Nelson Hotel at 401 East Locust Street. When this photograph was taken around 1958, a fire had recently occurred that gutted the place and the second floor. Next to Betty's are Sally's Lunch, a magazine stand, and the Columbian Hotel building. Both the Columbian and Nelson Hotels had reputations as brothels; above Betty's, the operation ran under the name S and L Sleeping Rooms. (ISB.)

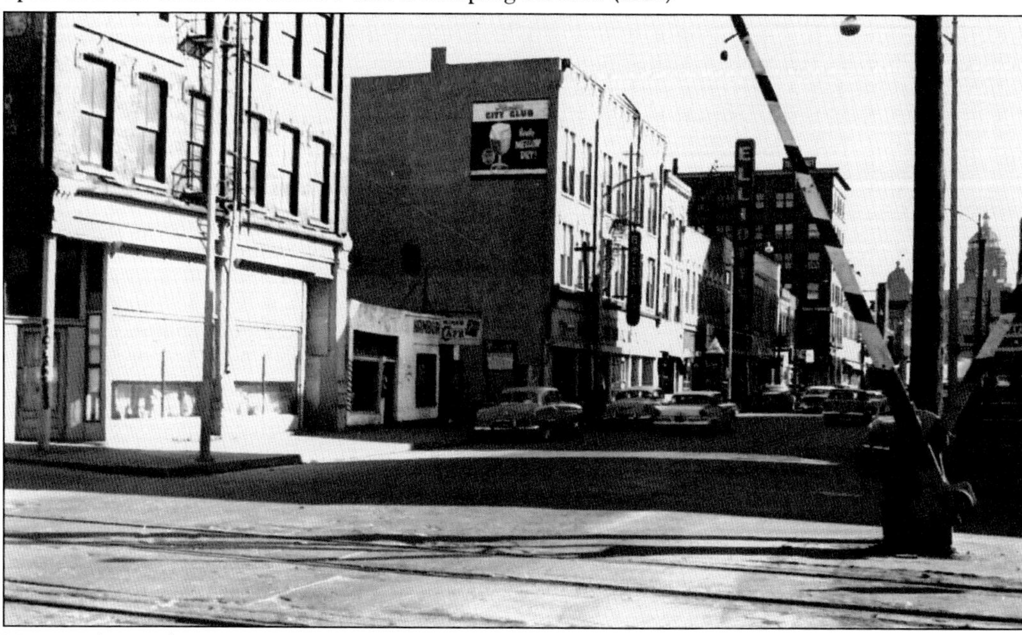

Here is the guide arms stand next to the railroad tracks that ran along East Fourth Street. The Stubbs Block, as it was called, included Betts and Son Hardware and Elliott Furniture Company. The building on the immediate left advertises Pro-Lak Yeast Feeds and has sacks of grains lined up inside its storefront. (ISB.)

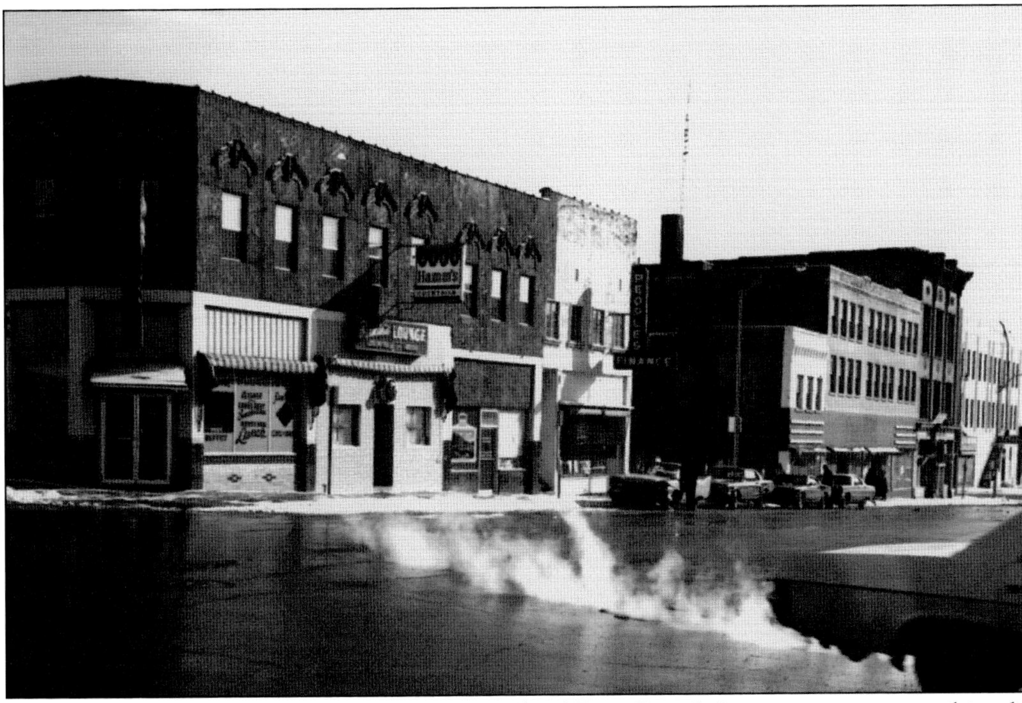

This photograph shows East Sixth Street south of East Grand Avenue as it appeared in the spring of 1975. A popular spot, Bernie's Restaurant and Lounge is on the corner, and behind it sits People's Finance. Bernie's was owned by Bernard J. Grandanette, who made the restaurant known for its kosher-style corned beef sandwiches. (ISB.)

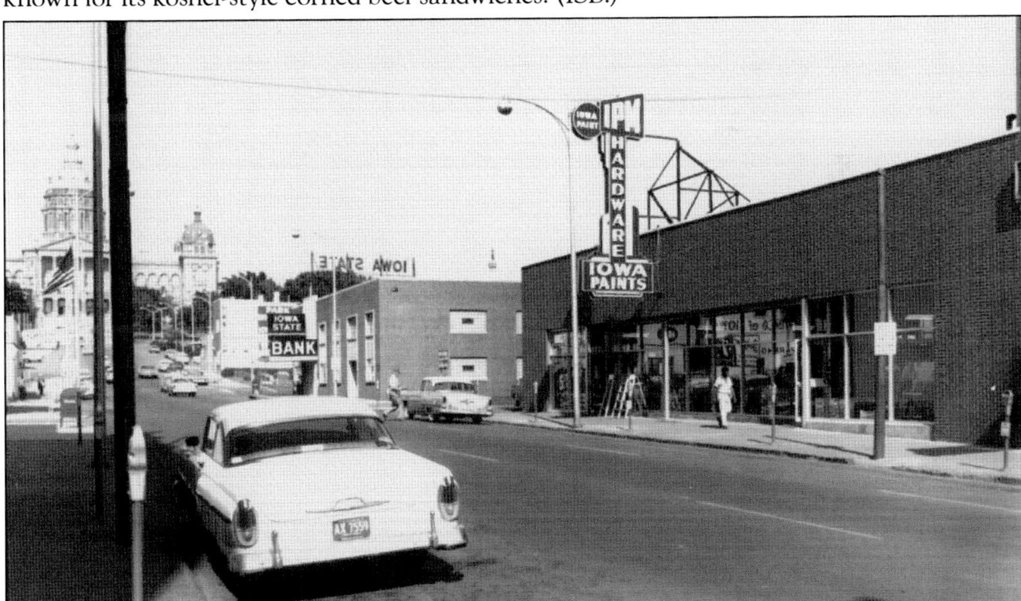

Iowa Paint Manufacturing (IPM) was founded in Des Moines in 1933 to serve professional painters in the area. By the late 1960s, the company had more than 10 locations across the Midwest and earned an almost $50,000 contract to supply the U.S. Army Corps of Engineers. The company is still in existence today but located in the western suburbs. (ISB.)

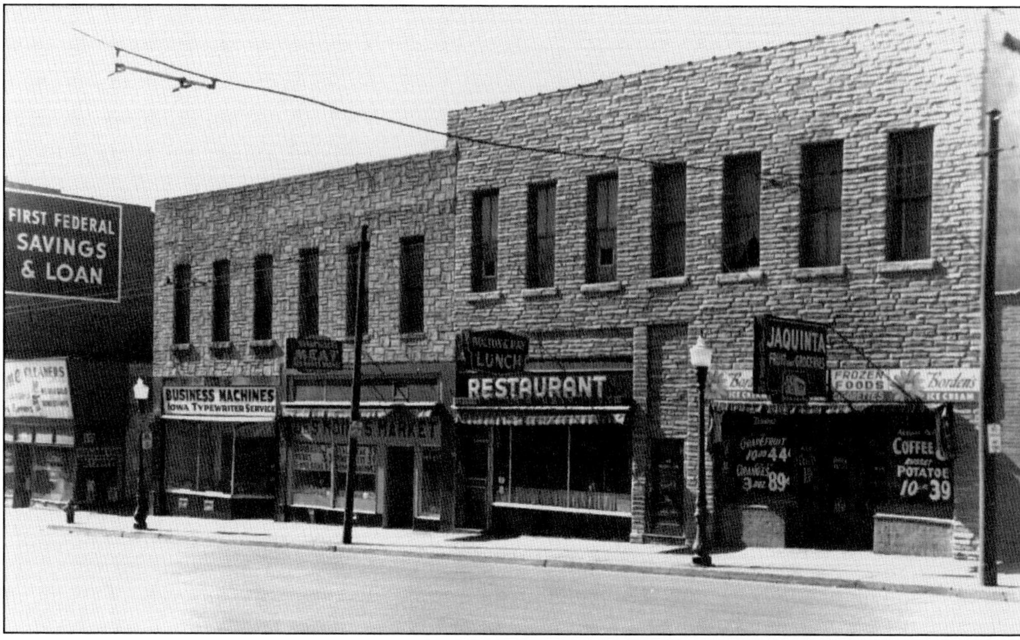

Storefronts and restaurants along East Sixth Street included the First Federal Savings and Loan; Neffenegger's Des Moines Market Meats; and Bolton and Hay. Jaquinta Fruit and Groceries is offering three-dozen oranges for 89¢, 10 grapefruits for 44¢, and 10 pounds of Russet potatoes for 39¢. The building farthest right is now a bath shop and a tea shop. (ISB.)

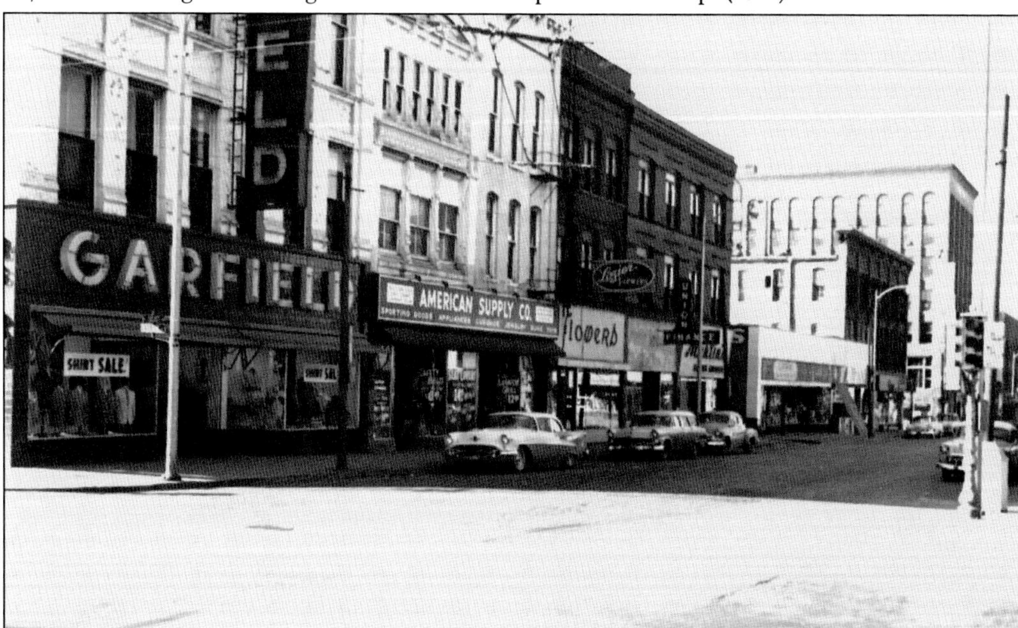

The single-story building in this photograph marks where the Lewis Opera House used to stand. The opera house hosted some of the biggest social events in Des Moines after it was built in 1887, a symbol that the east side had arrived. It burned to the ground only five years later. This photograph from 1958 shows the buildings around it that survived and storefronts filled with small business. (ISB.)

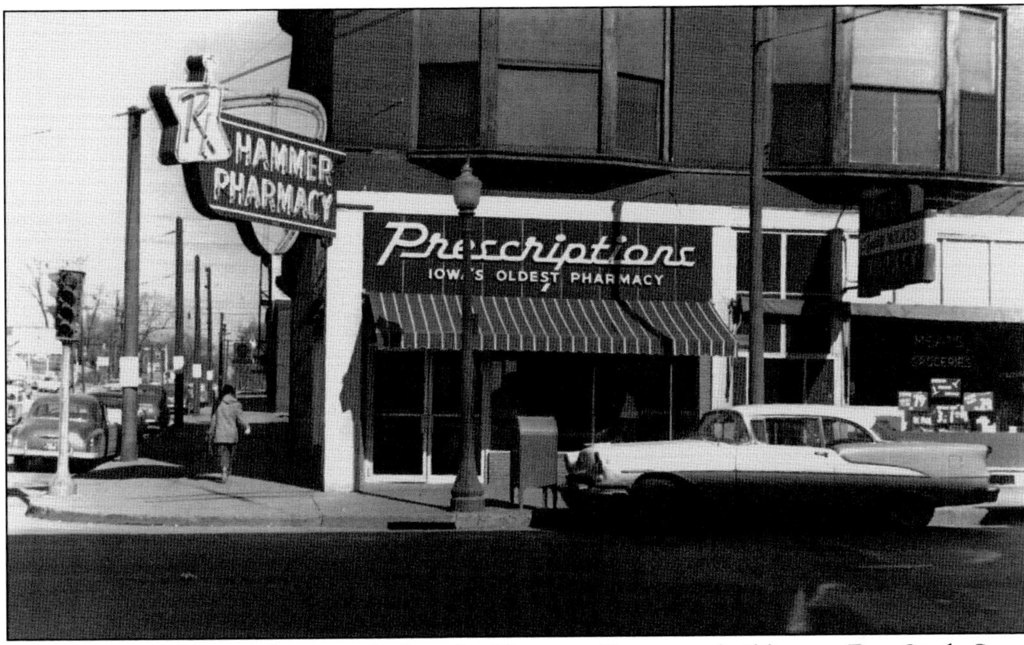

This photograph was taken just before the Hammer Pharmacy building at East Sixth Street and East Grand Avenue was refaced with siding in the late 1950s. The eastern storefront was occupied by Hast's Quality Meats. The corner neon sign advertising the business was removed in an effort to streamline the exterior of the building. (ISB.)

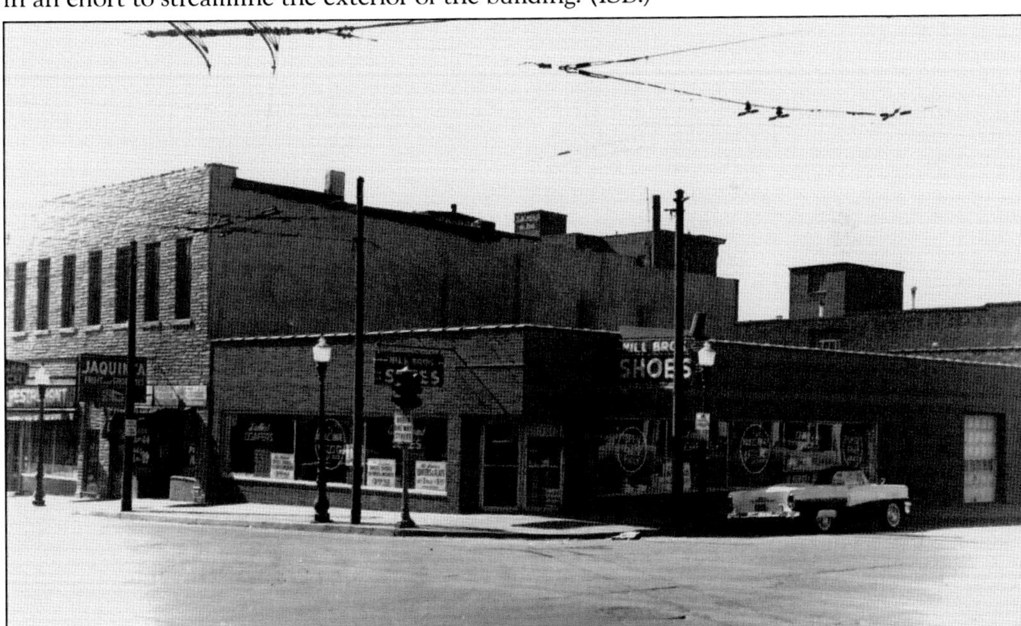

Hill Brothers Shoes occupied the eastern corner of East Sixth Street and East Grand Avenue, a building that Hammer Pharmacy on the opposite corner eventually took over as a satellite location for medical supplies and equipment. Note the signs advertising two pairs of shoes for $5 and "Open 9-9 Daily," a pressuring movement to remain open, even on Sundays, to keep up with mall competition. (ISB.)

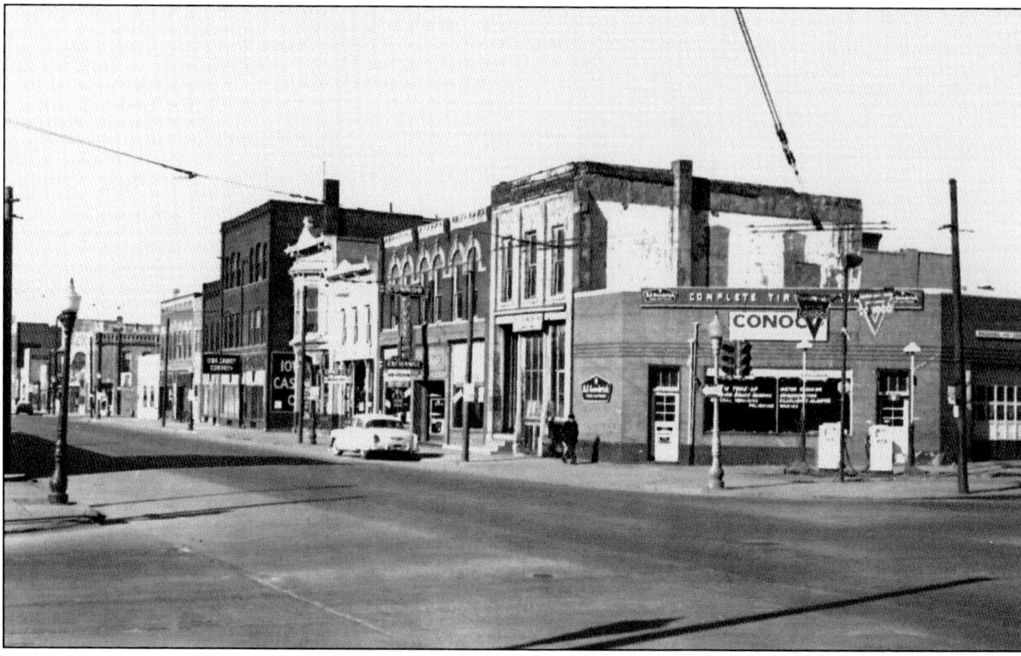

This photograph from about 1955 documents the north side of East Walnut Street. Although East Locust Street and East Grand Avenue earned much attention as the main thoroughfares to the state capitol, East Walnut Street to the south was filled with life as well. On the corner is a Conoco station, and farther down the block is the Iowa Casket Company. (ISB.)

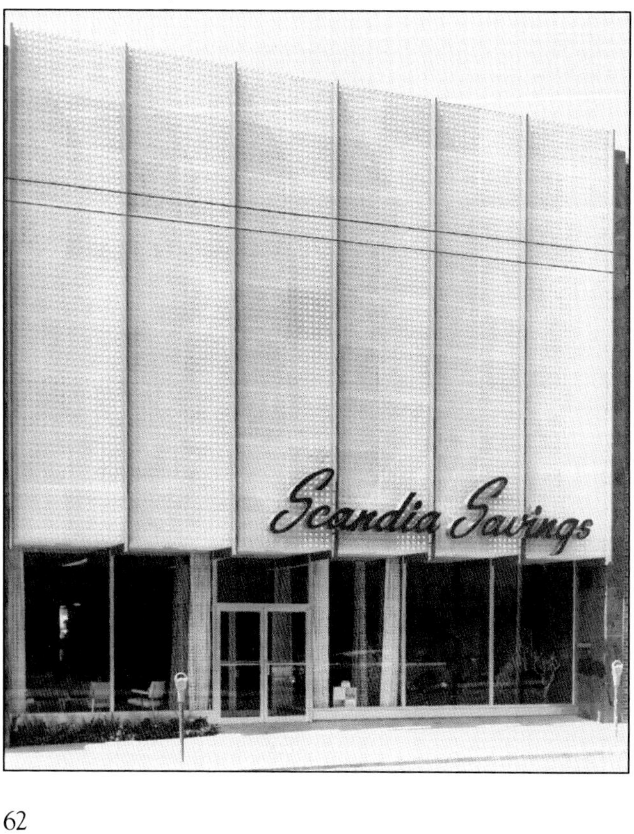

By the late 1950s, Scandia Savings and Loan had expanded its business and was doing quite well. Its success is evident in the changes it made to the exterior of the building it owned at 510 East Locust Street. The siding that was added lasted for more than 40 years until the building was sold and remodeled in 2007. (ISB.)

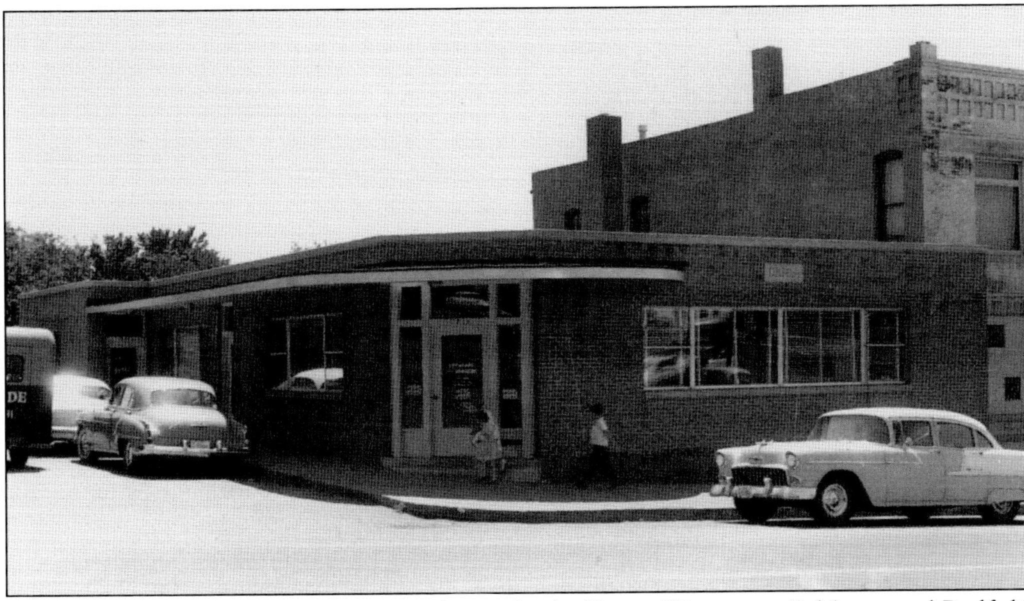

A mother leads her two children into the medical offices of Burgeson, Schlaser, and Redfield, M.D., located at 711 East Locust Street around 1958. Several offices occupied the building over the years, although its design never quite fit in with the historic row house it was attached to on the west. In 2008, it was purchased by the State of Iowa and torn down as part of the Capitol West Terrace improvements. (CDM.)

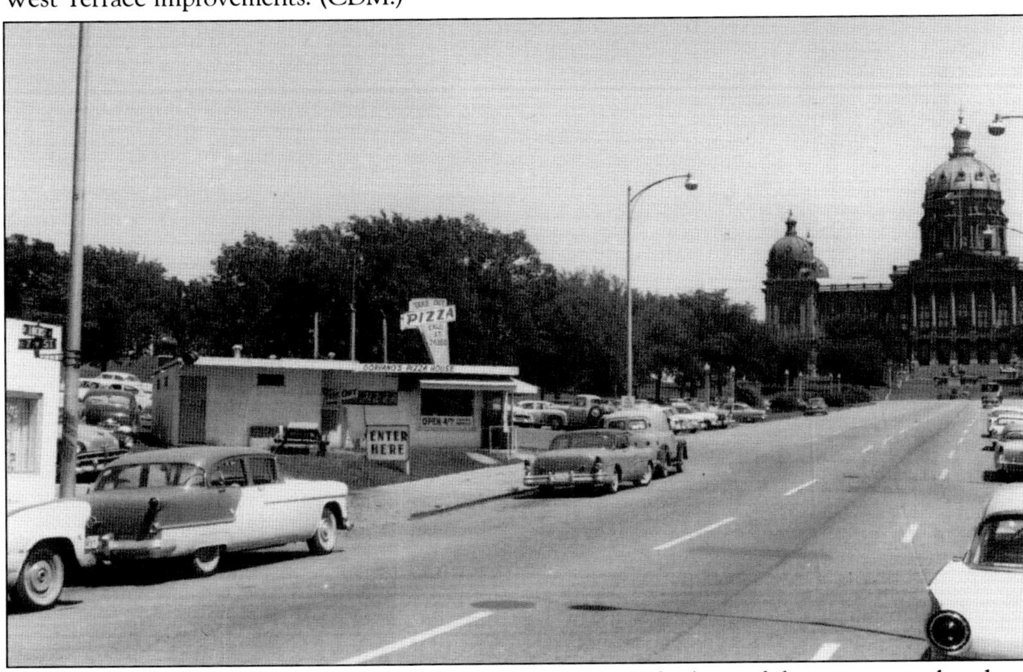

Gorvano's Pizza House at 650 East Locust Street sat just as the base of the state capitol and was surely a popular spot for legislators to frequent during session. This photograph, from about 1958, also shows East Locust Street extending all the way to the capitol building. Later the state closed East Locust Street east of East Seventh Street for parking. In 2008, the parking lot was replaced with Capitol West Terrace, a stately park and garden. (CDM.)

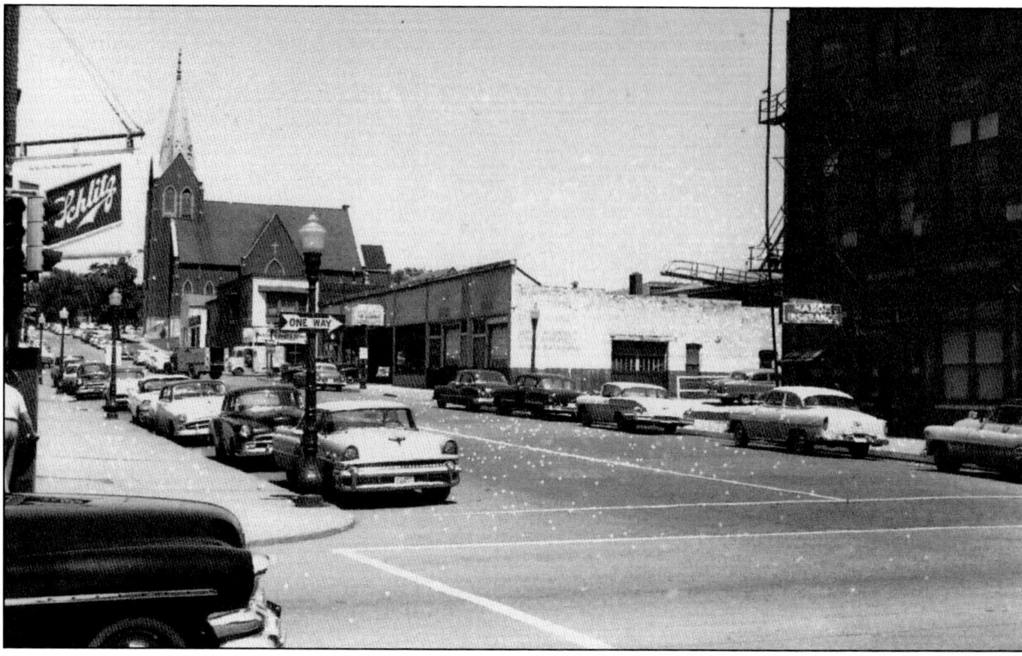

Here is East Fifth Street looking north from Locust Street around 1958. The tall spire of the Swedish Lutheran Church is an obvious marker. The Teachout building is on the right, and Locust Tavern (now Locust Tap) on the extreme left advertises Schlitz beer. (CDM.)

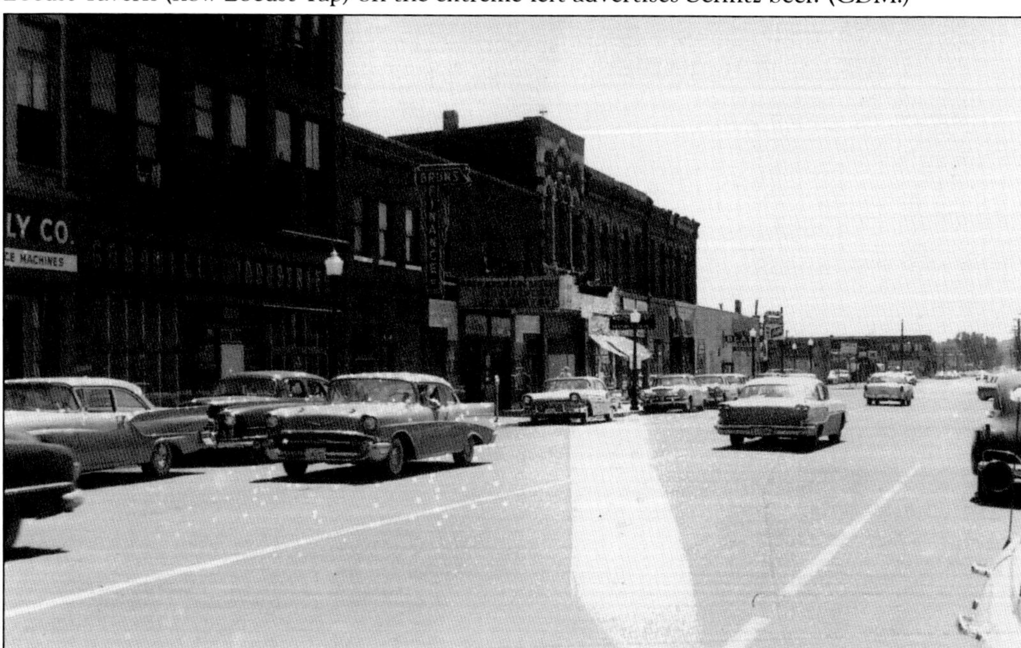

This photograph looks south from East Locust Street down East Fifth Street toward the east side of the street. Notable is the Iowa Theater, which states on its marquee, "Open Noon Fri Sat Sun Three Features & Cartoon." The Iowa Theater opened in May 1931, when several movie houses clustered south of East Grand Avenue on East Fifth and East Sixth Streets. Just to the south of the theater is the C. M. Ward druggist building. (CDM.)

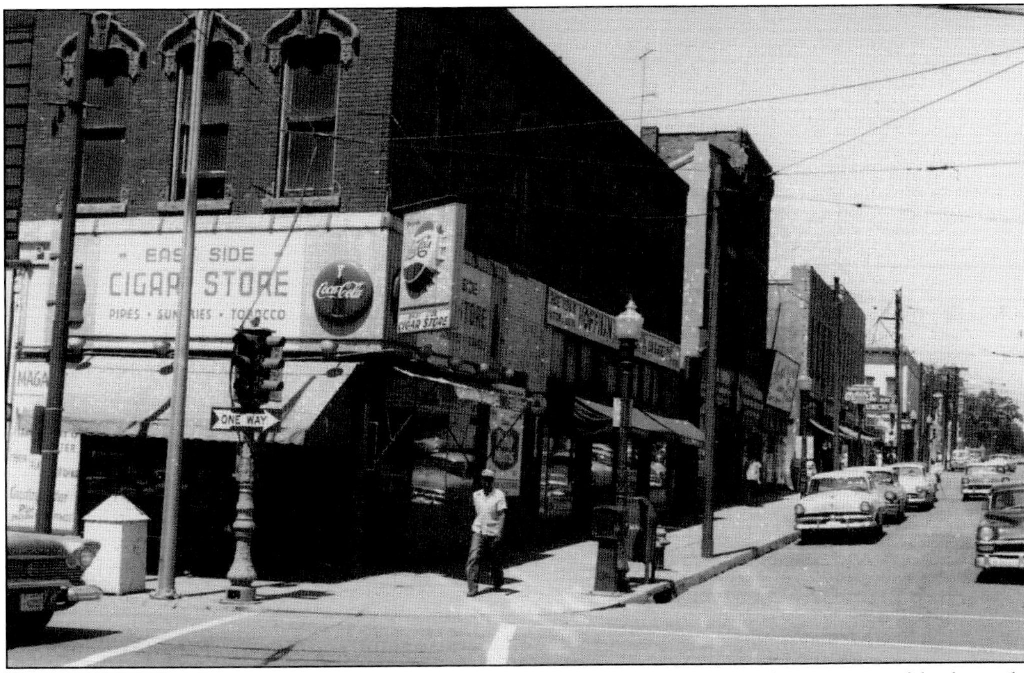

The East Side Cigar Store was one of two on East Sixth Street; the other was one block to the north and on the opposite side of the street. In 1958, businesses on the west side of East Sixth Street included Acme Cleaners, Des Moines Market Meats, Bolton and Hay restaurant, and Jaquinta's Fruit Market and Grocery. (CDM.)

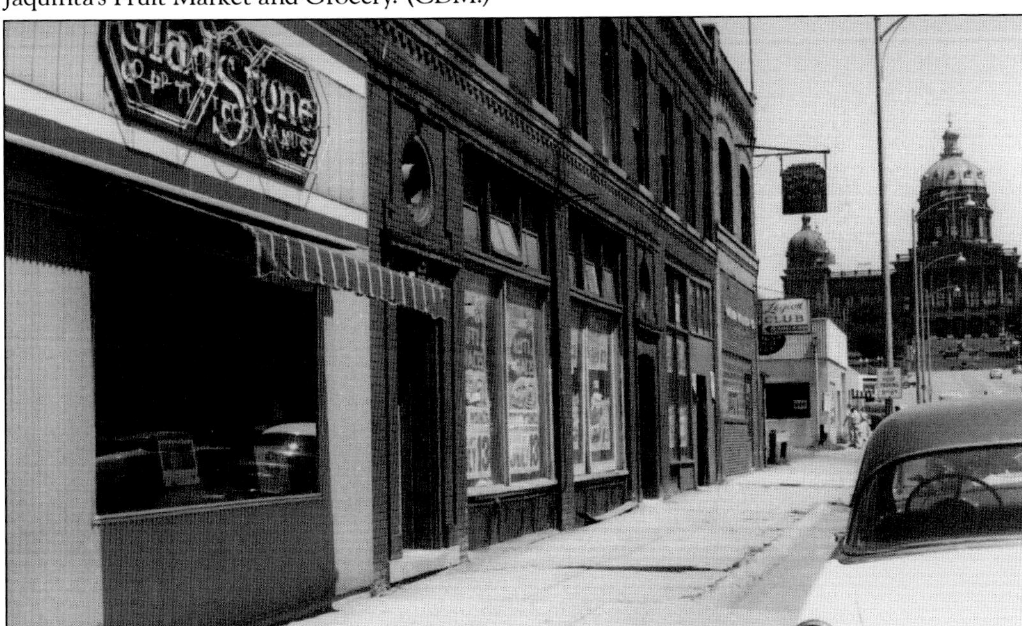

The 600 block of East Locust Street included Gladstone Opticians. W. F. Gladstone began his career as a traveling salesman for Geneva Opticals before opening his own business, which operated into the 1980s. Next to the Gladstone building was American Laundry Company; the posters in the windows next door advertise automobile races. (CDM.)

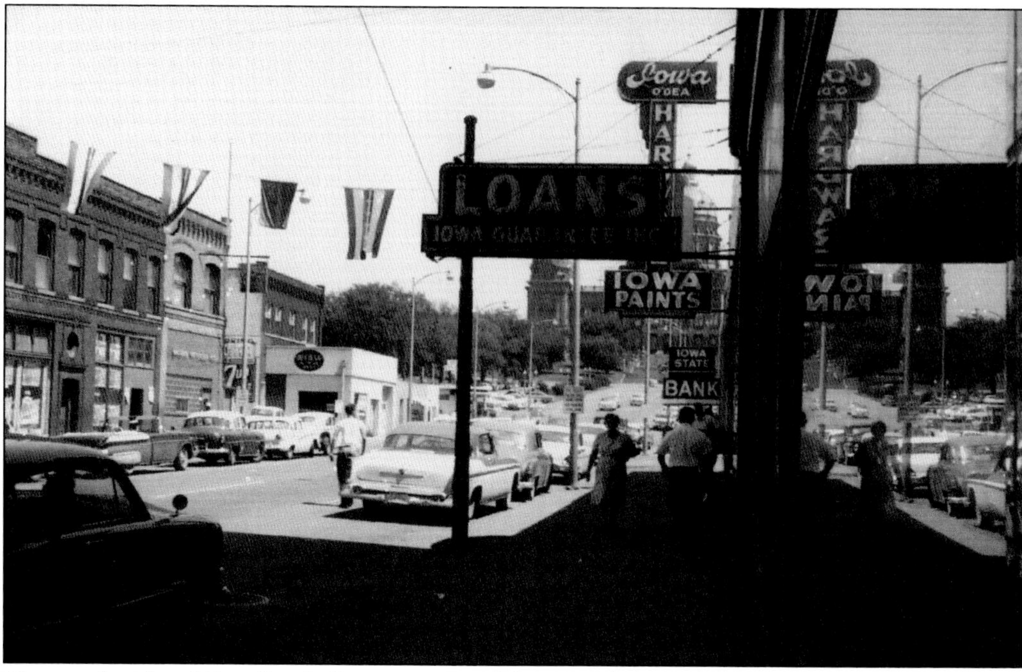

The south side of East Sixth Street is viewed here to the east. George O'Dea's stamp on the neighborhood is apparent with Iowa State Bank clearly situated in the background and O'Dea Hardware right in front. The flags hanging across the street indicate this photograph was taken around the Fourth of July in 1958. (CDM.)

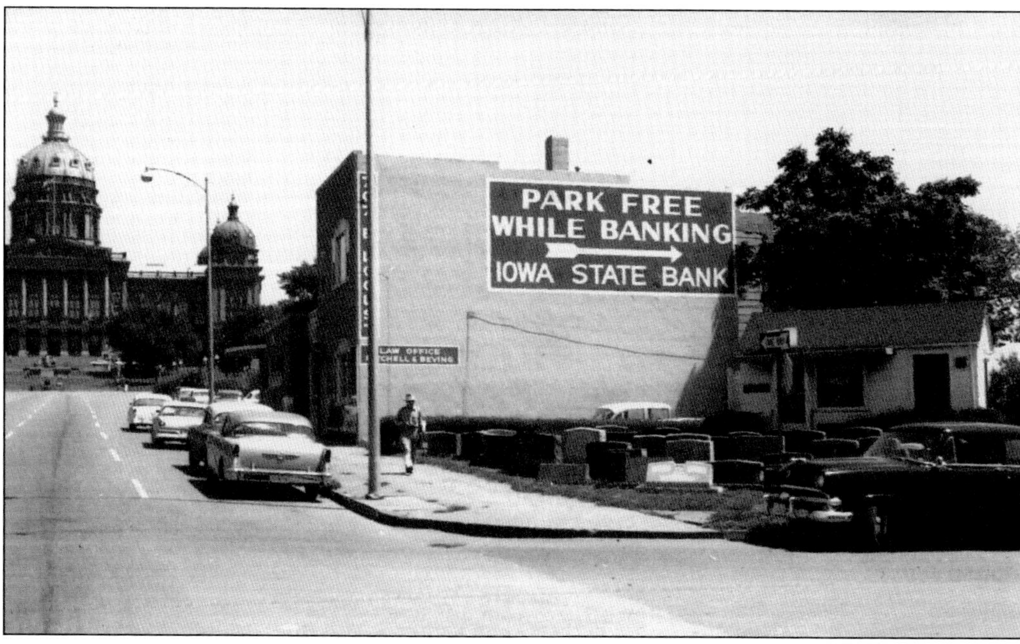

Capital City Monument Company occupied the southeast corner of the intersection at East Seventh and East Locust Streets at the time this photograph was taken in 1958. It is an interesting location, considering its proximity to the state capitol and also due to the fact that no cemeteries were in the immediate vicinity at this time. (CDM.)

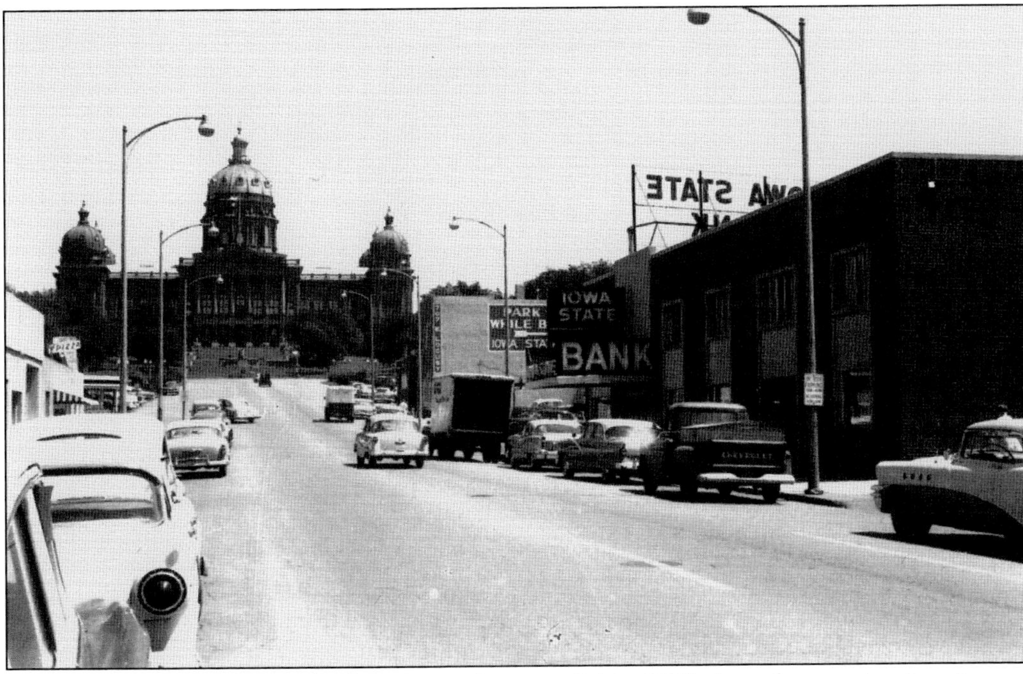

Iowa State Bank looks nearly the same today as it did in 1958, just after moving into its new location, shown here. Aside from expansion and modernization, the bank has been a fixture at this location, and its leaders were heavily involved in the redevelopment of the East Village from the late 1990s to today. (CDM.)

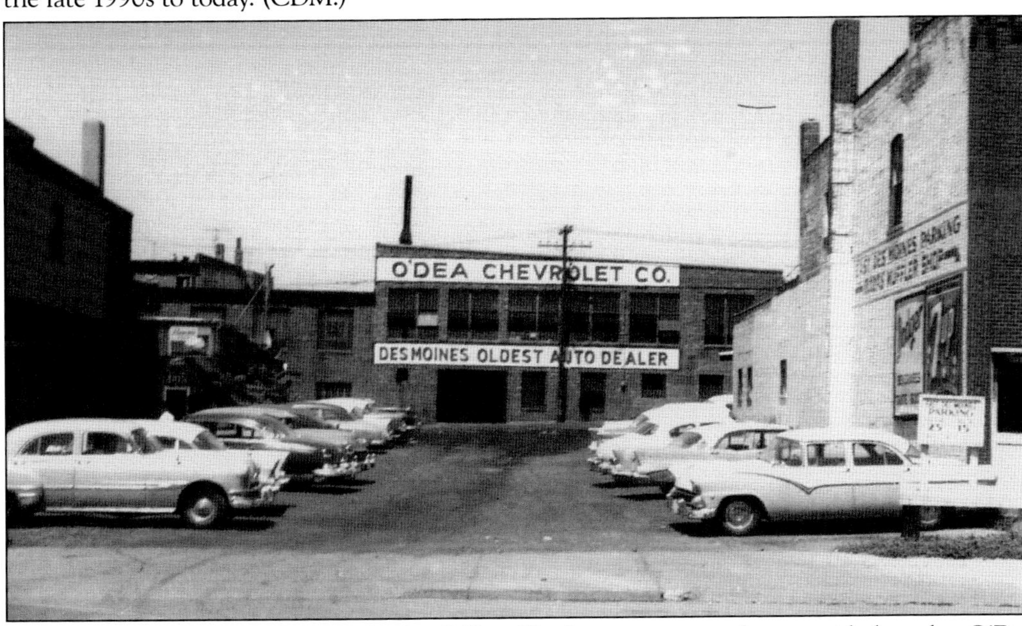

The O'Dea family owned not only the O'Dea Hardware store on the east side but also O'Dea Chevrolet car sales in the 600 block of East Grand Avenue. The O'Dea family was involved in east side business dating back to the mid-1880s and resided at 618 East Fifth Street. George O'Dea also founded Iowa State Bank in 1941, as well as the Capital City Broadcasting Company. He died in 1959. (CDM.)

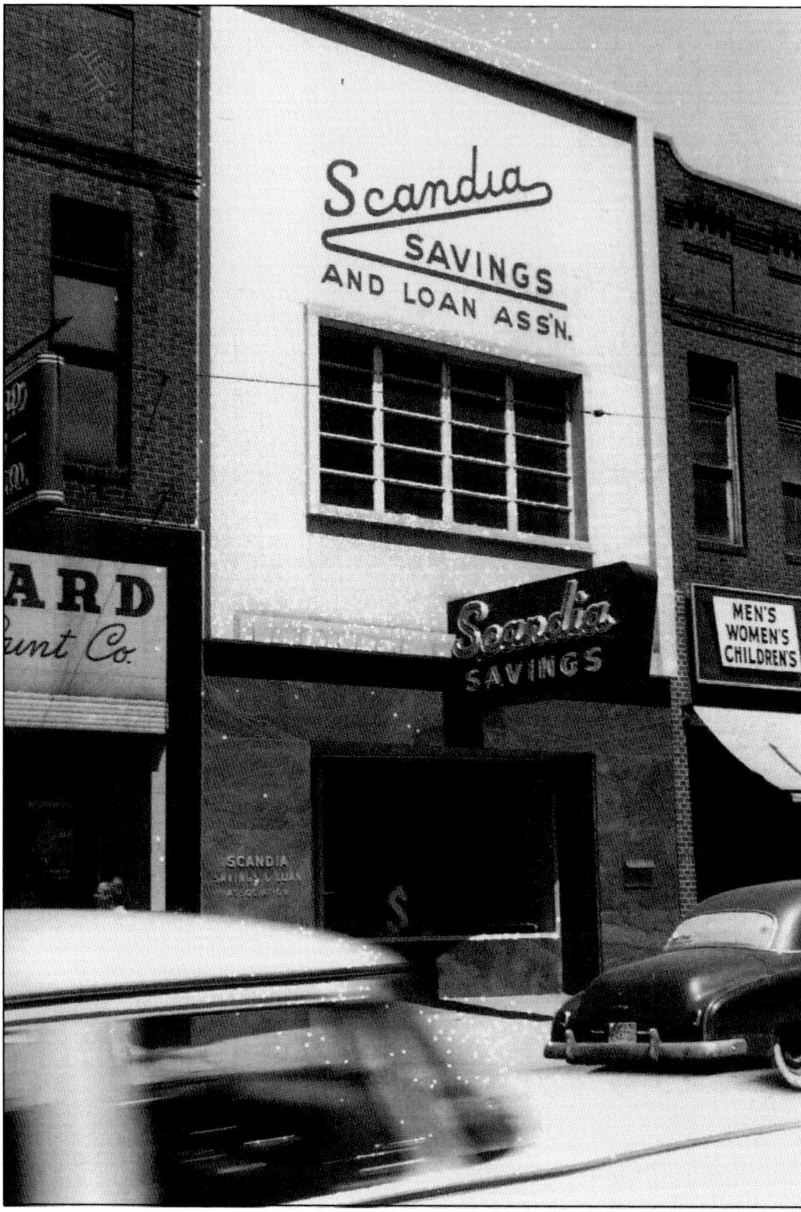

The Scandia Savings and Loan Association opened its doors on January 1, 1951, at this location at 518 East Locust Street, although its roots as a thrift institution go back to 1873. At that time, many banks and factories had closed, leading 21 young Swedish-speaking Scandinavians, all under 30 years old and living in east Des Moines, to form a mutual savings society. In 1973, the *Des Moines Register* reported on the Scandia Savings and Loan 100th anniversary: "From the old records, there are many interesting items, among them a description of the first safe. This was a wooden soap box, about 18 inches square and 12 inches deep. The corners were covered with strap iron and the lid was secured by means of hinges, hasp and padlock. All the valuable papers and small amounts of cash were kept intact in this crude wooden safe. To quote, from the minutes of the 50th anniversary meeting, 'The members surely had confidence in one another, and no fear of fire.'" (CDM.)

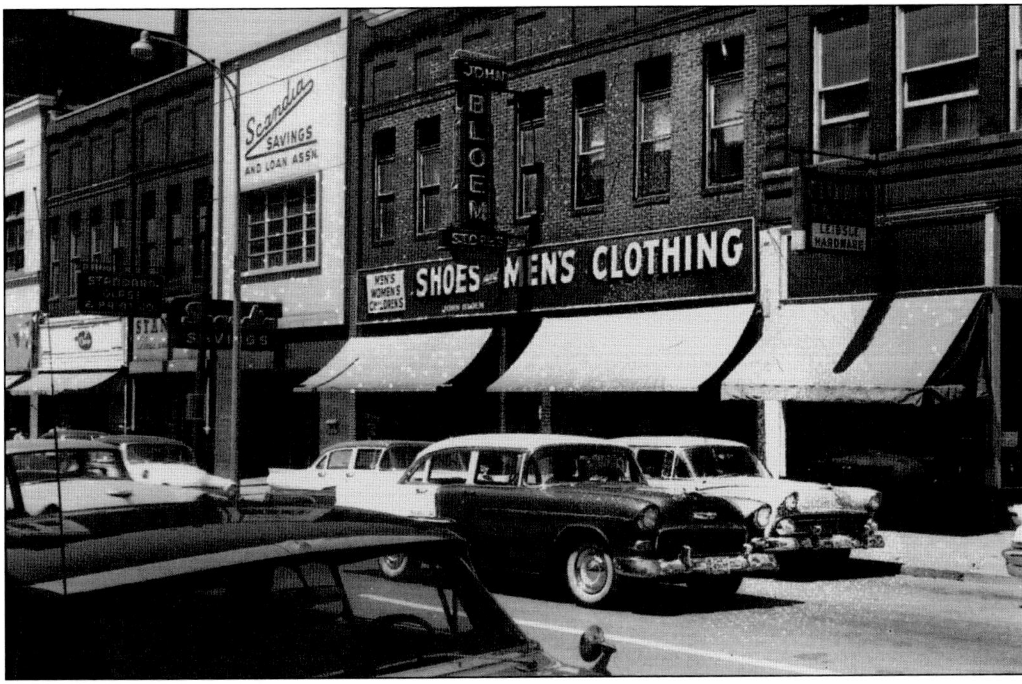

This 1958 photograph depicts the north side of a busy East Locust Street near East Sixth Street. Also shown are the Standard Glass and Paint Company, Scandia Savings and Loan Association, and Leibsle Hardware. Nearly every business has an awning hanging overhead, a subtle change that came as more stores tried to emulate the look of the popular shopping mall. (CDM.)

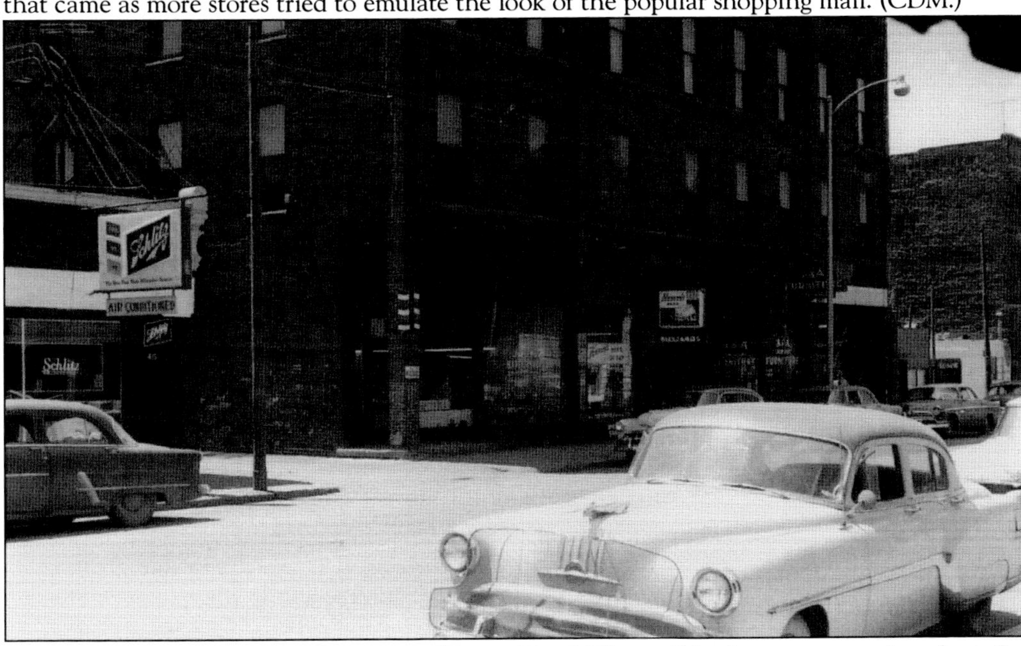

In 1910, the Columbian Hotel was one of five in East Village, all built to accommodate the influx of railway passengers from nearby depots. Located on East Locust Street between Fourth and Fifth Streets, the Columbian transformed into offices, apartments, and was even rumored to be a "house of ill repute" for a time. This block now houses the Blood Center of Iowa. (CDM.)

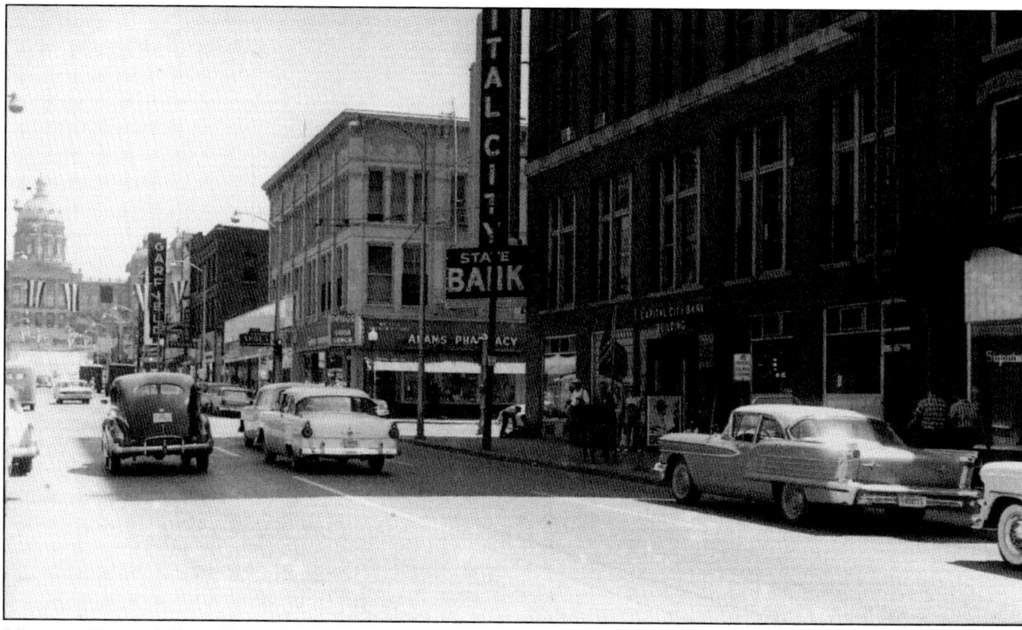

Here is Capital City State Bank around 1958. People standing alongside the building are waiting for the bus. The flag indicates a postbox, and a sign on the sidewalk states there is a military recruiting office inside the building. Capital City State Bank operated out of the first few floors of the seven-story building; the remaining floors included various offices, such as the East Des Moines Commercial Club. (CDM.)

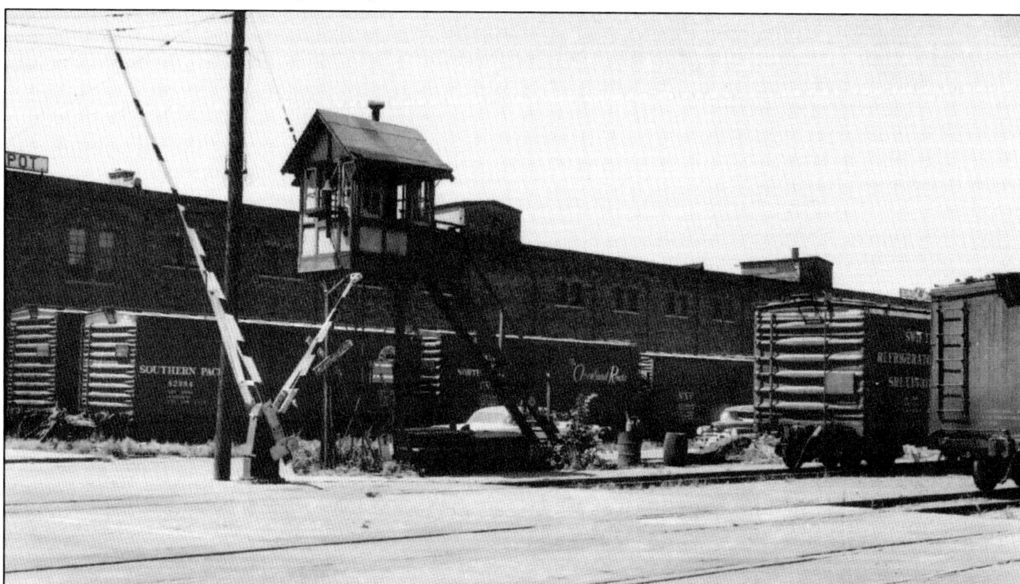

The Chicago and North Western Railway freight depot was located on East Fourth Street between East Locust Street and East Grand Avenue. Built in 1900, it served industry in the area, mainly the large lumber companies next door—Jewett and Queal, but it served also grain companies and John Deere tractors and equipment. The tower is a watchman's shanty in which the operator controlled the manual crossing gates to protect street traffic from train movements. The shanty had a coal-burning stove inside for winter months. (CDM.)

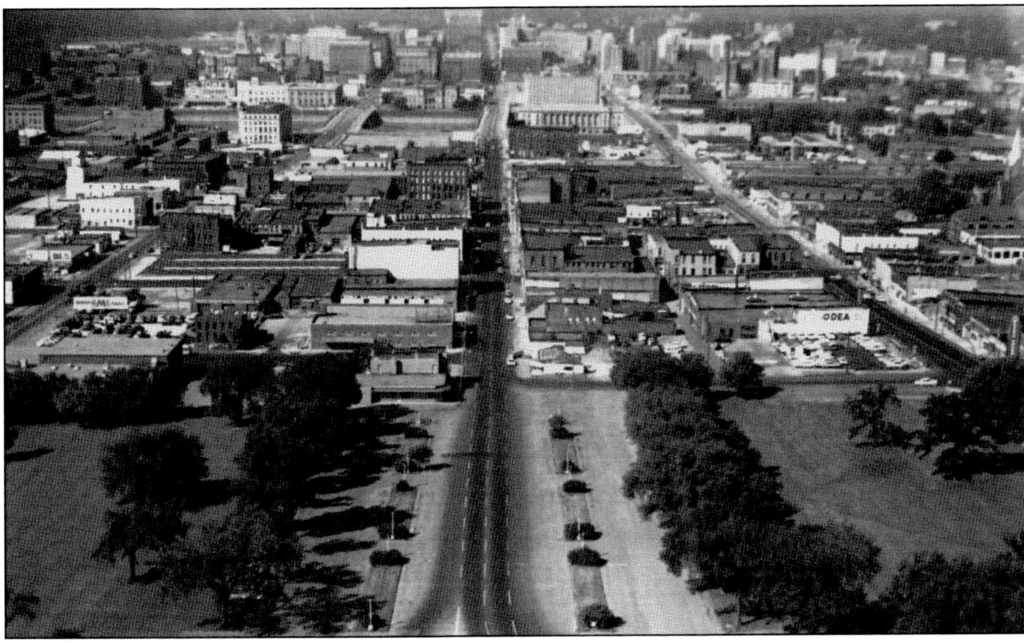

The photographer of this picture must have been standing at the very top of the state capitol dome to get a wide, bird's-eye view of the east side. At the time, East Locust Street extended all the way to the capitol as a one-way street. That later changed as the capitol required more parking for legislators and state workers. (ISB.)

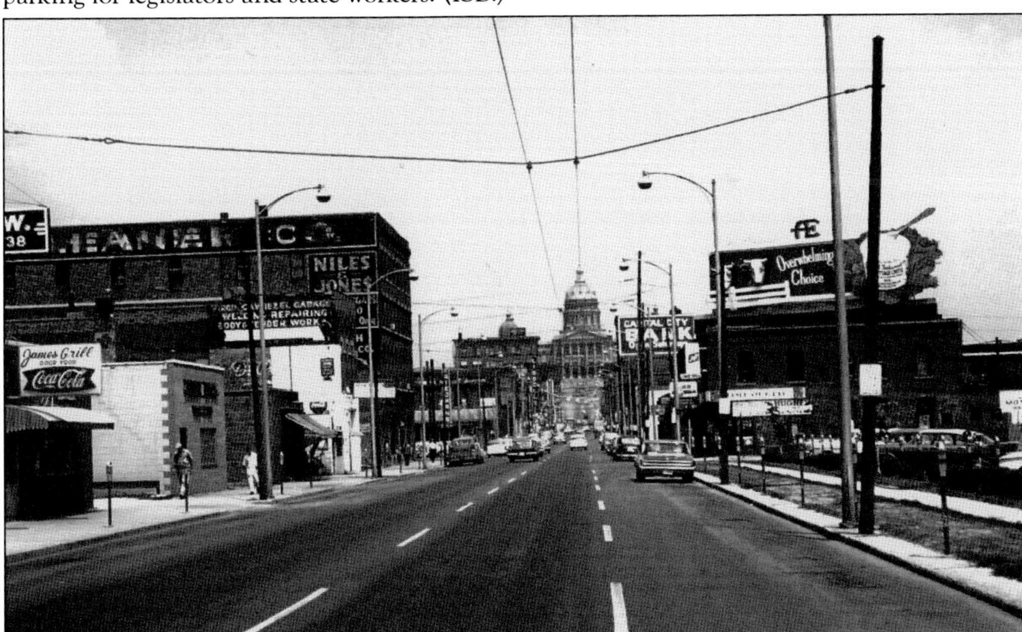

The neighborhood entered a new phase in the early 1960s, as malls became popular and convenient, and mom-and-pop operations became nearly obsolete. The grandiose Waterbury Chemical Company building on the left was occupied by a cleaning company at this time. Note the wires over the street to service the curb liners, which did not end their run in Des Moines until 1964. (CDM.)

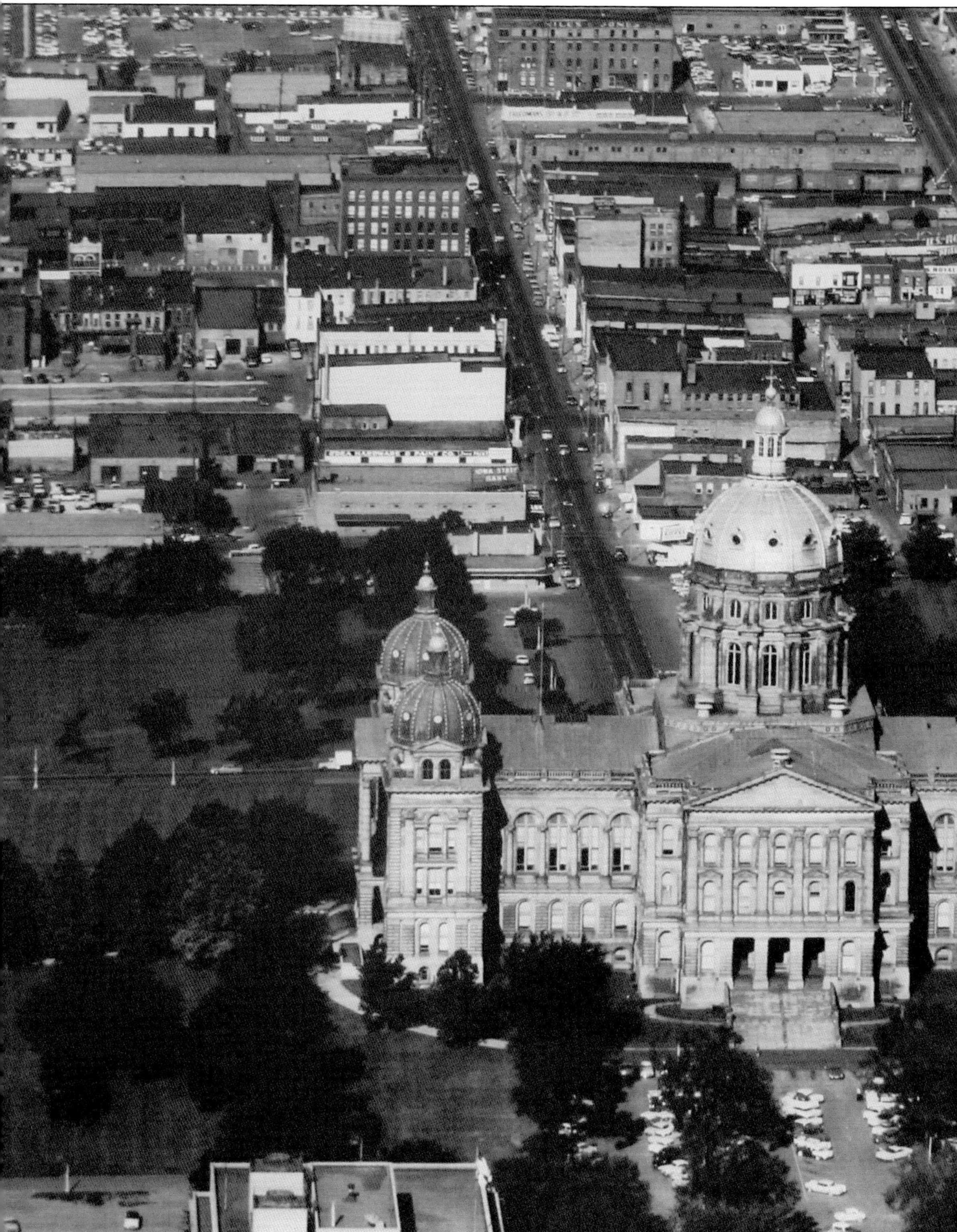

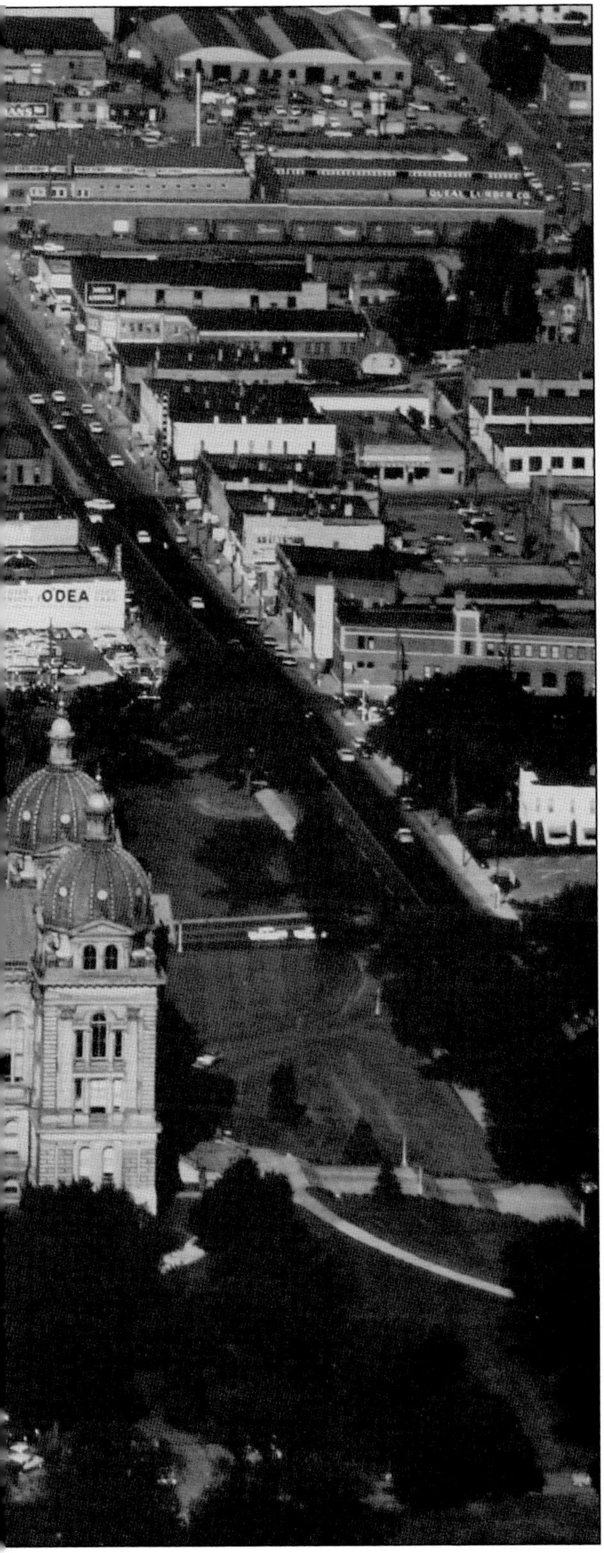

Topographically, the Iowa State Capitol sits high on a hill overlooking Des Moines, which is just how its planners intended. This is a great view of the capitol and its relation to the neighborhood around it about 1960. Capital City State Bank, Iowa State Bank, O'Dea Hardware, and O'Dea Chevrolet all appear in the photograph. The Waterbury Chemical Company building is still there and had the name Niles and Jones painted across the top. Parking was becoming an issue in the neighborhood, and it is apparent here that the few lots available were not enough to accommodate the cars. A few years after this photograph was taken, the state began buying up more land around the capitol so that it could construct more state office buildings. (SHSI.)

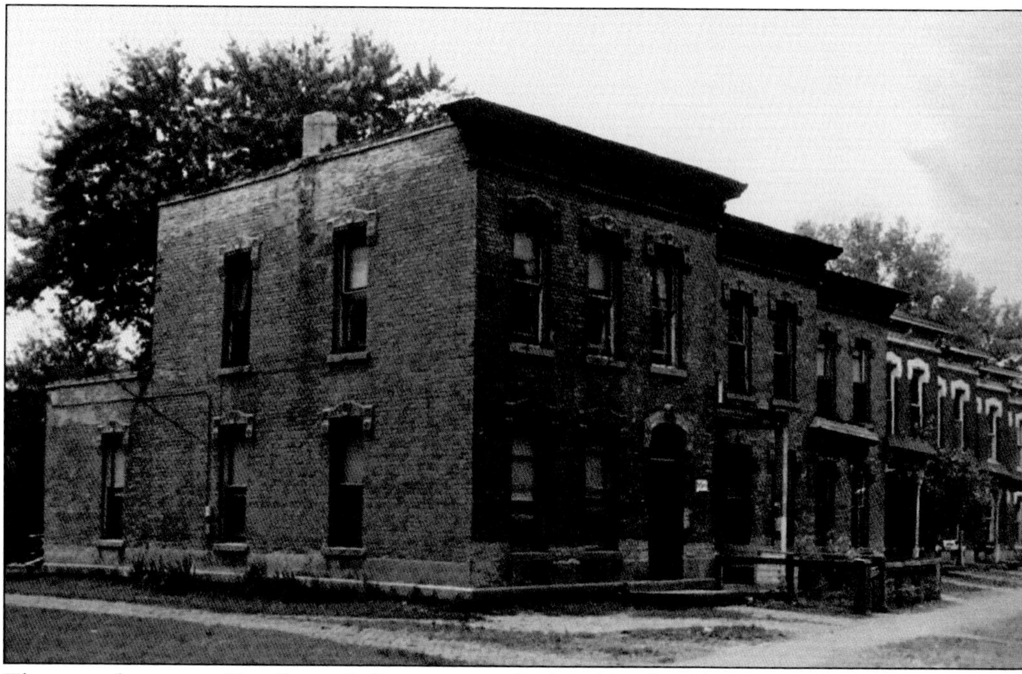

These row houses on East Seventh Street were scheduled for demolition for the River Hills Urban Renewal Project in 1963. Some 256 families were displaced as part of the project, and many of them were minority or low income. Residents complained that city officials were indifferent to the plight of the groups affected by the project and the new freeway. (SHSI.)

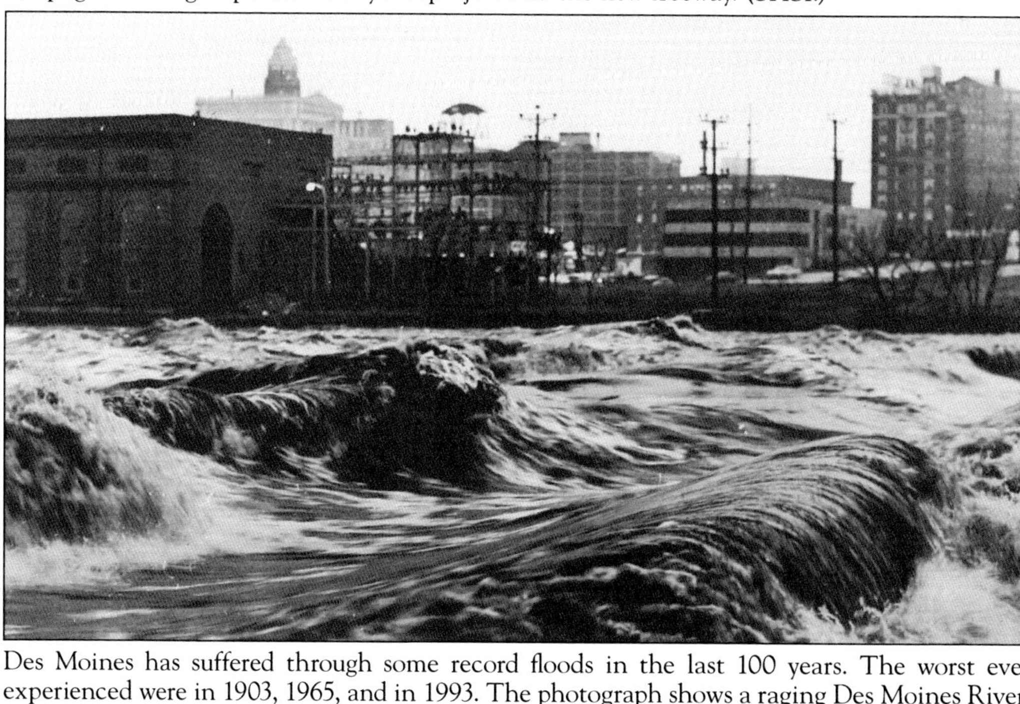

Des Moines has suffered through some record floods in the last 100 years. The worst ever experienced were in 1903, 1965, and in 1993. The photograph shows a raging Des Moines River, as is flowed through downtown on April 12, 1965. It was taken by a member of the 234th Signal Battalion Corps Iowa army. (DMPL.)

The Capital City State Bank building was constructed in 1902, and the *Des Moines Tribune* reported, "The erection of the seven-story brick building by the Capital City State Bank, at the corner of Fifth and Locust streets, has firmly anchored the center of business in East Des Moines." The bank also offered Des Moines's first drive-up teller. The building was demolished in 1981. (Kirk Blunck.)

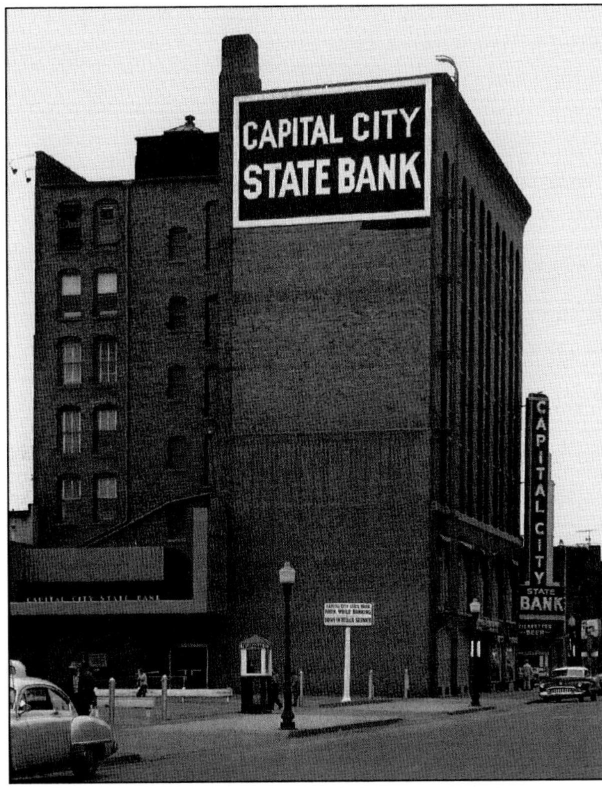

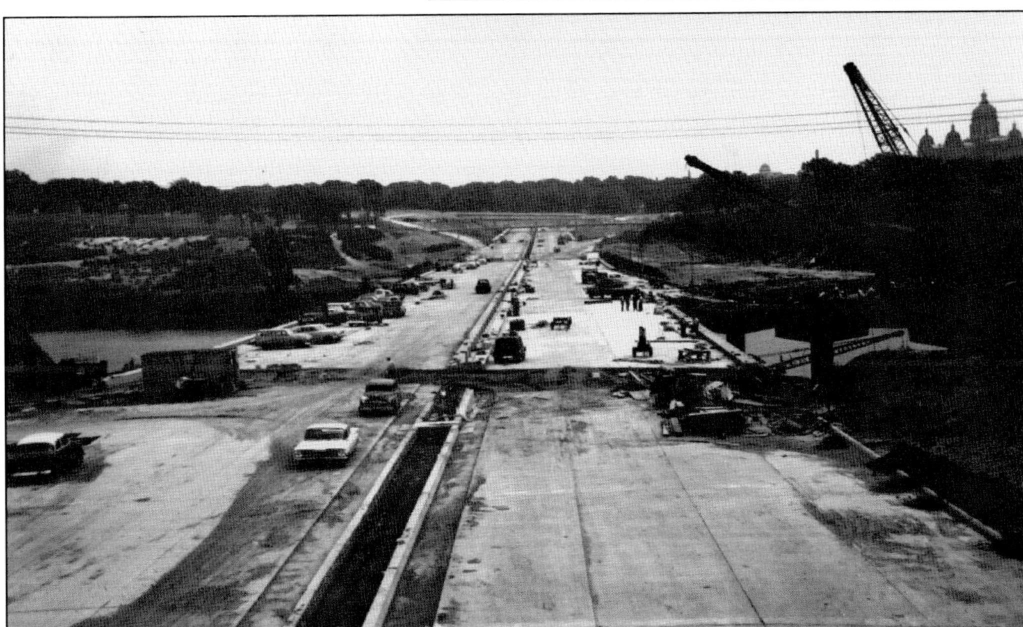

This September 16, 1963, photograph shows the MacVicar Freeway, or Interstate 235, under construction looking east from the Second Avenue bridge. It was Iowa's first urban freeway project and was built between 1961 and 1968 at a cost of $57 million. Many homes were relocated or torn down to make way for the massive construction project. (SHSI.)

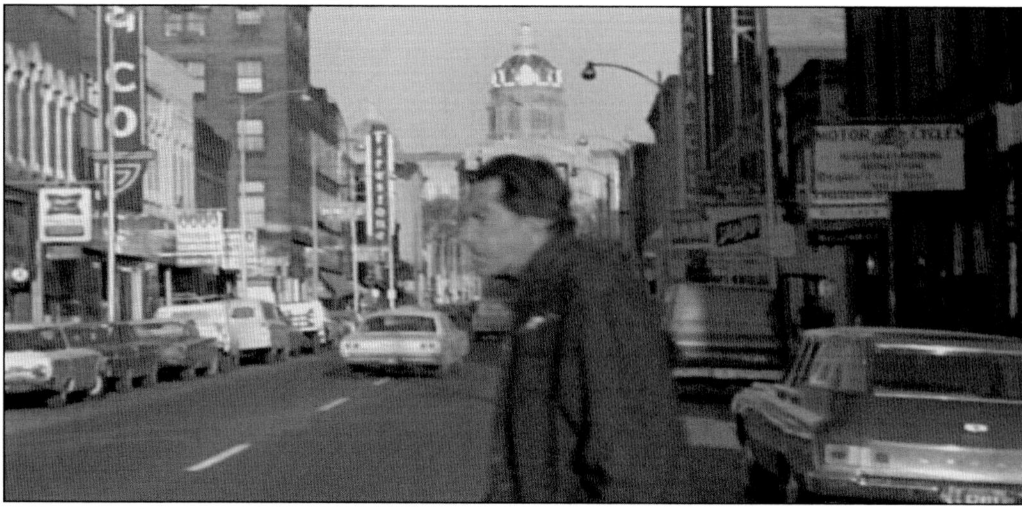

In 1966, production began in Des Moines for the film *The Hostage*, starring Harry Dean Stanton, in an early role, and John Carradine, pictured here. Carradine's character Otis P. Lovelace was a vagrant suspected of kidnapping a boy. Apparent in this image, captured from the film, is the impression of East Village as the "bad" side of town, where vagrants were often found. The film was the first ever to use Des Moines as its setting. (Crown International Pictures.)

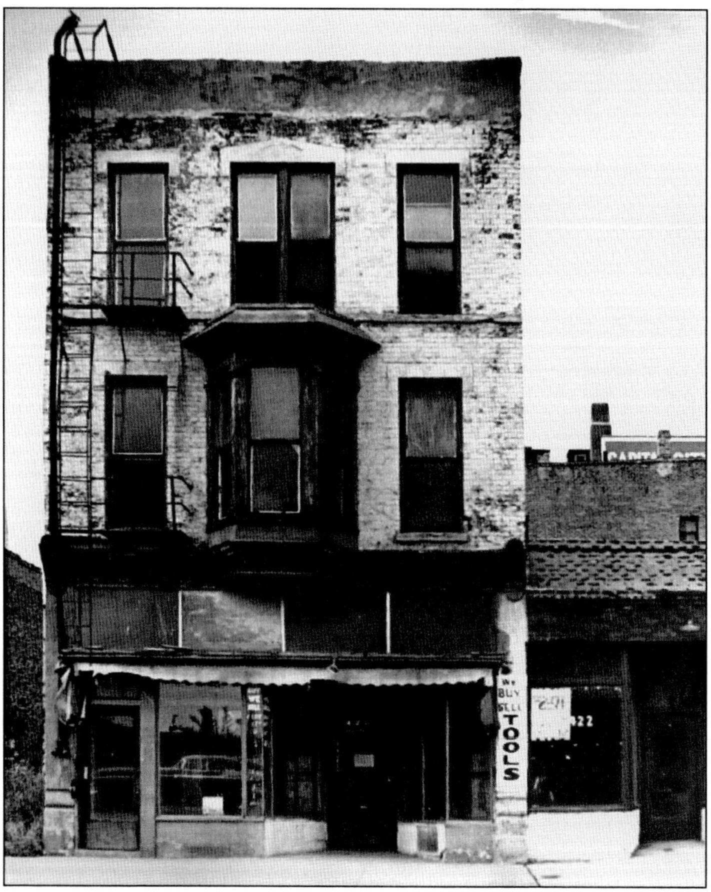

Dr. T. K. Brooks came to Des Moines in 1845 and built the first brick house on the east side at 420 East Walnut Street sometime between 1891 and 1901. This photograph was taken in 1967, shortly before the building was condemned and razed. If Brooks had had his way, Des Moines, or at least its east side, would be known as Brooklyn. (SHSI.)

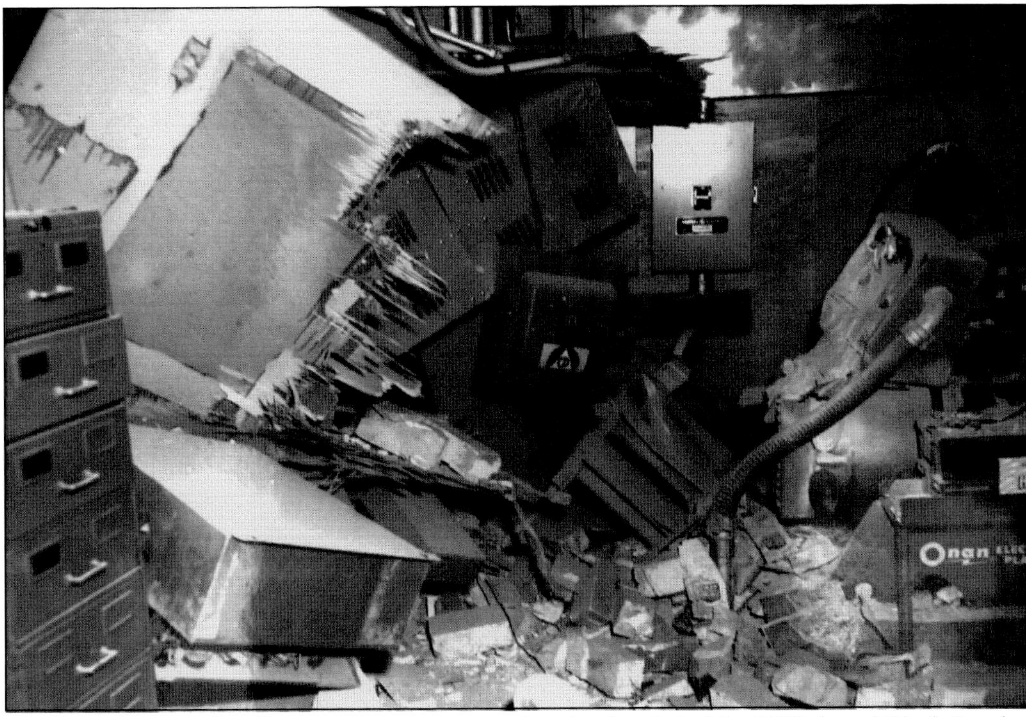

The Des Moines Police Department was targeted with a bomb in May 1970. Local Black Panther activists were suspected of the crime, but it was never proven. The blast ripped a hole in the building's foundation and destroyed about a dozen vehicles parked immediately outside. Only one person suffered minor injuries. (SHSI.)

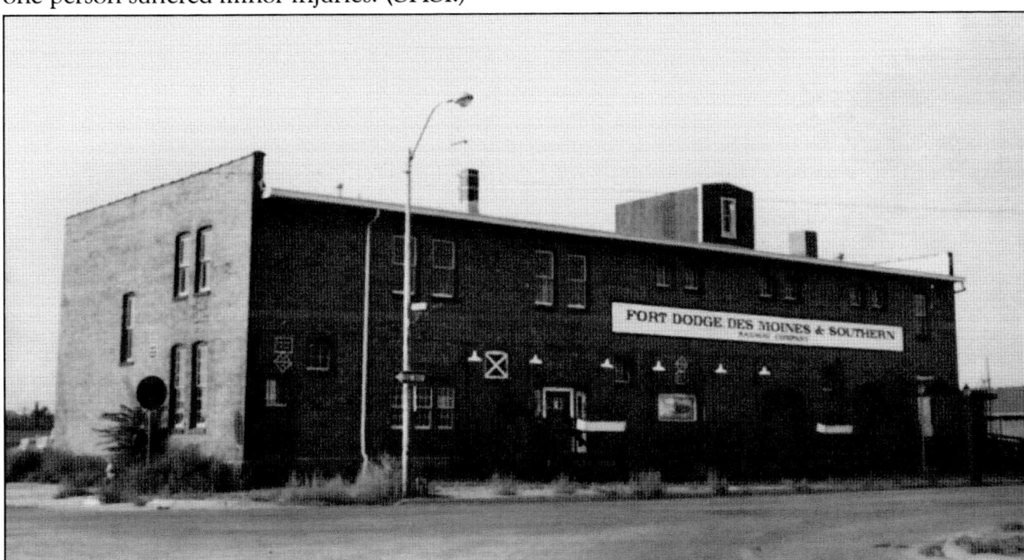

Built in 1903, the Des Moines Western Railway freight house is significant for its contribution to the growth of the city. It was built by local businessman F. M. Hubbell to help expedite the process of receiving goods into the city via rail. From the 1930s through the 1950s, it served as a passenger depot. After that, it housed a series of restaurants and is currently the home of the Iowa Bar Association. This photograph shows the building in 1970. (SHSI.)

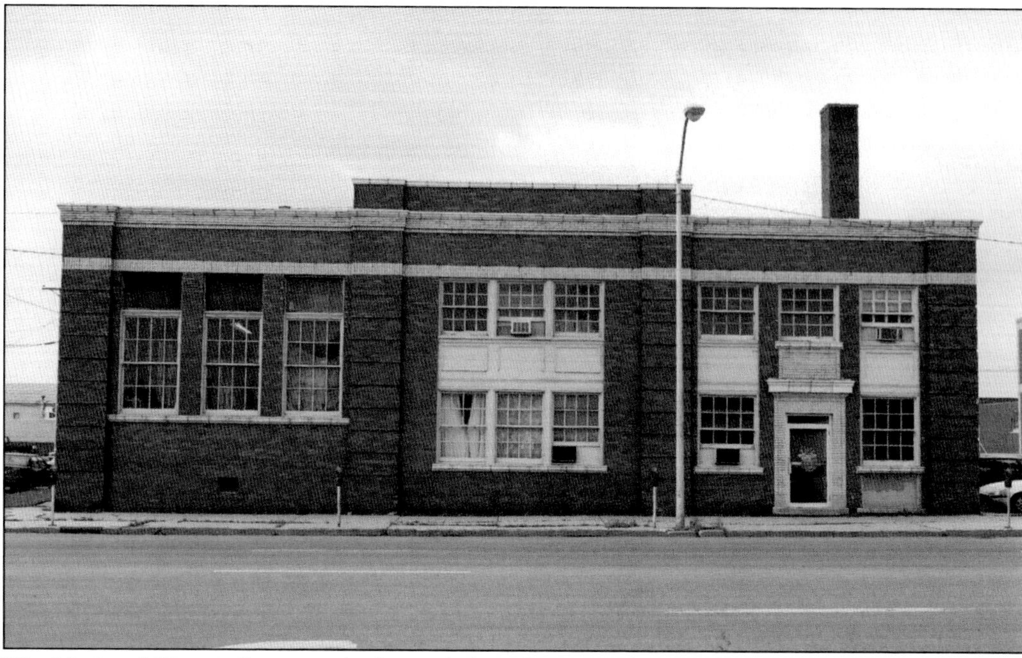

The National Biscuit Company had grand plans for expanding its Des Moines factory operation, so it built this as a second production site on East Court Avenue in 1920. Changes within the company and a delayed timeline eventually left the building to serve as a warehouse and garage, but it was never involved in production. Today it is owned by the Salvation Army. (CDM.)

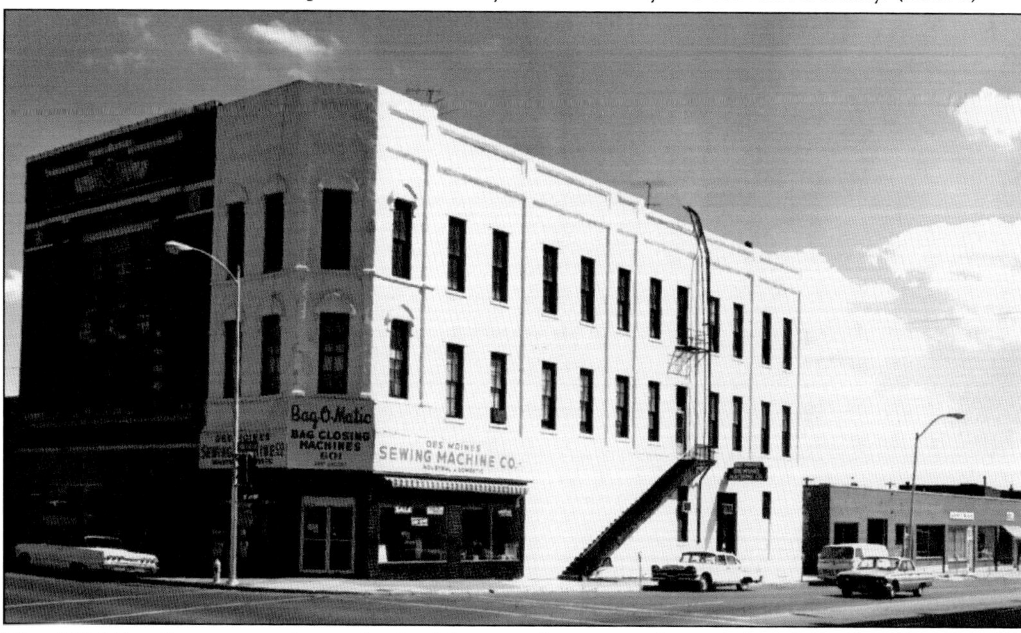

The 1906 Sandborn map shows the building on the corner here as having a drugstore on the street level. What is interesting is that it also lists two other drugstores on the same corner at East Sixth and East Locust Streets. This photograph was taken in 1971, when it was used by the Des Moines Sewing Machine Company. The adjacent building to the east is the Masonic temple. (ISB.)

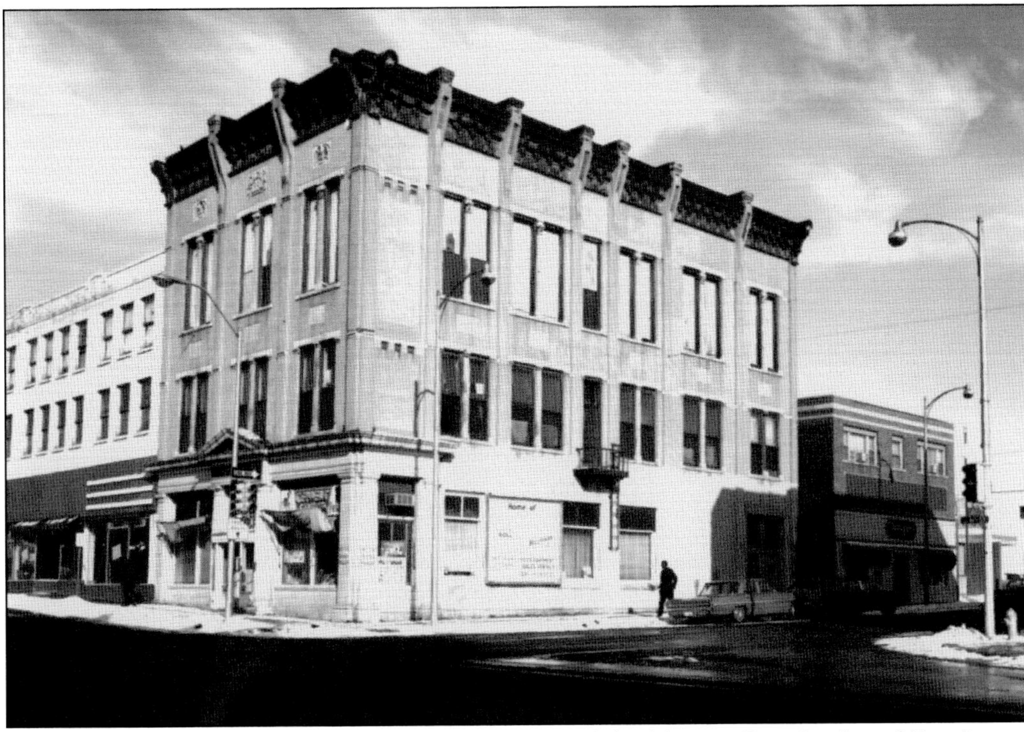

This 1971 photograph of the original Iowa State Bank building at East Sixth and East Locust Streets housed Geppert Studio at this time. The sign in the window reads, "Black & White Roll 8 for 60¢, 25 billfolds $1.00." The building was torn down to make way for the State Historical Building in 1985. (ISB.)

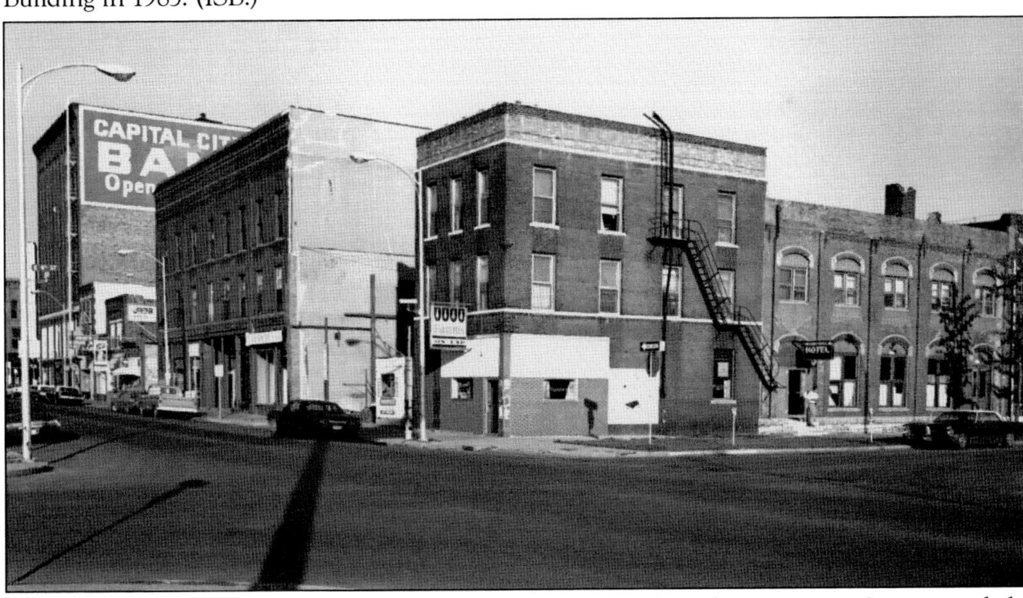

The Nelson Hotel, shown here at the corner of East Fourth and East Locust Streets, and the Columbian Hotel just up the block were built to accommodate railway passengers. However, when this photograph was taken in 1971, both establishments had quite the reputation as "houses of ill repute." This entire block was torn down in the 1980s for a new bank. (ISB.)

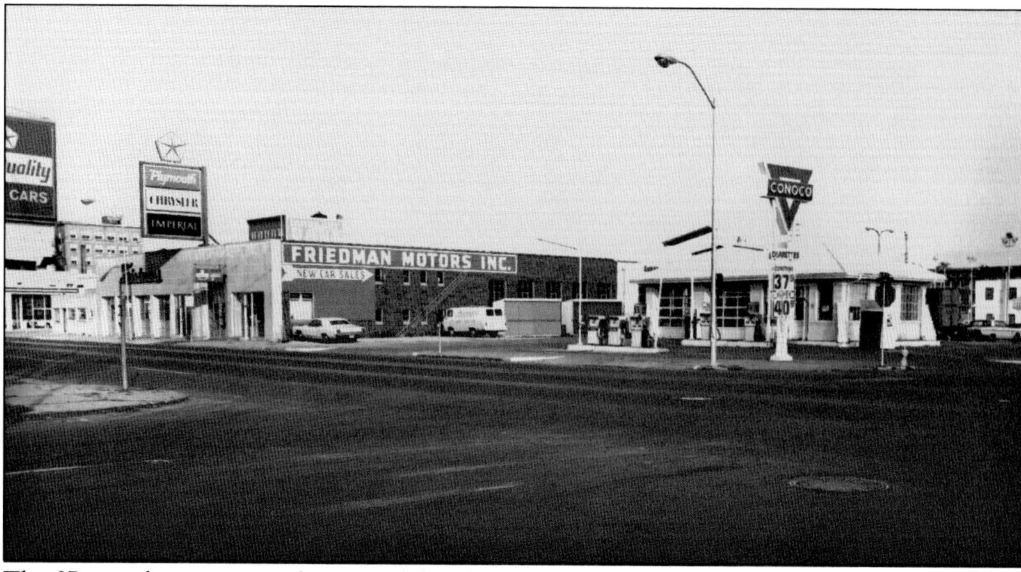

The 37¢ gasoline price on the sign of this Conoco station at 203 East Grand Avenue indicates the photograph was taken prior to the gasoline crisis that began in 1973. The station was erected in 1933 for Continental Oil. Friedman Motors had expanded its operation and its real estate by the time this photograph was taken around 1971. (ISB.)

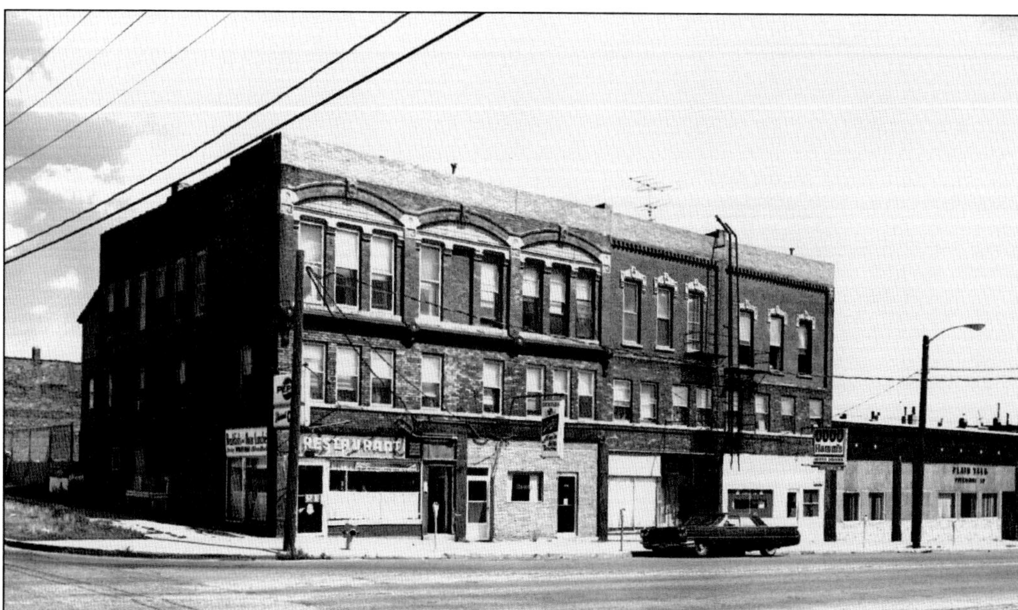

This building stood at the corner of East Sixth and Des Moines Streets, and at the time the photograph was taken around 1971, it housed Jim's 606 Tavern and Visions Café on the street level with housing above. Note the sign on the north side of the building advertising "Breakfasts and Noon Lunches . . . serving Wonder Bread." The Wonder Bread/Hostess baking and distribution center was just up the block. (ISB.)

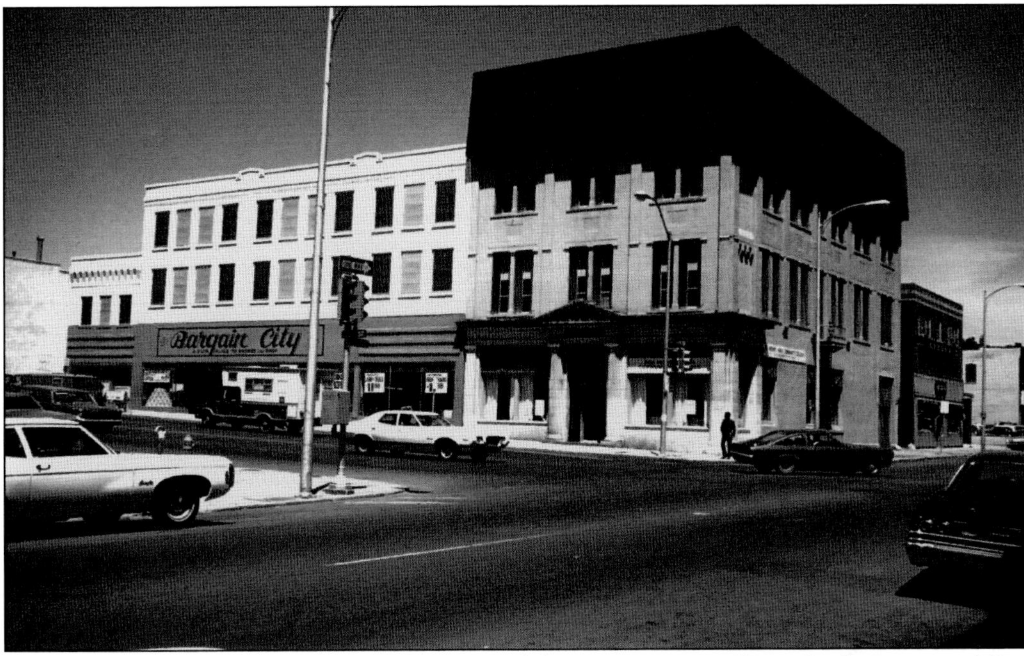

This photograph shows the northeast corner of the intersection of East Sixth Street and East Locust Street. The building in the foreground was erected in 1950 to serve as the first home of Iowa State Bank. In the late 1950s, the bank moved to the corner of East Seventh and Locust Streets, leaving this building open for various offices, including classes for the Des Moines Area Community College. (CDM.)

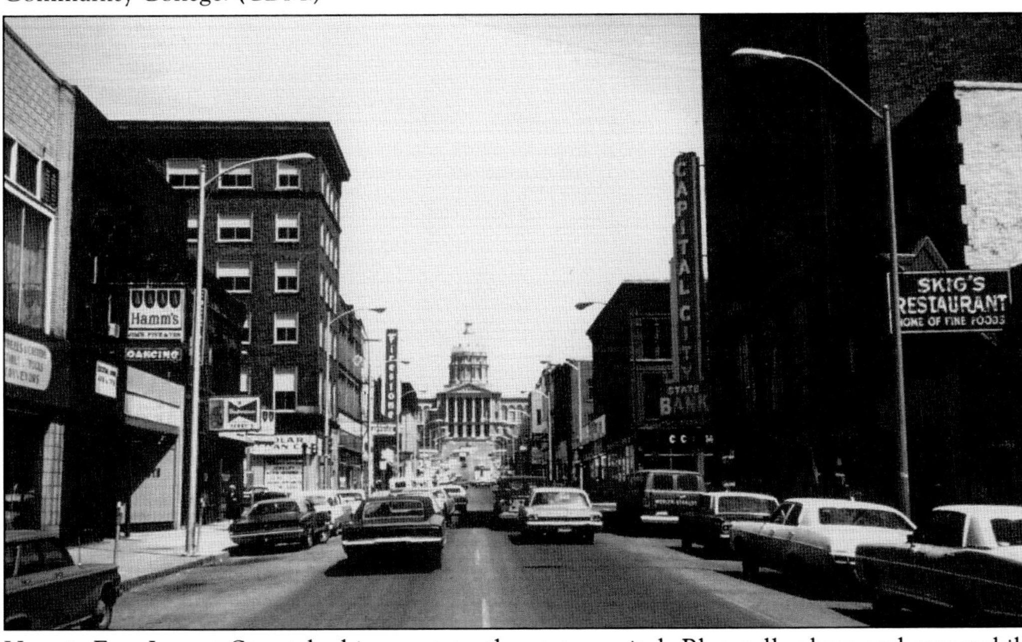

Here is East Locust Street looking east to the state capitol. Blue-collar bars and automobile repair and parts shops had already started sprinkling in when this photograph was taken about 1973. Despite Skig's Restaurant: Home of Fine Foods, the transition of the neighborhood during this period is apparent. (CDM.)

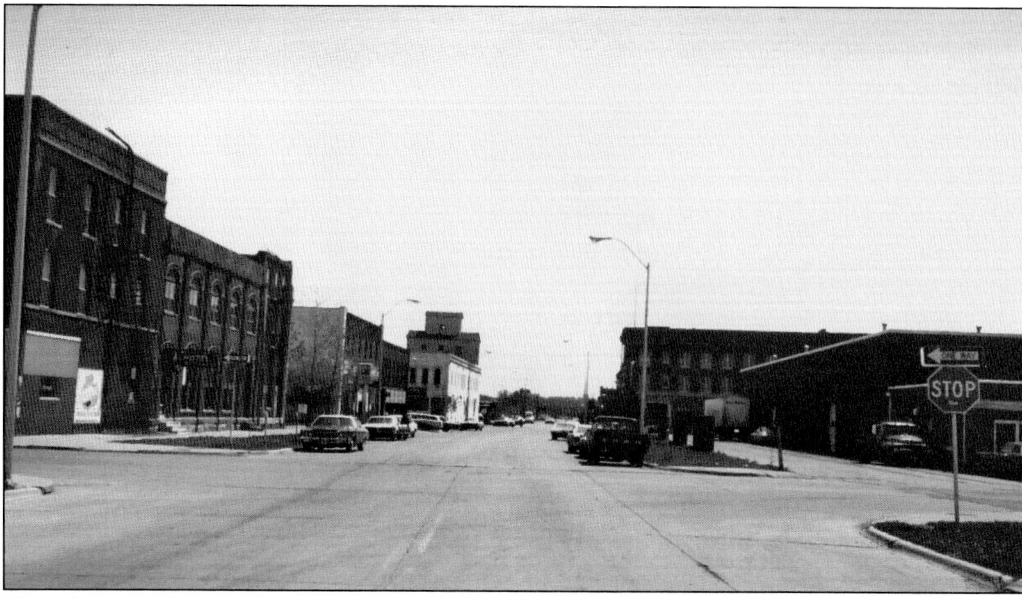

This photograph was taken on East Fourth Street just north of East Locust Street looking south. The building in the left foreground is the former Nelson Hotel, established to service passengers of the Chicago and North Western Railway line that ran the length of Fourth Street. (The passenger depot sat between Locust and Walnut Streets; the freight depot sat between Grand Avenue and Locust Street on East Fourth Street.) In the background is the tower for the Sargent Feed Mill Complex. (CDM.)

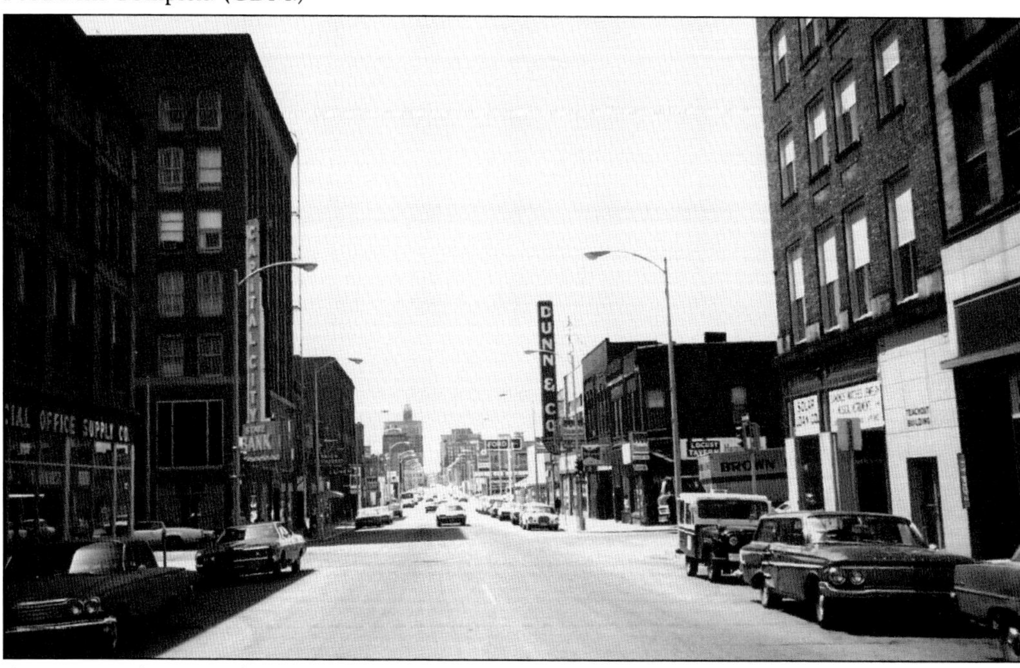

A view to the west down East Locust Street reveals a more commercialized neighborhood with less retail. Small taverns and restaurants are still here, but the area has already started its transition. The McCoy building on the left houses Commercial Office Supply Company on the first floor. Dunn and Company down the block sells wheels and casters. (CDM.)

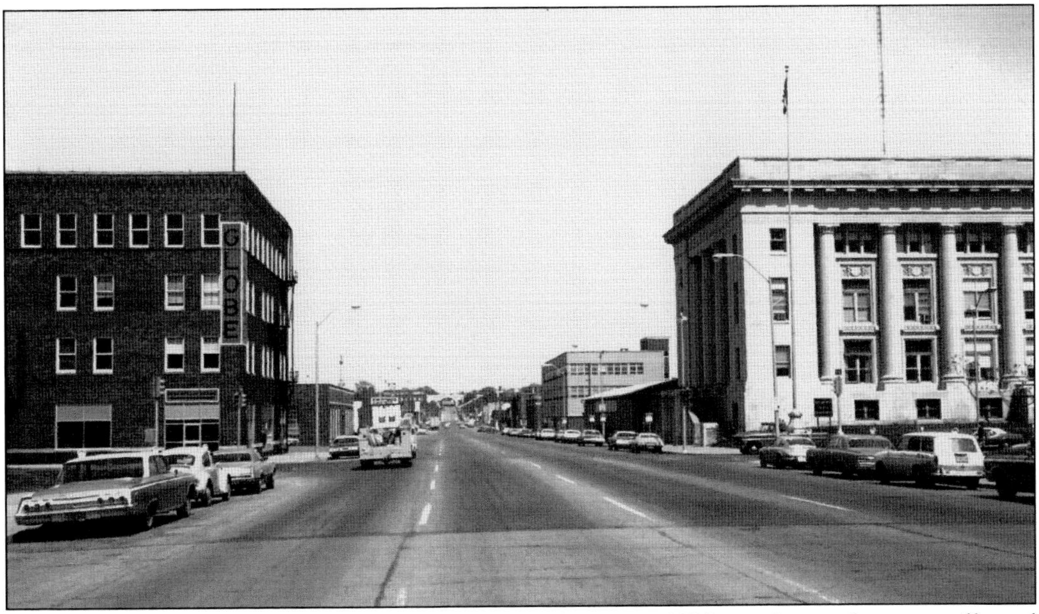

The Globe Machinery Company began in Des Moines in 1893, producing factory, mill, and mining supplies and equipment. This photograph shows the Globe manufacturing plant at East First Street and East Court Avenue. The building was demolished in 1996 to accommodate expansion of the federal courthouse. The company is known today as SVI, Inc., and continues to supply parts to its original hoists, some of which continue in service. (CDM.)

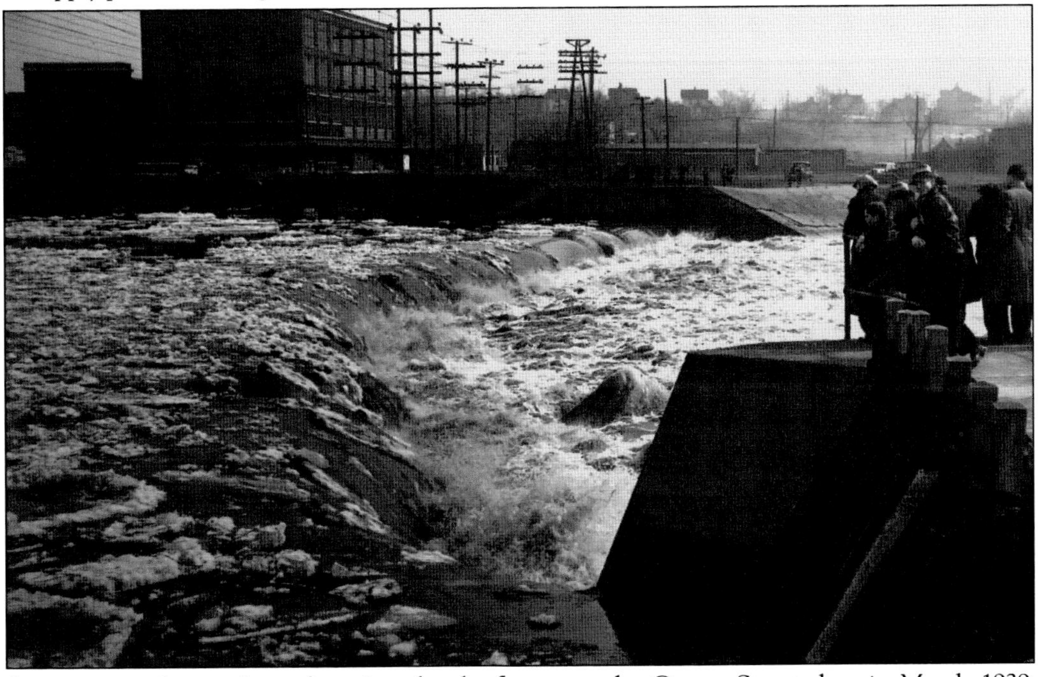

Spectators gather and watch as ice chunks flow over the Center Street dam in March 1939. A rapid spring thaw broke up ice jams to the north, and the Des Moines River swelled. The Des Moines branch of Swift and Company meatpacking can be seen on the west side of the river. (SHSI.)

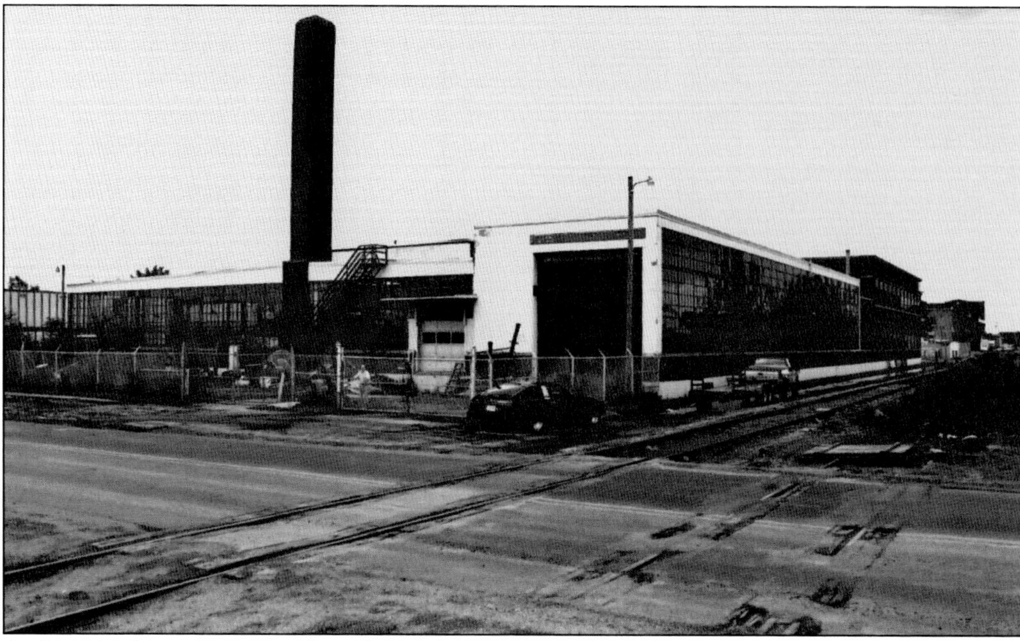

A throwback to the east side industrial era, many of the factories remain standing but long abandoned or are in transition today. This building, just south of Court Avenue on Southeast Sixth Street, was completely remodeled in 2006 and now houses Two Rivers Marketing. This area, becoming known as Lower East Village, is targeted for aesthetic improvements and commercial and residential development. (CDM.)

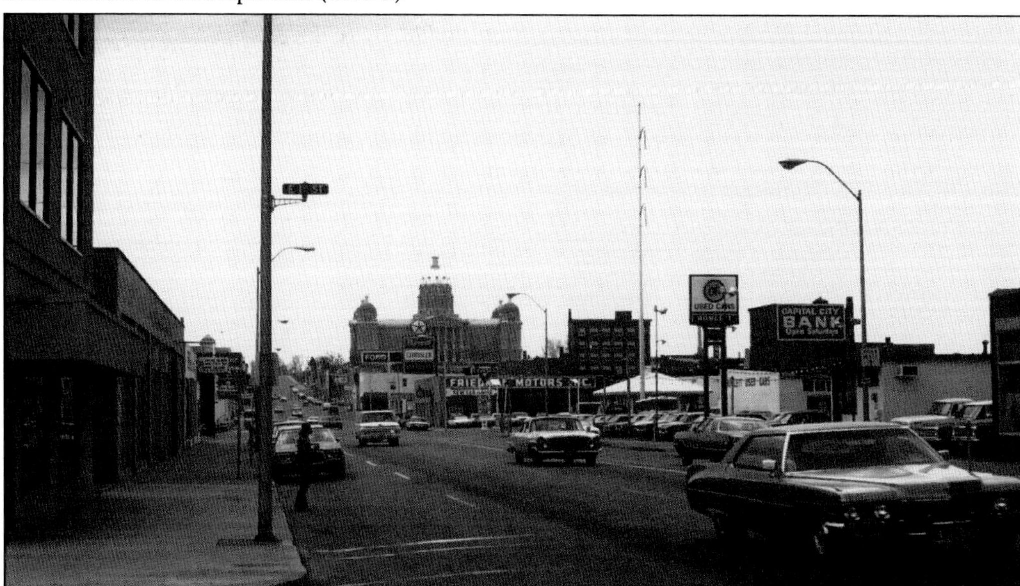

Taken around 1978, this photograph looks east down East Grand Avenue, which is lined with car dealerships and service shops. Capital City State Bank and the Teachout building tower are in the middle right, with the state capitol looming in the background. The Conoco station boasts 39¢ gasoline. Here now, on the left-hand side, is a state parking lot. The photograph was taken from where Brenton Skating Plaza is now. (CDM.)

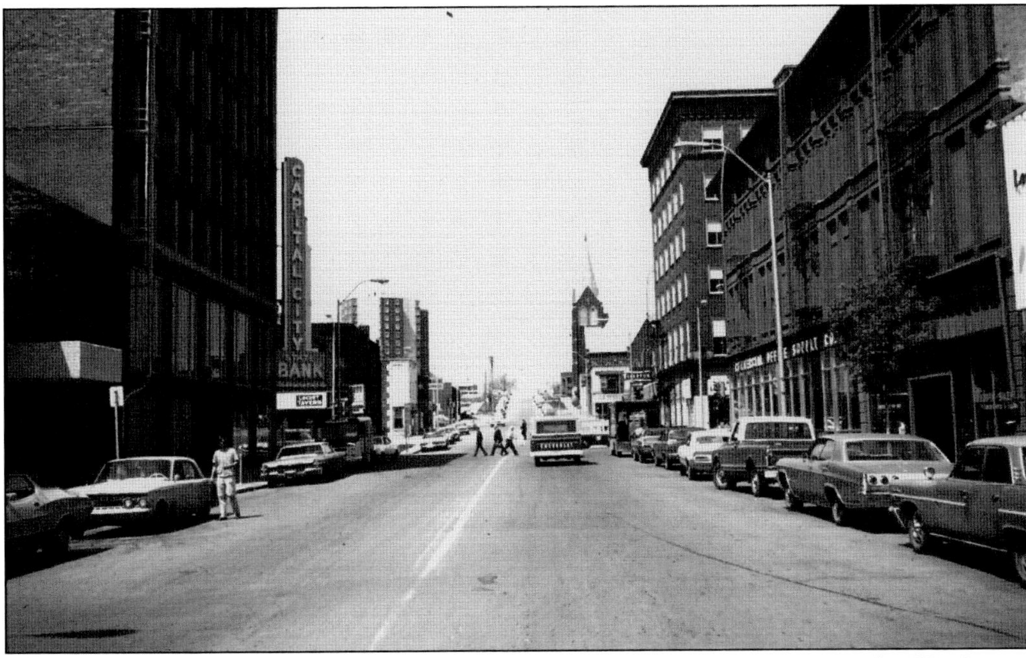

This is East Fifth Street looking north from just south of Locust Street around 1978. Capitol City State Bank is on the left, and Commercial Office Supply Company is on the right. In the back left is what, at that time, was the Horace Mann Home for the Aged, built in 1970. It is now Prime Towers and continues to be a residential living facility for retirees. (CDM.)

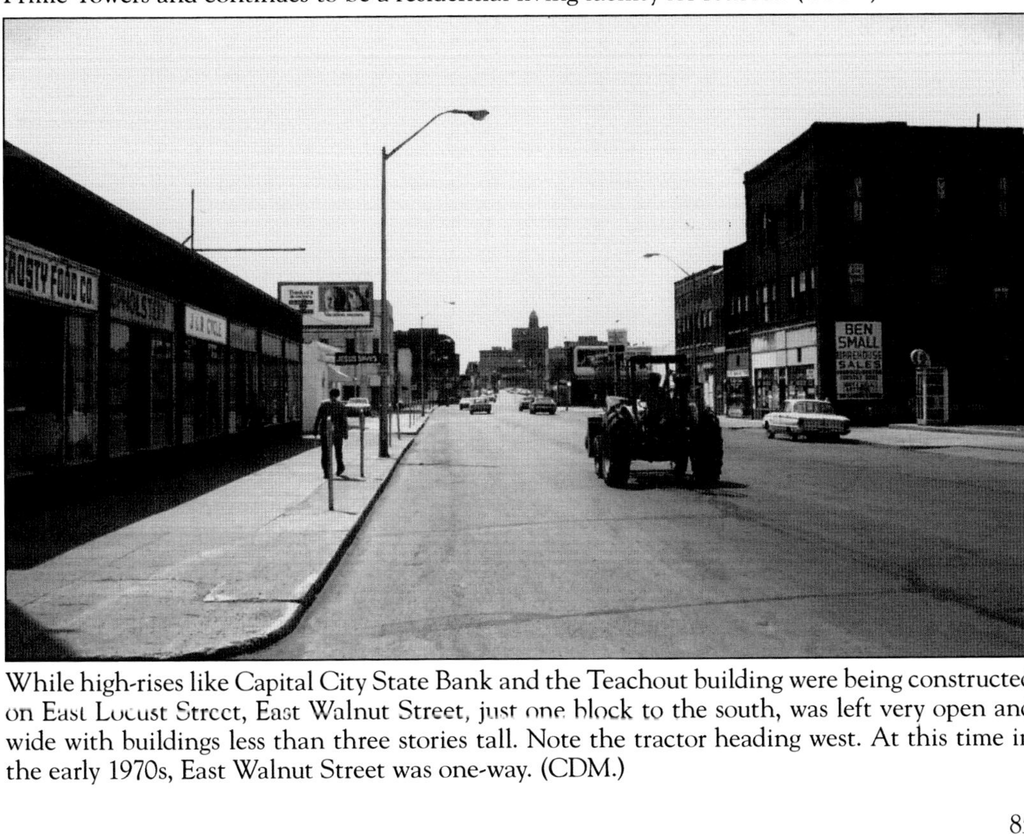

While high-rises like Capital City State Bank and the Teachout building were being constructed on East Locust Street, East Walnut Street, just one block to the south, was left very open and wide with buildings less than three stories tall. Note the tractor heading west. At this time in the early 1970s, East Walnut Street was one-way. (CDM.)

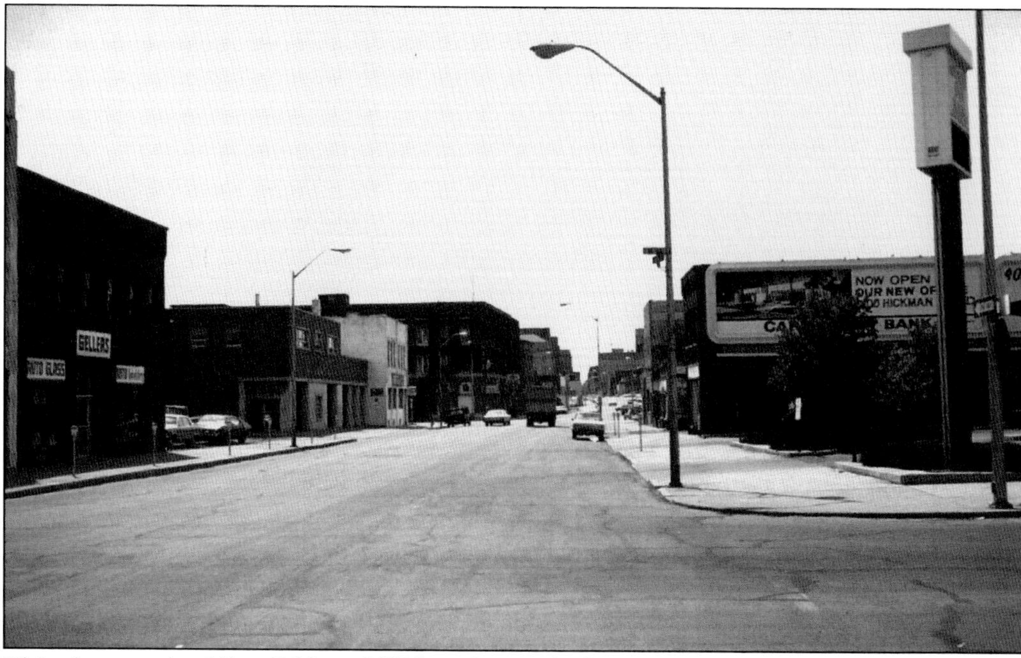

This photograph of East Fifth and Walnut Streets looking west in 1973 shows Des Moines Fire Station No. 2, which is no longer there. Newspaper reports around this time cited incidents of violence at the Northwestern Tap Room on the first floor, further earning the poor reputation of the area. Longtime business owner Jerry Geller's shop is on the left; the parking lot of Capital City State Bank is on the right. (CDM.)

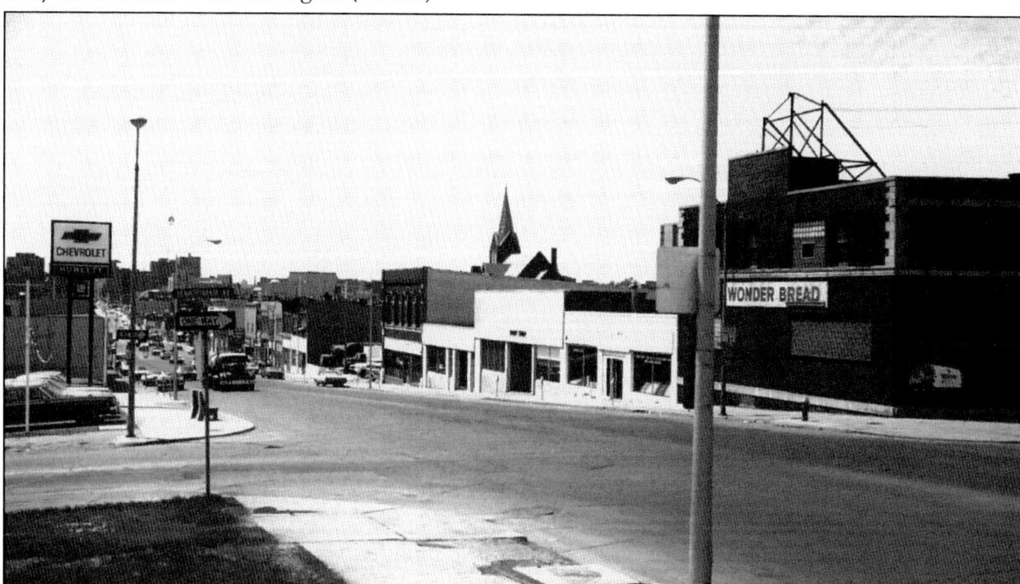

This photograph shows the block of businesses along East Grand Avenue looking west from East Seventh Street. At this time, Howlett Chevrolet (formerly Friedman's Chevrolet) operated its sales with a large car lot on the corner at left. Wonder Bread/Hostess also maintained a bakery and distribution center in Des Moines. Interestingly, the inventor of the bread slicer, Otto Rohwedder, was born in Des Moines. His invention made Wonder Bread famous. (CDM.)

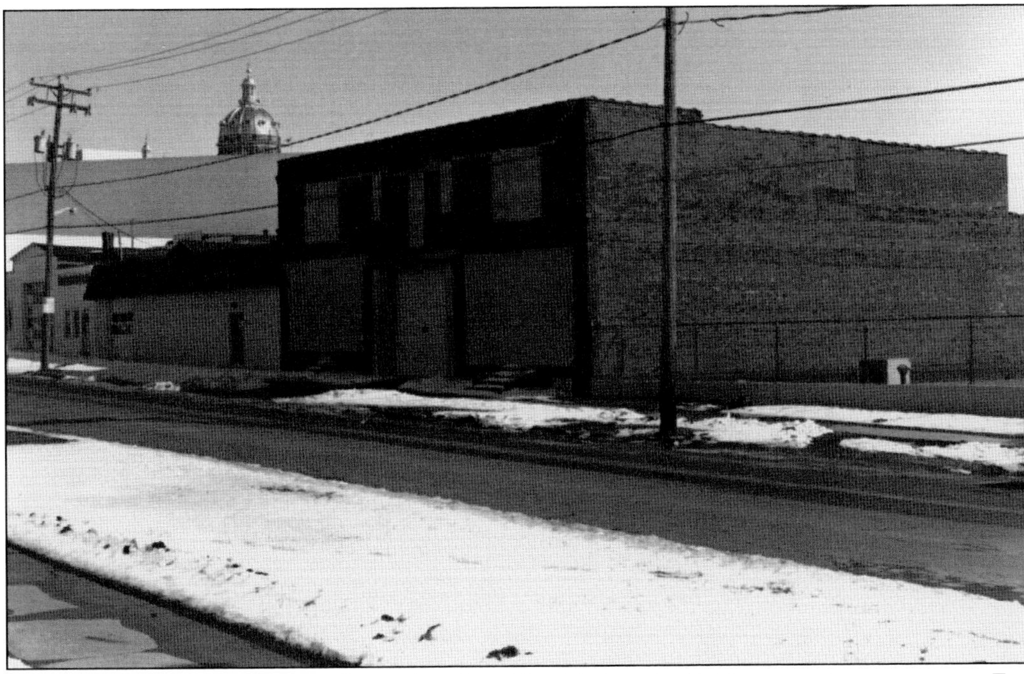

The Northland Dairy Plant relocated to East Des Moines in 1926, occupying quarters at East Sixth and Des Moines Streets. The original building is gone, but this one, which served as stables for the delivery horses, remains just across the street. A fire here in October 1940 killed 22 of the horses. This photograph, taken in the late 1970s, shows the building boarded up and abandoned. (JB.)

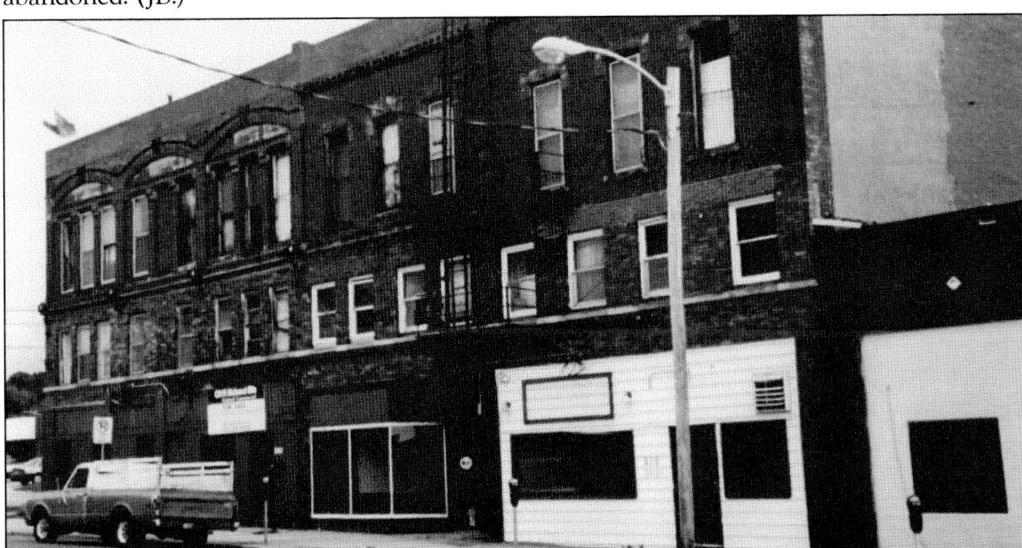

A 1975 study of this building, constructed in 1880 in the Victorian commercial style, was deemed "not architecturally significant" although it contributed to the "visual quality of its surroundings." It was built by H. E. Dillon as a business block during a boom in East Village development. Due to its age and disrepair, the building was taken down in 2002, and the site is now a parking lot. (State Historic Preservation Office.)

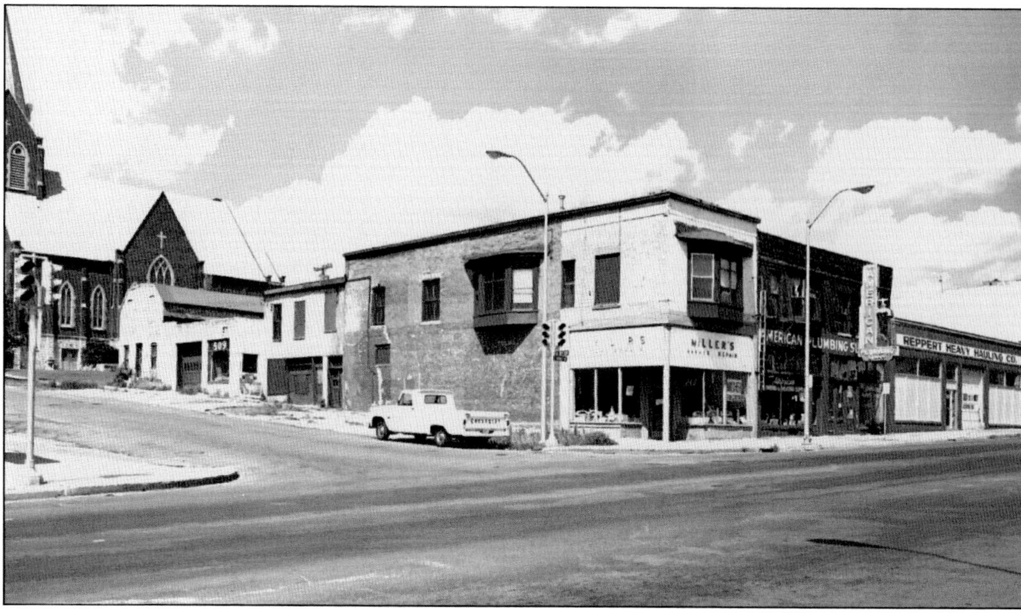

Miller's Washer Repair at 500 East Grand Avenue advertises "Alum Tubing," "Copper Tubing," and "Rinse Tubs." Although the washers seen through the windows seem to date to the 1950s (complete with hand wringers), the photograph was taken in 1971. Today the location is home to Eden, a bath shop opened in 2004. (ISB.)

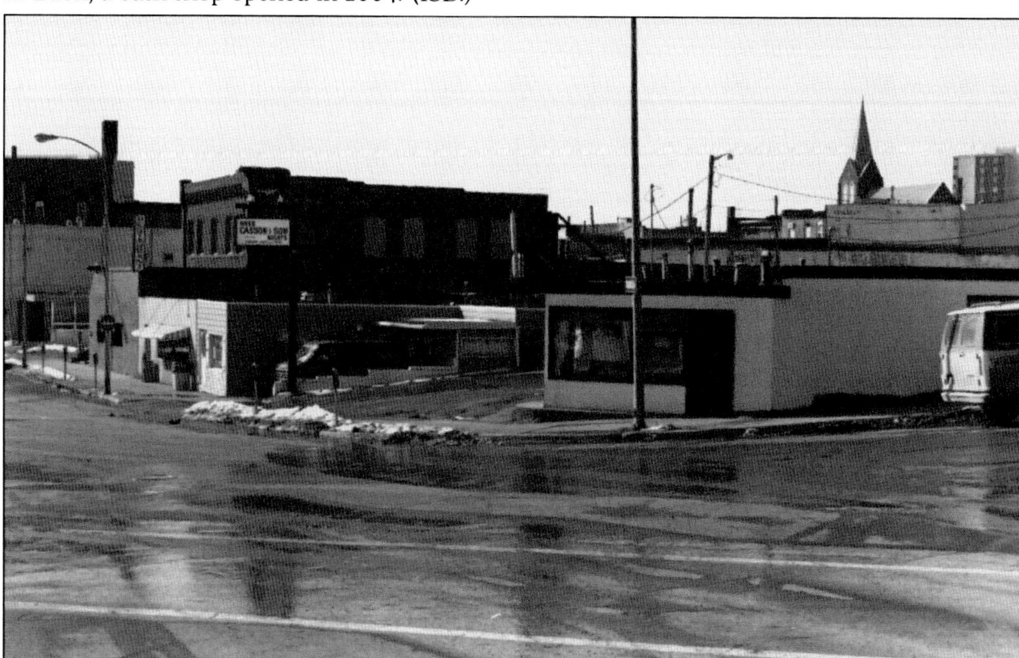

This 1973 view looks to the west down East Locust Street from Pennsylvania Avenue and East Seventh Street. Russ Casson and Son Meats appears next to the Gustaveson restaurant and barbershop. On the corner is a pizza house. This block was cleared in the mid-1980s for the construction of the State Historical Building. In the background, the steeple of the Capitol Hill Lutheran Church is clearly visible. (JB.)

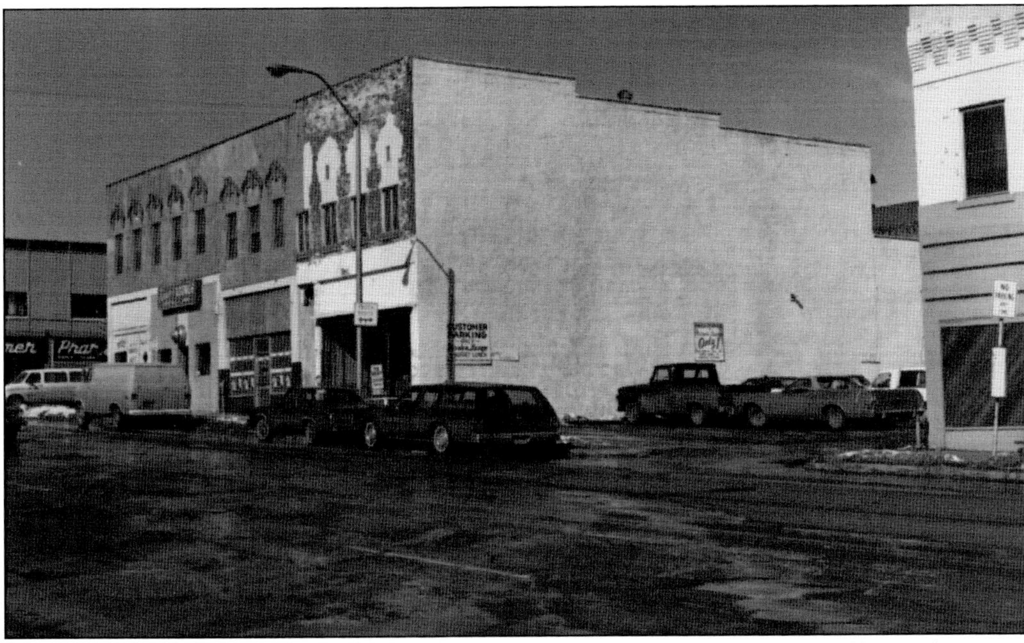

This view looking to the northeast of East Sixth Street includes Bernie's Buffet and Lounge. Even before these buildings were removed, it appears some effort was made to modernize the windows, as seen in the gap between the short windows above Bernie's and the decorative plaster caps floating on top. The building to the south went a step further and completely filled in the upper half of the window space, not bothering to make it any less obvious. (JB.)

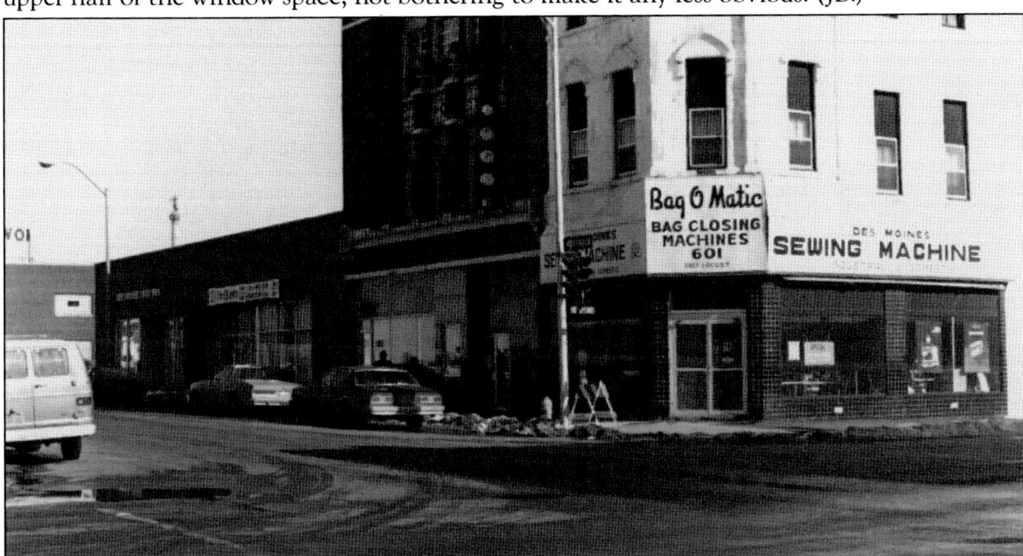

The Des Moines Sewing Machine Company occupied the southeast corner of East Sixth and Locust Streets from the 1960s until the building was vacated and torn down in 2000. Still in business today, the company deals, distributes, and repairs a variety of sewing machines, including the prominent "Bag O Matic" Bag Closing Machines and rare antique models. The building to its left is the Masonic temple, and beyond that is the Don Quixote Mexican Restaurant and State Employees Credit Union. The photograph was taken in the late 1970s. (JB.)

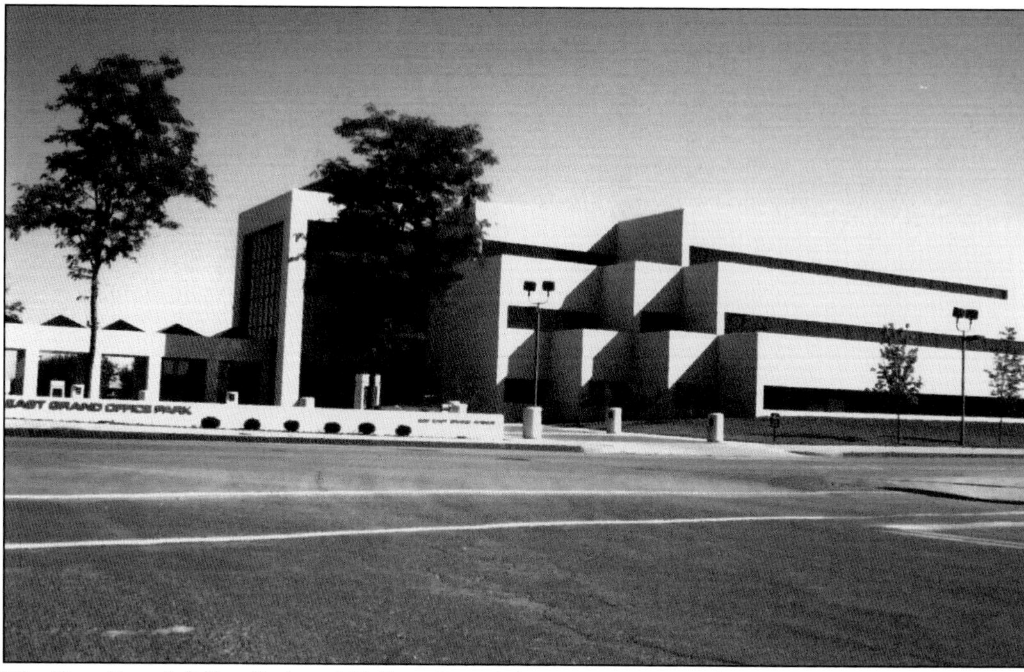

The East Grand Office Park at 200 East Grand Avenue was erected in 1987 in the middle of the movement to tear down the old and build new. Two large modern buildings, plus parking, take up more than a city block. The State of Iowa rents offices in one building, and the other is leased to individual businesses. (CDM.)

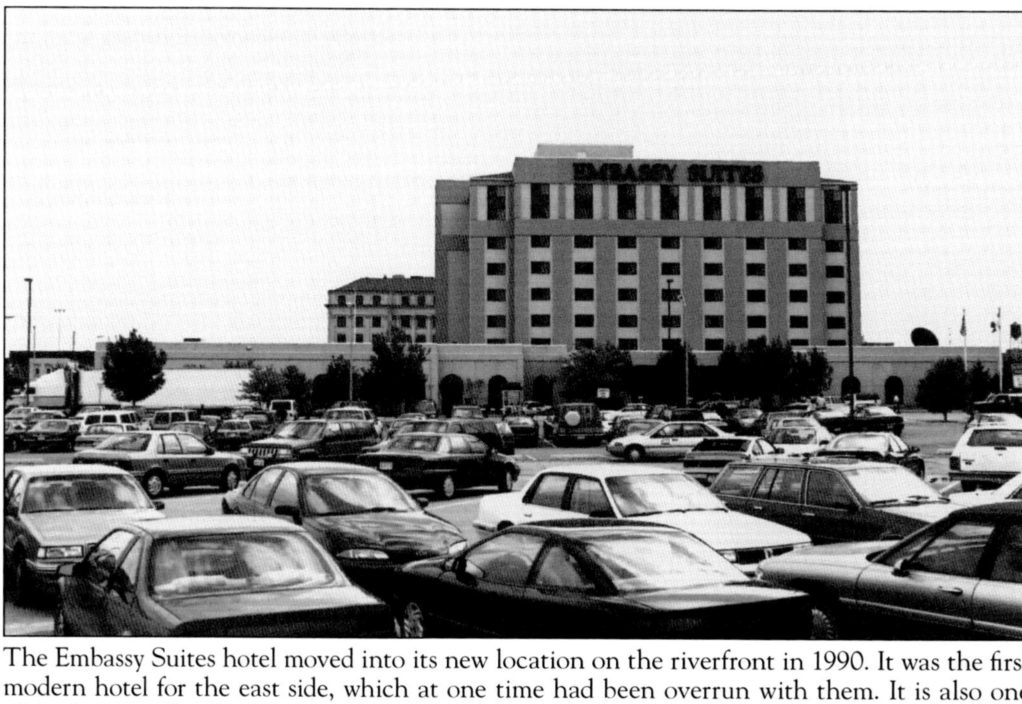

The Embassy Suites hotel moved into its new location on the riverfront in 1990. It was the first modern hotel for the east side, which at one time had been overrun with them. It is also one of the last new hotels to go up in the downtown area. Just outside its doors sits the Simon Estes Amphitheatre, a popular entertainment venue in the summertime. (CDM.)

Five

Renaissance

The City of Des Moines was faced with either tearing everything down and rebuilding, or making the most of what remained in the first step toward revitalizing the east side. In 1997, the City of Des Moines, the Des Moines Development Corporation, and the State of Iowa worked together to formulate the Des Moines: Capitol Gateway East Urban Design Plan. The plan stated, "Having undergone several decades of disinvestment, the East Side currently suffers from negative perceptions. Empty parcels of land, a few boarded-up properties and limited street activity are misinterpreted as inhospitality or lack of safety." One of the first and most noticeable improvements came in 2002 with the addition of streetscaping. New lights were added, greenery beds and benches lined the sidewalks of East Locust Street, and the investment to renovate historic properties was an idea catching on. Businesses also came back. Retail businesses brought a youth and vibrancy that the area had never felt before. The name East Village gave it a hip identity that caught on quickly. Suddenly everyone wanted to live in an urban, refurbished prewar loft and be able to walk to work. Artists moved in, gays moved in, young people liked the nightlife, and retirees liked upscale condominium living. Today it is a model of success that has driven further urban development throughout the entire downtown area and would make its predecessors proud.

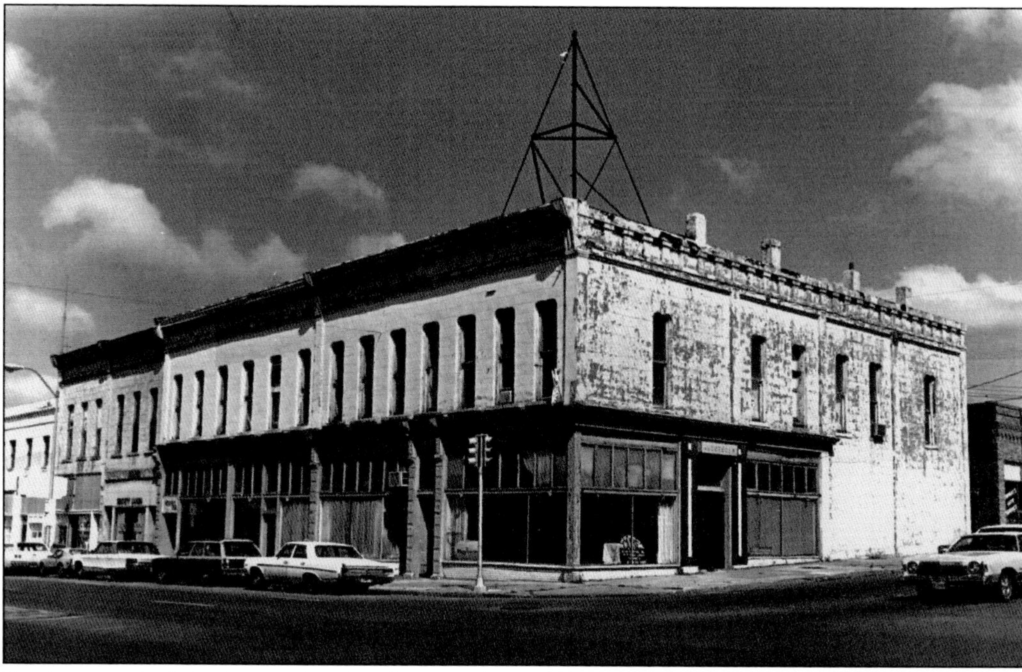

Jim Boyt took this picture shortly after purchasing the Anderson's Furniture building in 1976. The Anderson name is still visible above one of the doors, but the building is now home to a retail shop, an art studio, and a nonprofit organization. The structure on the top of the building is what remained of the large Anderson Furniture sign. (JB.)

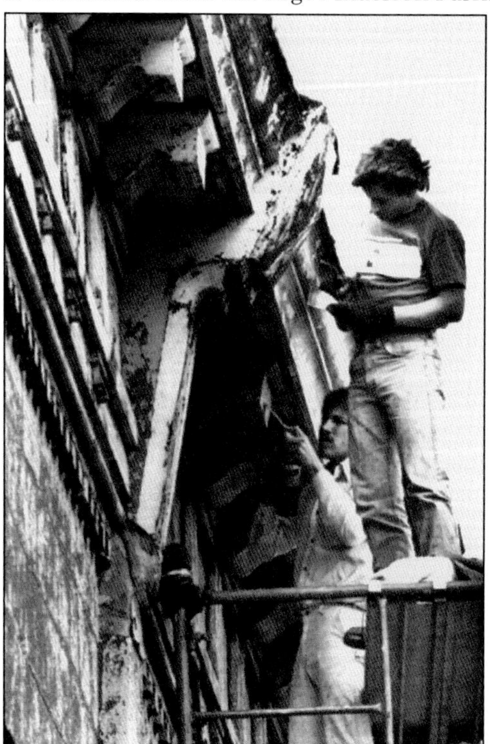

Workers begin the painstaking process to remove paint from the cornices of the Anderson Furniture building in 1976. Boyt spent many years researching the building's history so he could return it to a close version of its original. The building is now listed on the National Register of Historic Places. (JB.)

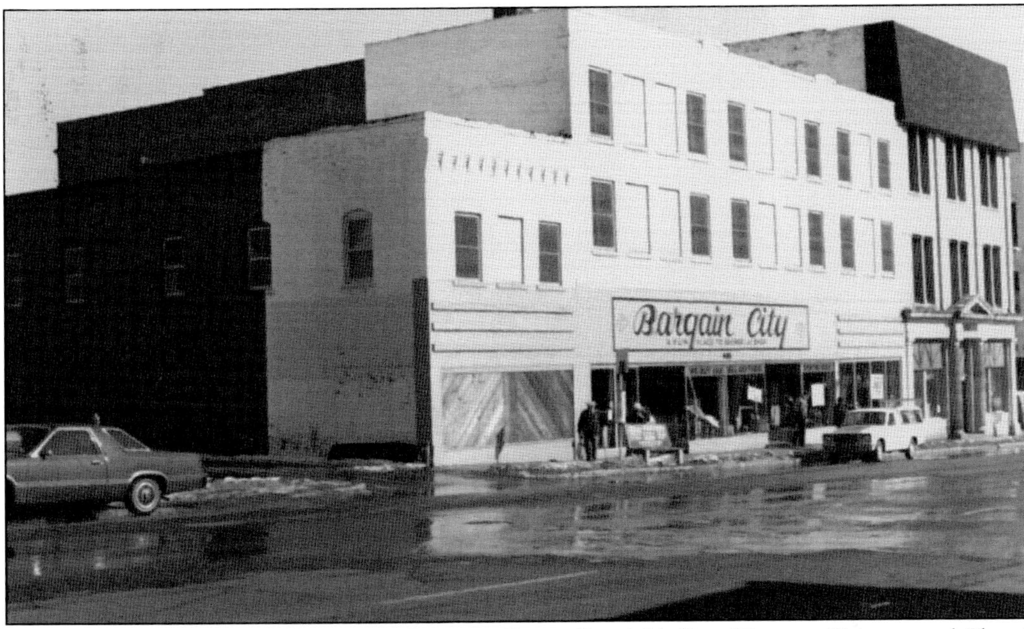

A precursor to today's dollar stores, Bargain City offered "A Fun Place to Browse and Shop." The storefront also notes it buys and sells anything, indicating it was a consignment shop. The building to its right is the Des Moines Area Community College. Both of these buildings were torn down in the mid-1980s as part of the construction of the State Historical Building. (JB.)

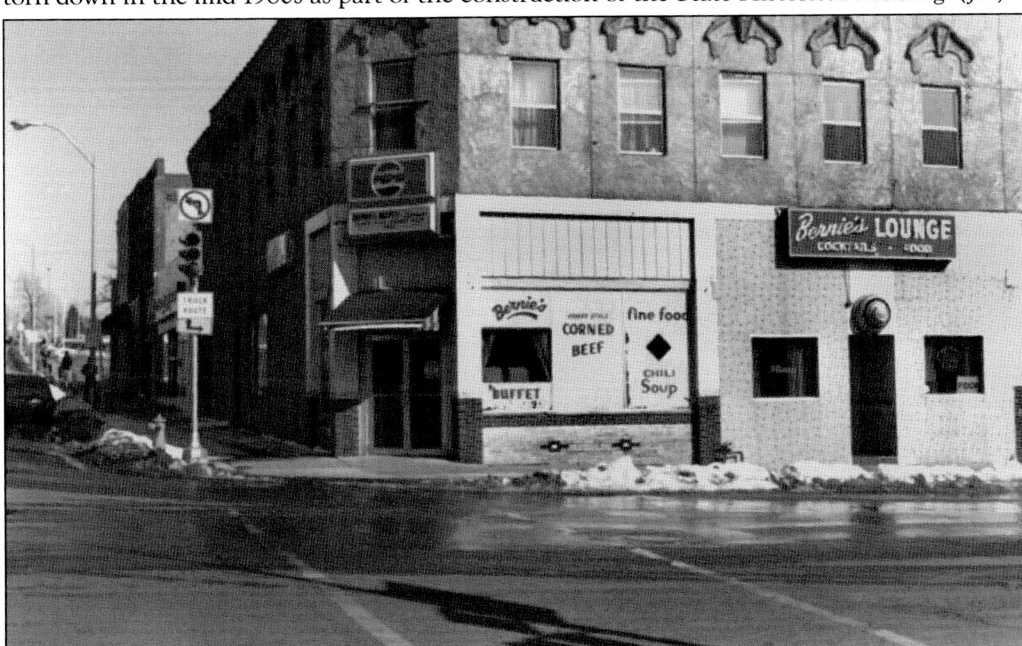

Bernie's Buffet, on the southeast corner of East Sixth Street and East Grand Avenue, was a favorite spot for neighborhood businessman Jim Boyt, who enjoyed dining there. The restaurant offered "kosher style corned beef" and chili as its specialties. The corner restaurant was removed to make way for the State Historical Building, but longtime neighborhood owners and residents remember it fondly. (JB.)

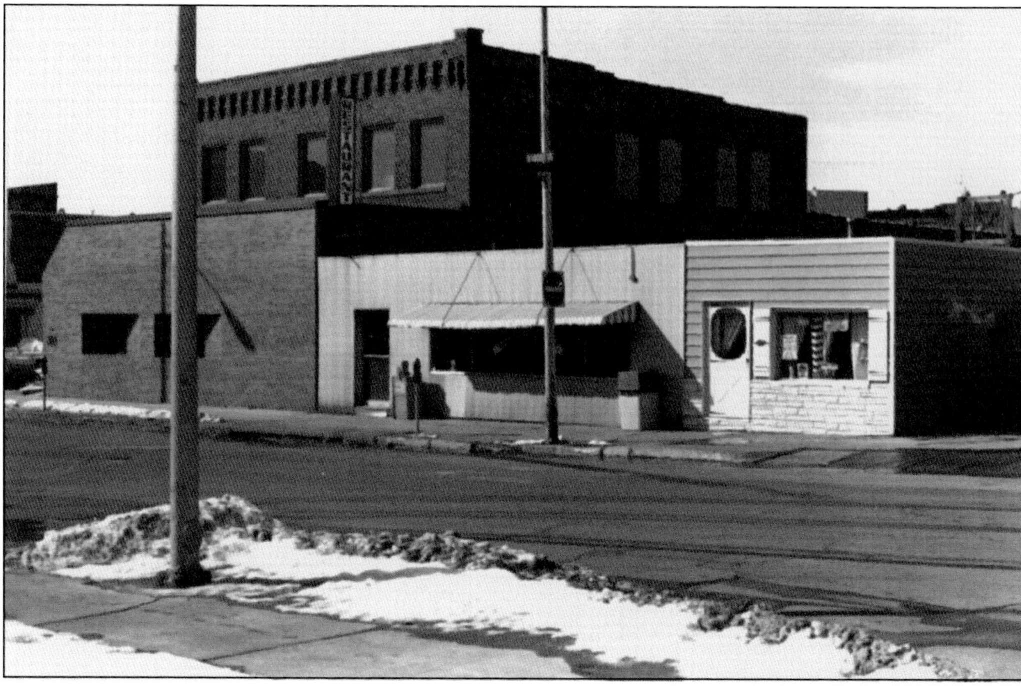

An attempt to modernize an old building resulted in an awkward pairing of old and new when it became an office building in the late 1970s. The restaurant in the middle is Gustaveson's, and a barbershop sits on the end. Gustaveson's is particularly notable as a longtime East Village establishment. It is listed in the 1958 City Directory and remained in this location until the block was cleared for the State Historical Building in the mid-1980s. (JB.)

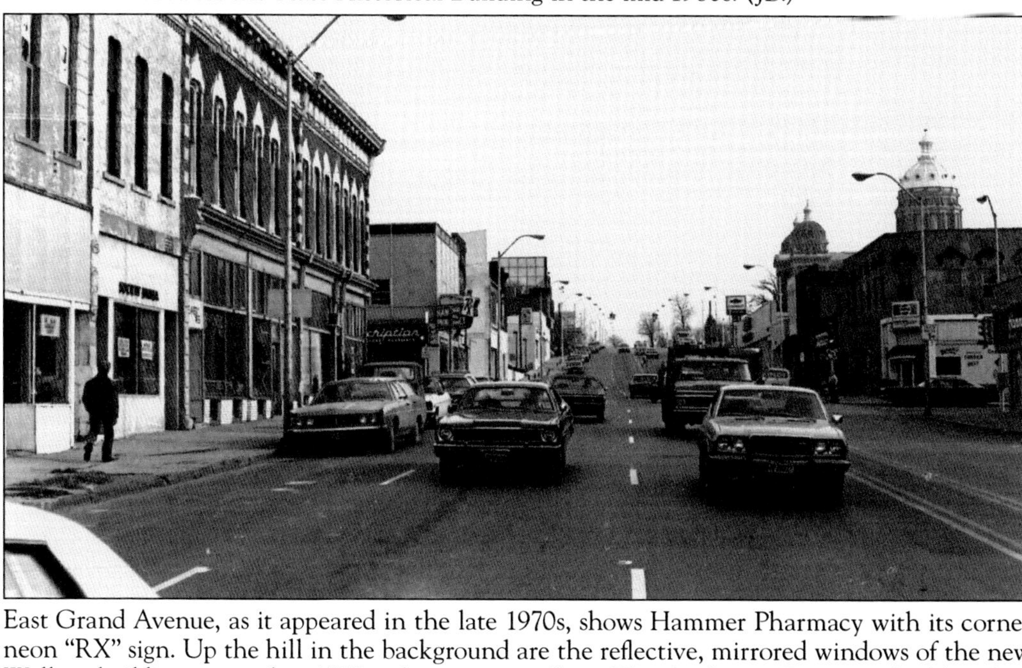

East Grand Avenue, as it appeared in the late 1970s, shows Hammer Pharmacy with its corner neon "RX" sign. Up the hill in the background are the reflective, mirrored windows of the new Wallace building, erected in 1978 to house state offices. The Anderson Furniture building had been purchased by Jim Boyt, who was working to restore the upper windows at this time. (JB.)

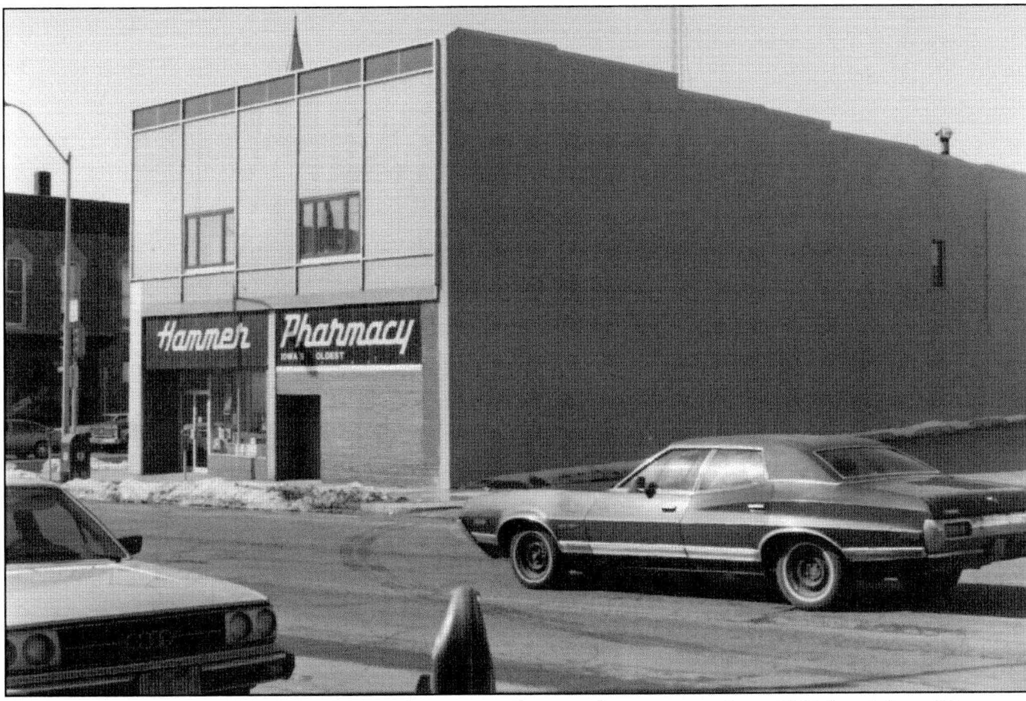

Hammer Pharmacy is Iowa's oldest pharmacy, having been started in 1872 by Alvin Hammer. The business moved to this building shortly after its erection in 1899 by Seymour Johnson, who constructed it as a double storefront, one of which is still very visible here. This photograph depicts an attempt to modernize the appearance of the building by adding aluminum siding in 1956. (JB.)

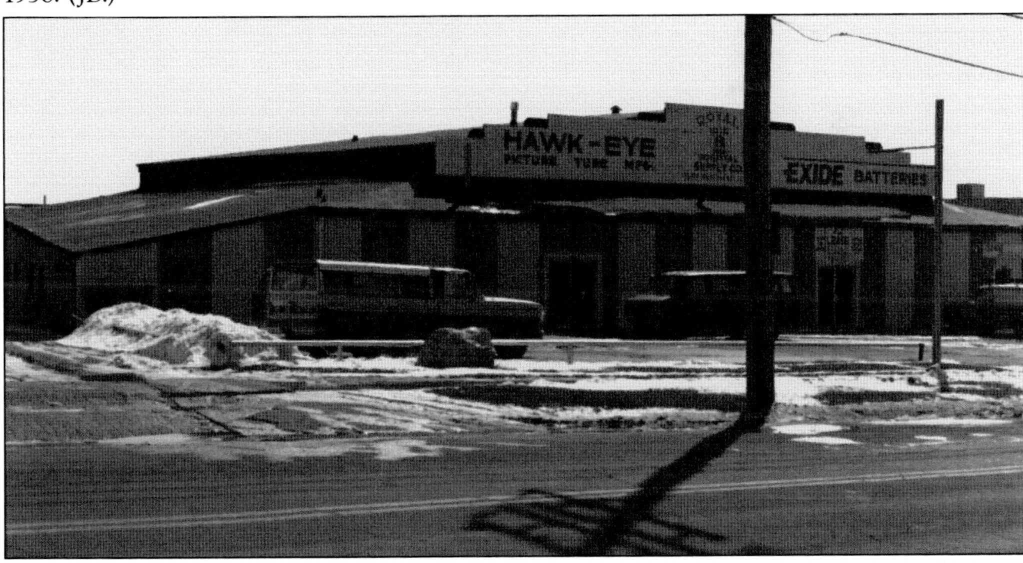

The Royal Hospital Supply Company building on Des Moines Street seems curiously out of place as a downtown "mini-mall." Just as out of place is the collection of businesses located there, including Hawkeye Picture Tube Manufacturing and Exide Batteries. The building no longer stands, having been demolished when a new state parking ramp was built on part of this location. (JB.)

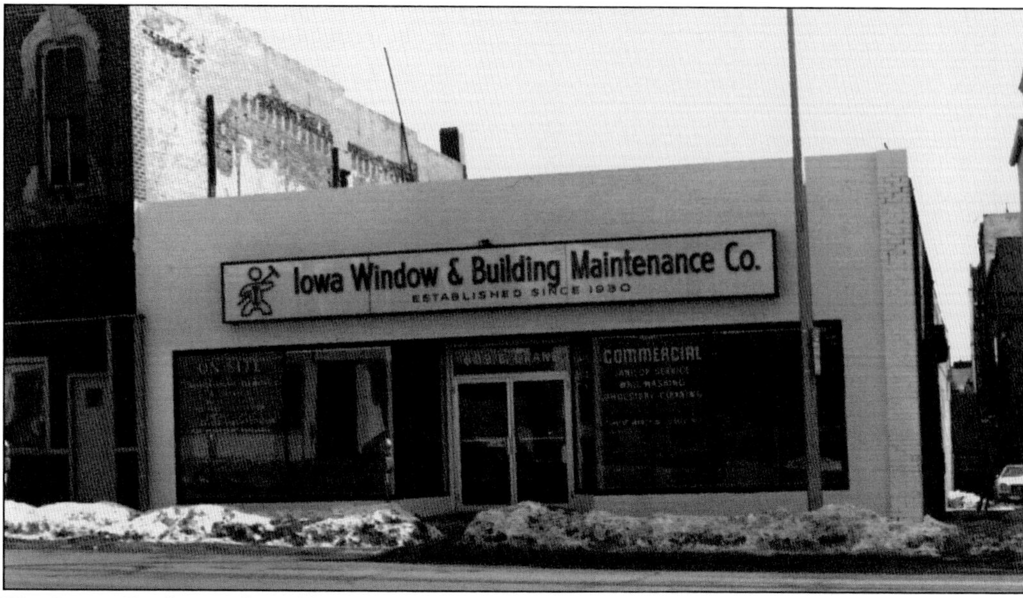

The Iowa Window and Building Maintenance Company at 609 East Grand Avenue is pictured here. Its windows advertise commercial janitor service, wall washing, upholstery cleaning, and interior window coverings. The building is on the site of what is now the State Historical Building. Note the building on the far left with the upper floor crumbling; at street level, there are obvious signs of attempted improvements. (JB.)

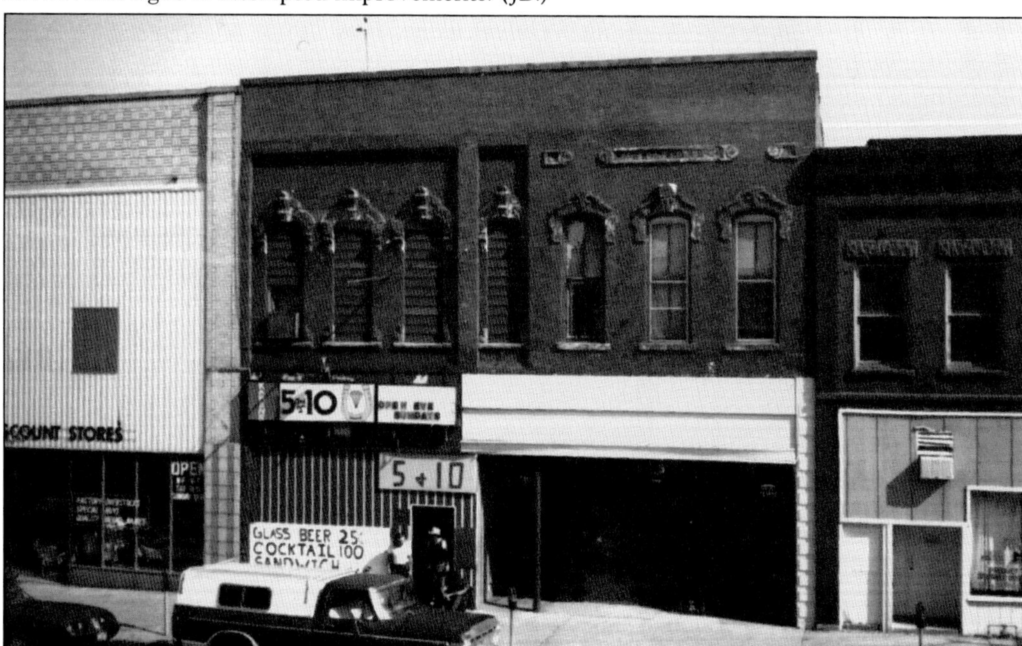

It is easy to see why people may have been fearful to visit the east side of downtown. The structures at 428 and 430 East Locust Street appear to be well worn in this late 1970s image. Built in 1882, 428 East Locust Street survives today. It was built as a permanent home and hall for the Skandia Society, a collective of Swedish immigrants who lived in the area. Today these two storefronts are occupied by a restaurant and a culinary supply store. (JB.)

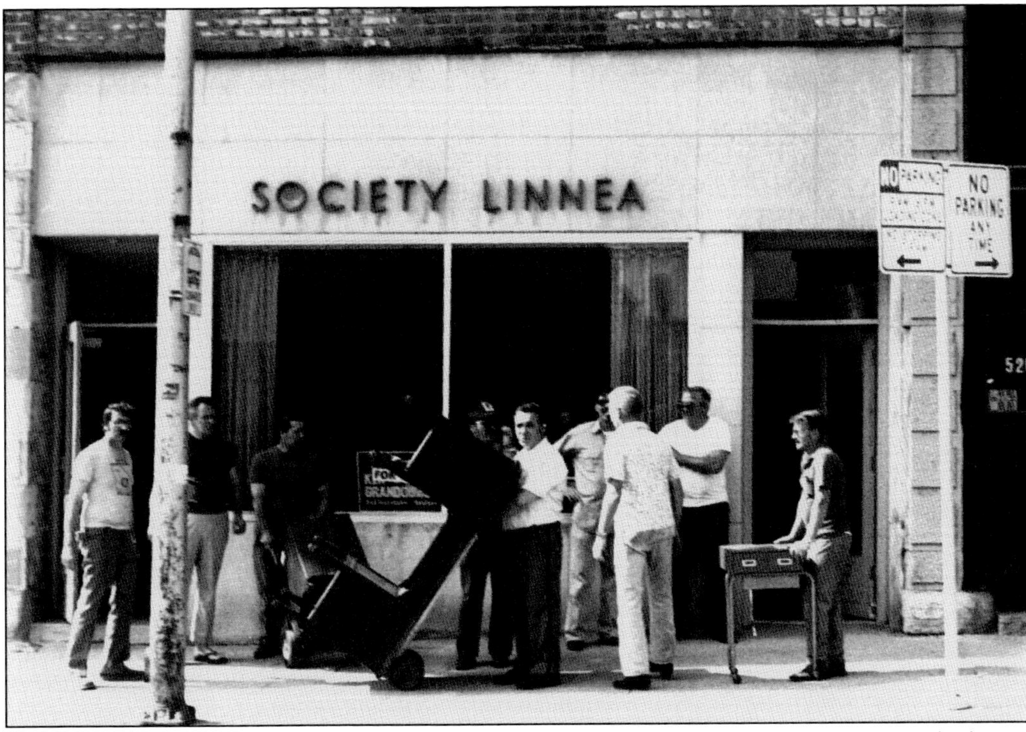

Although the sign on 518 East Grand Avenue says "Society Linnea," the photograph depicts the members of the postal union who moved in during later years and used it as a social hall. Another testament to the strength of the Swedish community in East Village, Society Linnea formed in Des Moines in 1906 to honor Swedish heritage. The society honored Charles Linnaeus (1707–1778), the Swedish father of modern botany. (JB.)

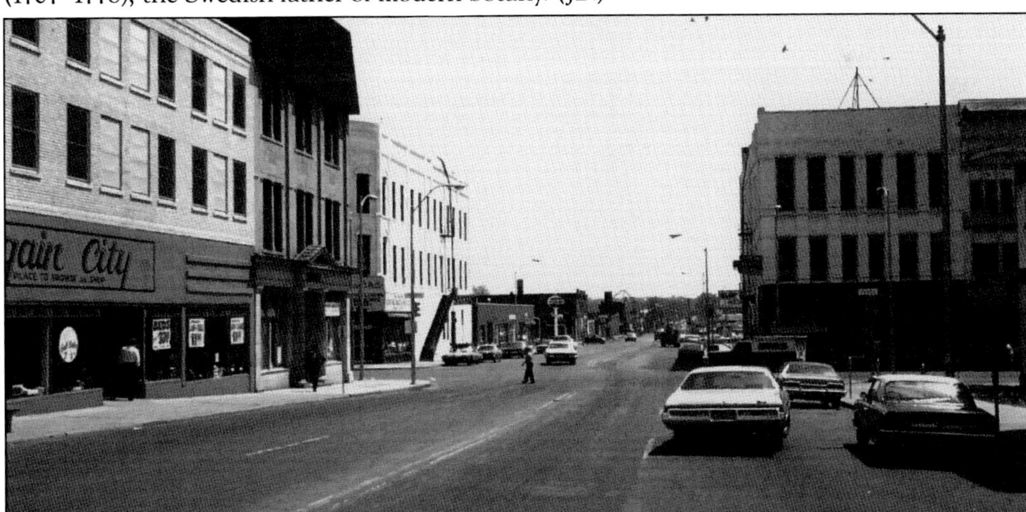

East Sixth Street had changed considerably by 1978, particularly on the west side of the street, where some buildings had already been cleared. The area was showing its age, as evidenced by the concentration on street-level retail, with upper floors in such disrepair that they were uninhabitable. (CDM.)

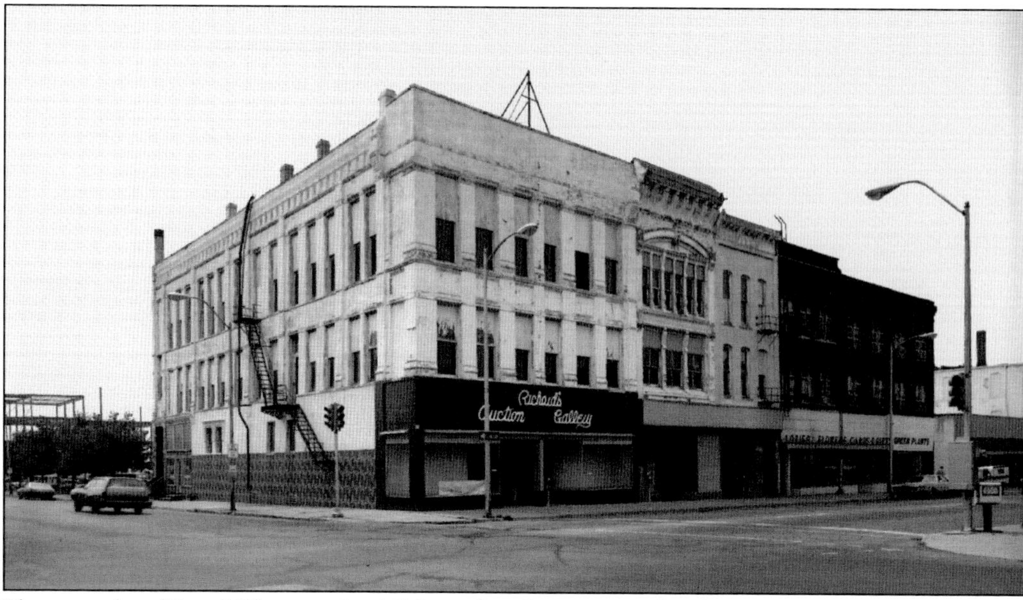

Photographs of East Village in the 1980s and early 1990s are hard to come by, and this image of the 500 block of East Locust Street shows why. Most of the buildings were vacant and uncared for, even though many of them were more than 100 years old at the time. All of the buildings shown here came down for a new office and retail building. Note the construction in the background of the Court Avenue office park. (HABS.)

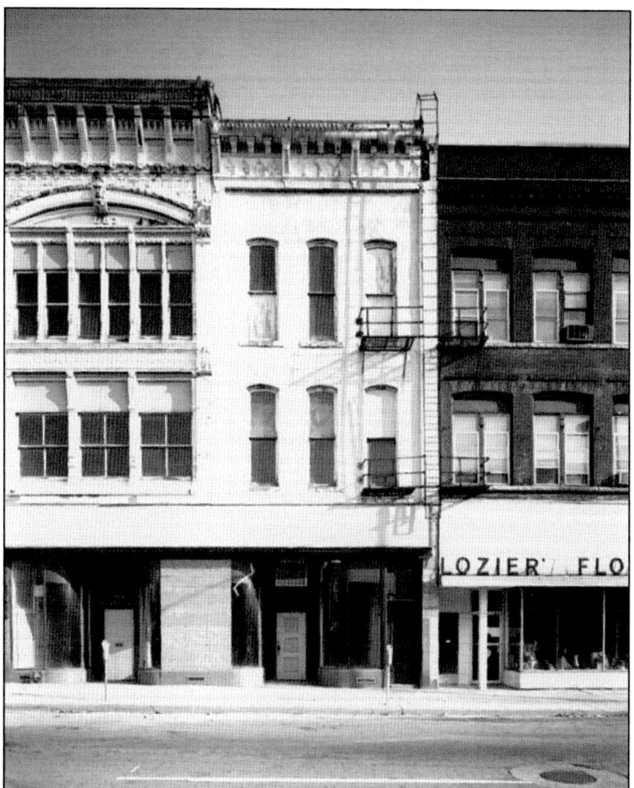

In 1983, the City of Des Moines participated in the Library of Congress Historic American Buildings Survey. The building in the middle was known as the C. F. Wheeler Grocery, although it housed a number of retail stores since being built in 1880. At the time of the survey, the building at 521 East Locust Street was vacant and was torn down shortly after, along with the buildings adjacent to it. (Photograph by Larry Day; HABS.)

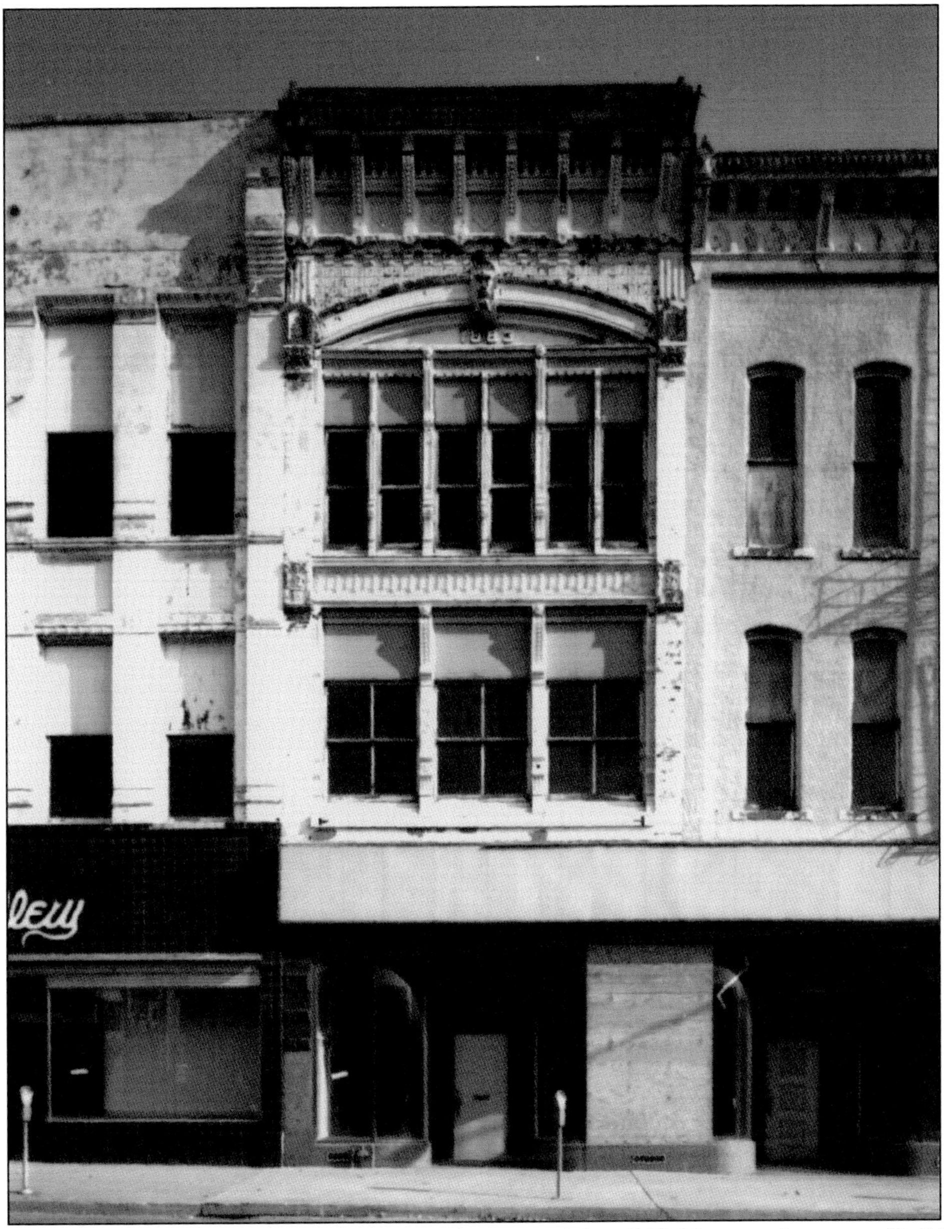

The Garton Bakery and Confectionary was also part of the 1983 Historic American Buildings Survey and stood at that time as one of the last remaining Victorian commercial buildings in Des Moines at 523 East Locust Street. Samuel B. Garton was born in County Surrey, England, on February 3, 1848. When he was six years old, he was brought to America by his parents, who first settled in Indiana and two years later moved to Iowa. He operated the bakery and confectionery between 1883 and 1913. In 1914, he was elected to the office of state representative and served one term from 1915 to 1917. The F. W. Woolworth Company operated out of 521 and 523 East Locust Street from the late 1920s until the 1950s. After that, businesses came and went until finally the building was abandoned and left to the condition apparent here. Survey data forms reveal that ornate woodwork remained on the second and third floors, which were used as apartments as far back as the time of the Garton family, who lived above their business. (HABS.)

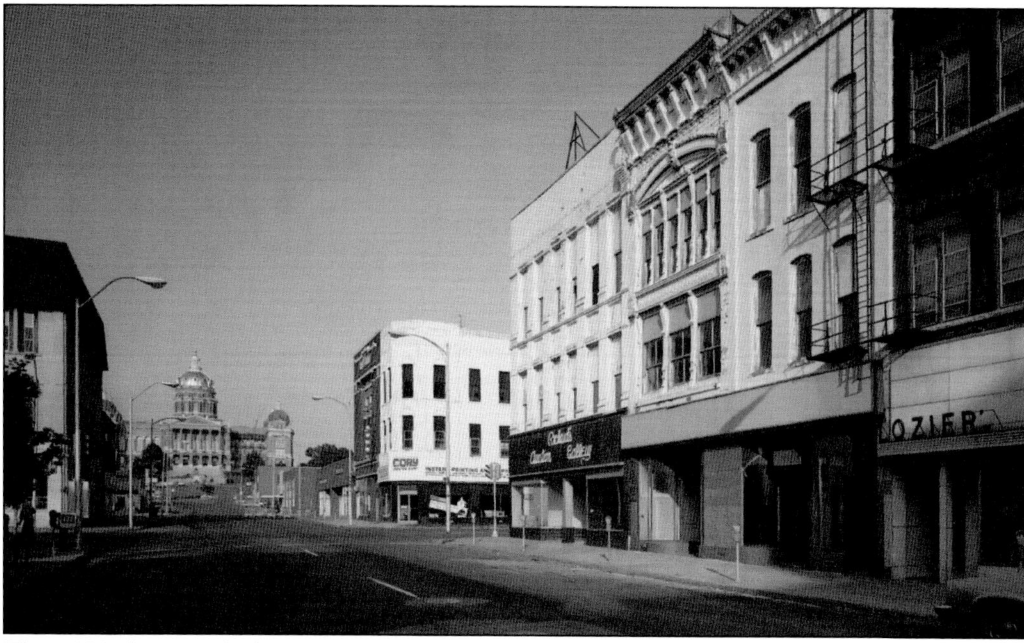

This 1983 photograph shows a view to the east down East Locust Street of the commercial block when studied as part of the Historic American Buildings Survey. None of the buildings on either side of the street remain. The survey documented the achievements in architecture, engineering, and design in the United States. (HABS.)

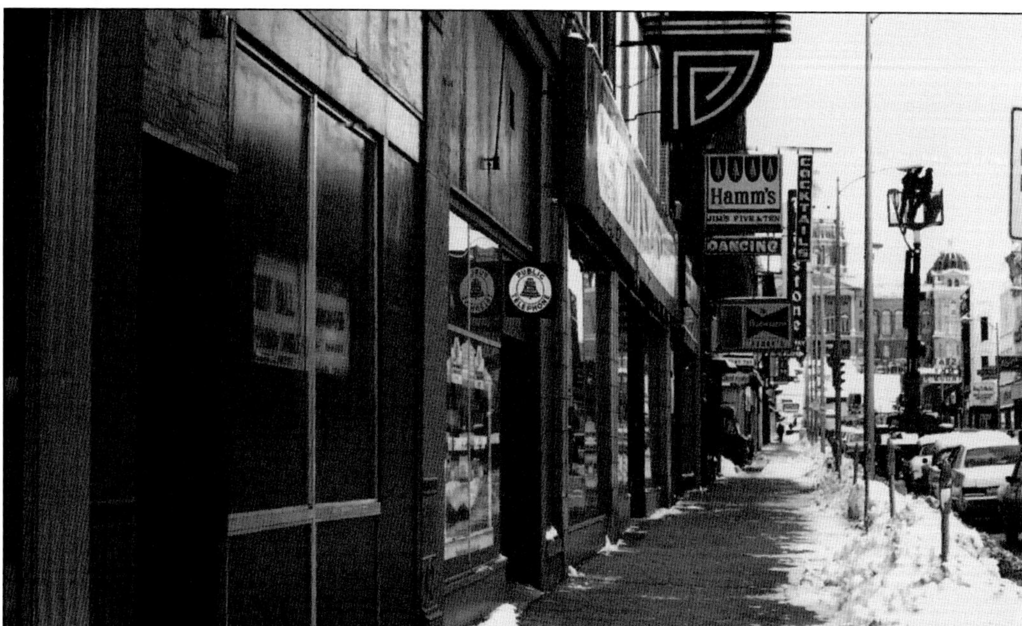

This photograph was taken in the 400 block of East Locust Street, the north side of the street, and was used by the city as it reviewed its signage ordinance, an early indicator that the neighborhood was in for stricter enforcement. Signs were all but eliminated until beautification efforts in late 1990s called for an exception that would heighten the pedestrian walkability of the historic neighborhood. (CDM.)

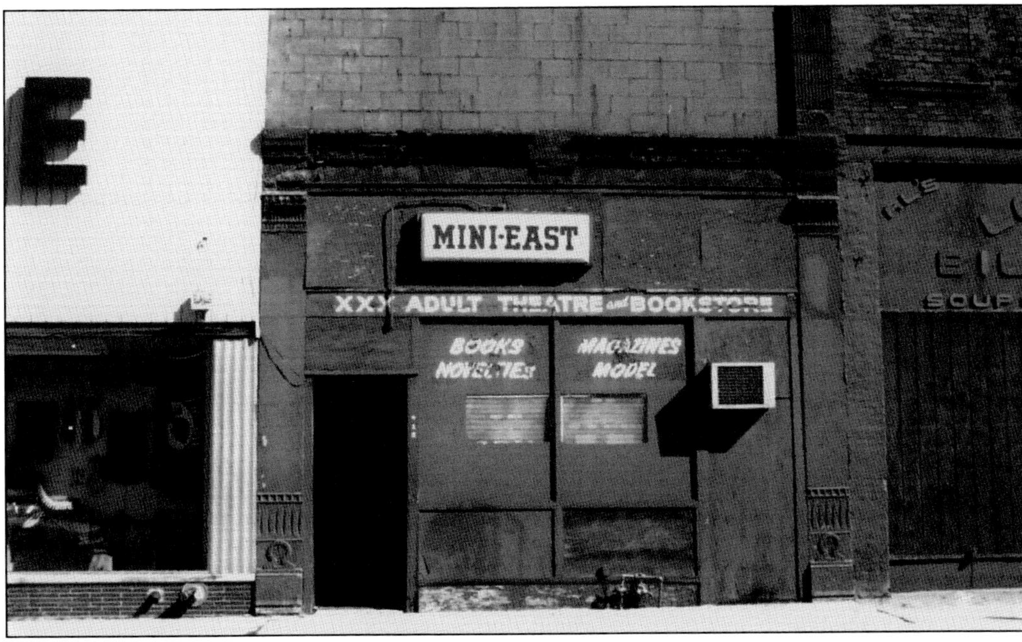

Pictured are Betts Hardware, which is selling ammunition and army surplus prominently in its front window; the Mini East XXX Adult Theatre and Bookstore; and Al's Locust Street Billiards. The photograph shows how run down East Village had become in the 1980s. Crime increased in the neighborhood at the time. (CDM.)

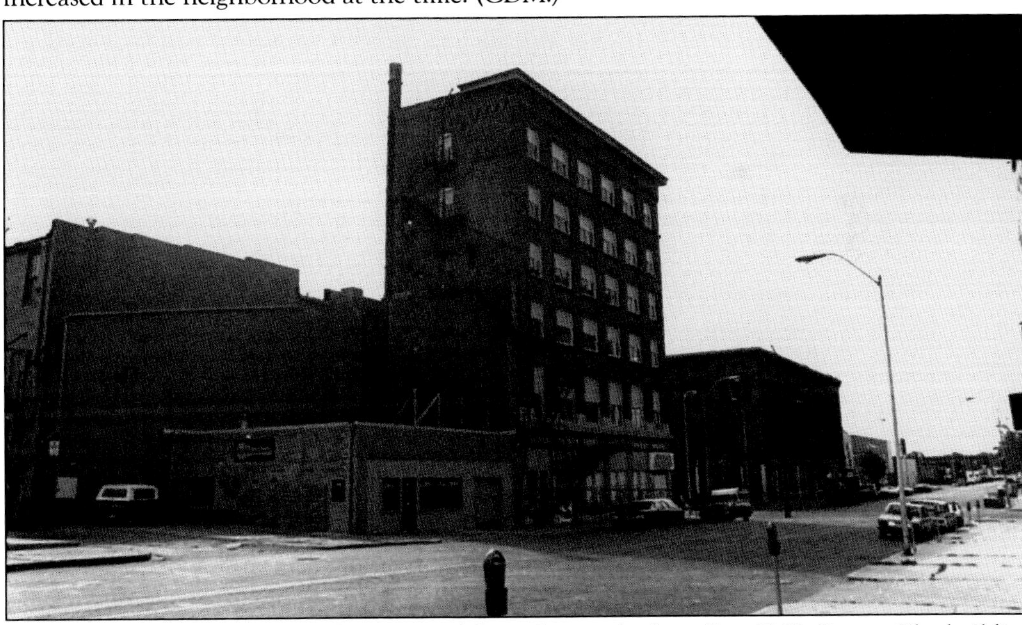

The Teachout building is seen here viewed from the north along East Fifth Street. The building adjacent is a locksmith's shop. The intersection of East Fifth and East Locust Streets seems all but deserted at the time of this photograph in the 1980s. The locksmith building is still there but has been updated and modernized and formerly housed a restaurant. The Teachout building was restored in the late 1990s, although its outward appearance here retains much of its historic character. (Kirk Blunck.)

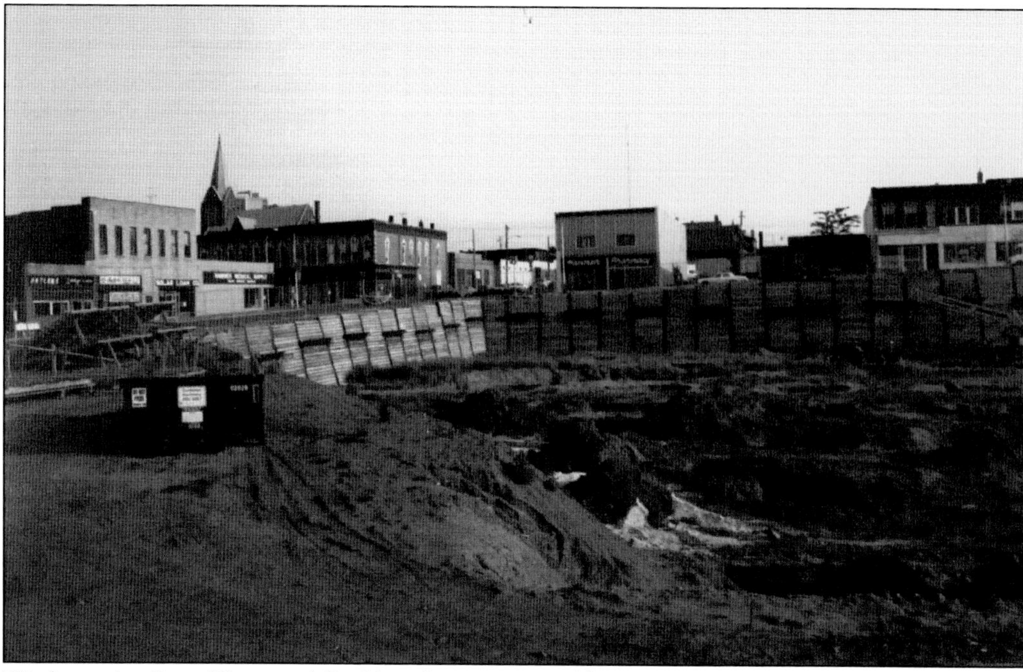

Work on the State Historical Building began in 1985 by Weitz Construction. The entire block was purchased by the state and then demolished for the modern building. It was another coup for the east side and became its first tourist attraction since the state capitol was built. (SHSI.)

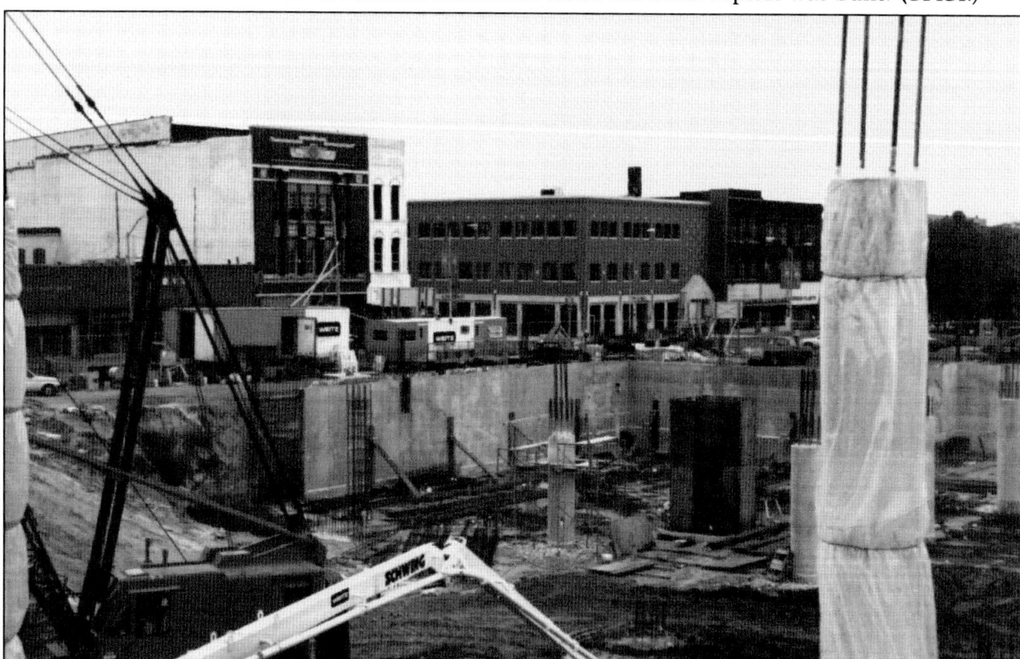

This photograph shows the southwest corner of the construction of the State Historical Building. The Masonic temple and Des Moines Sewing Machine Company are still present across the street. A new office and retail building had just been completed to the west. Adjoining that new building is the Lozier florist business. (SHSI.)

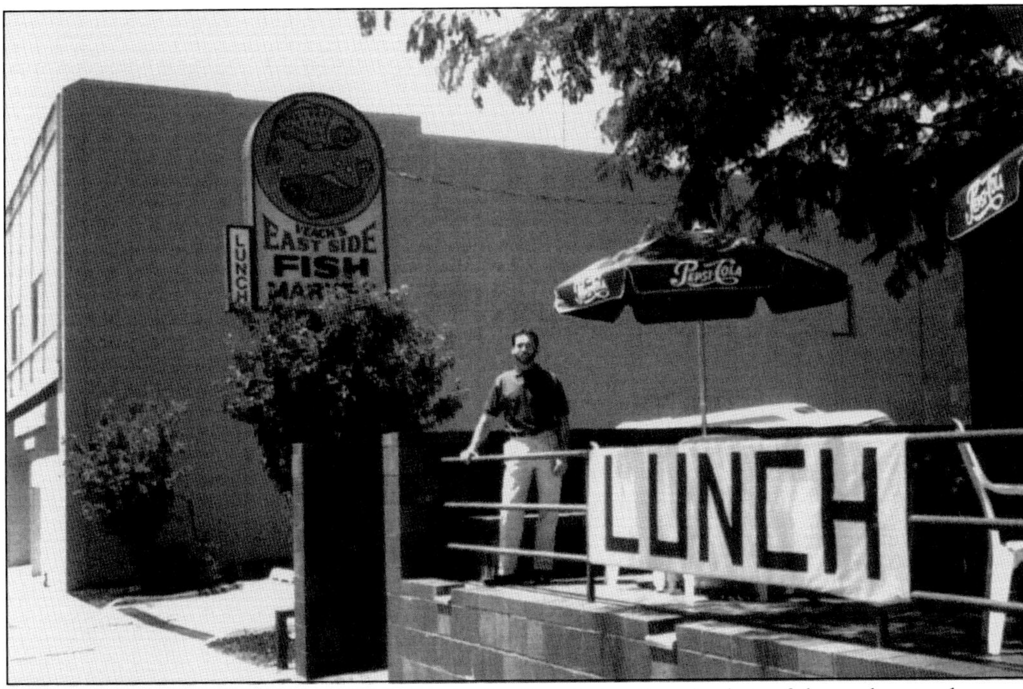

When its former structure was torn down, the Veach family rebuilt its fish market in the same location and reopened in the 1990s with a greater focus on serving its fresh fish. The building looks very much the same today, although the business was gone by 1999 and an architectural firm had moved in. (FEH Associates/Denny Sharp.)

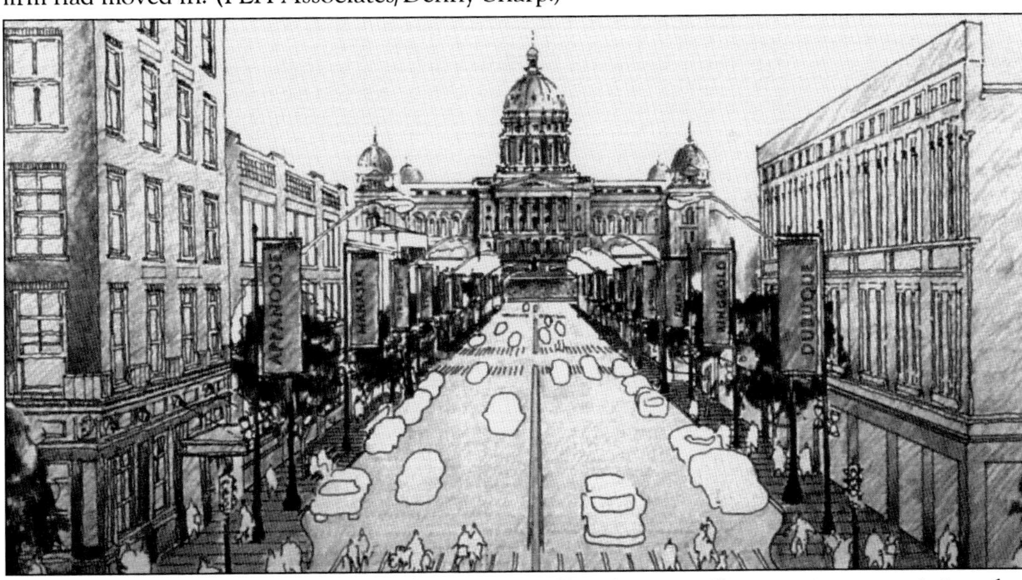

In September 1997, the city, state, and Des Moines Development Corporation commissioned an urban design plan. This drawing represents the beautification of East Locust Street. The plan states, "Every city should have a memorable street which embodies or symbolizes the city overall. When one thinks of Paris, the Champs Elysee comes to mind. In Boston, it's Commonwealth Avenue. Locust Street should be perceived in the context of such great streets." (Brooks Borg Skiles Architecture Engineering LLP.)

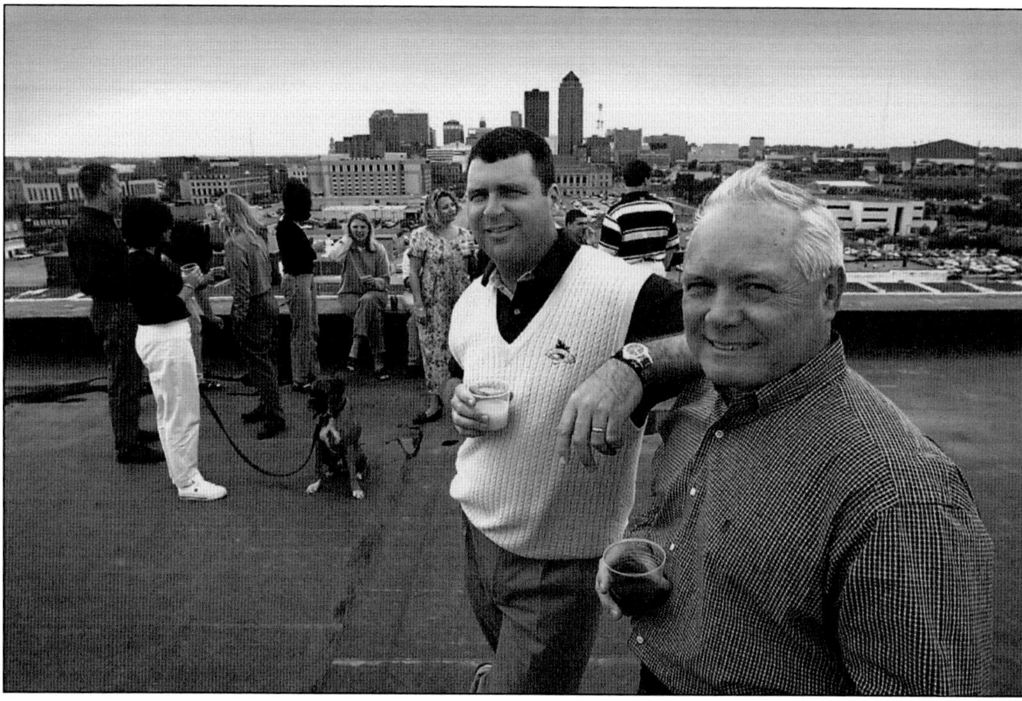

Tom Dunphy, left, and Jarrett Cowden founded Two Rivers Marketing in East Village in 2000. Its home was the Teachout building, where its raw space appealed to the young workers they wanted to attract. "It's like 1892, but wired with fiber optics and Mac G4s all over the place," Dunphy commented. This photograph shows Two Rivers Marketing employees enjoying a rooftop after-work party atop Teachout. (DMBR.)

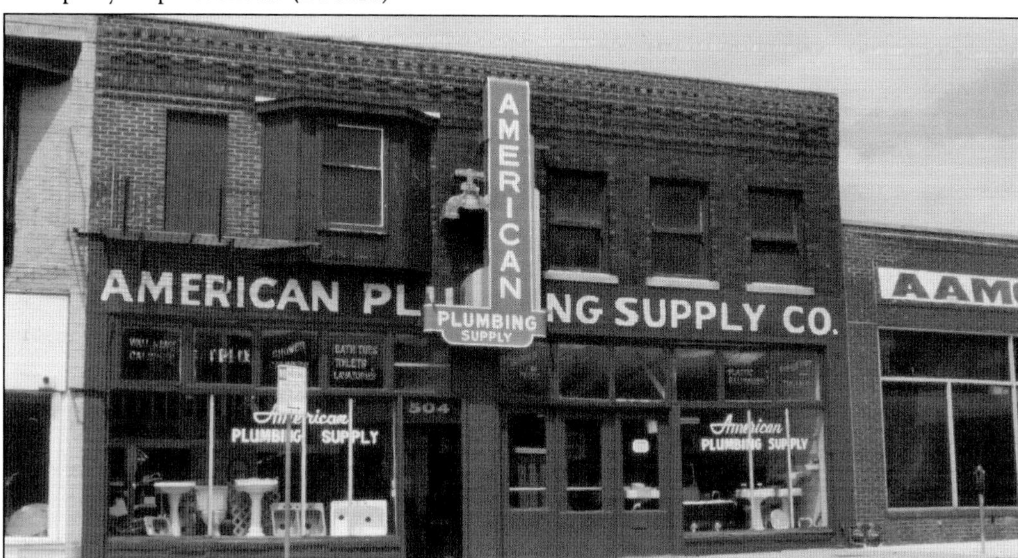

The American Plumbing Supply Company looks nearly the same in 2000 as it did the day the business moved in, in 1938. It is a popular spot for people restoring old houses who are looking for period fixtures or hard-to-find parts. The business is now owned by David Lekowsky, son of Harlan Lekowsky, whose father started it. (JDL.)

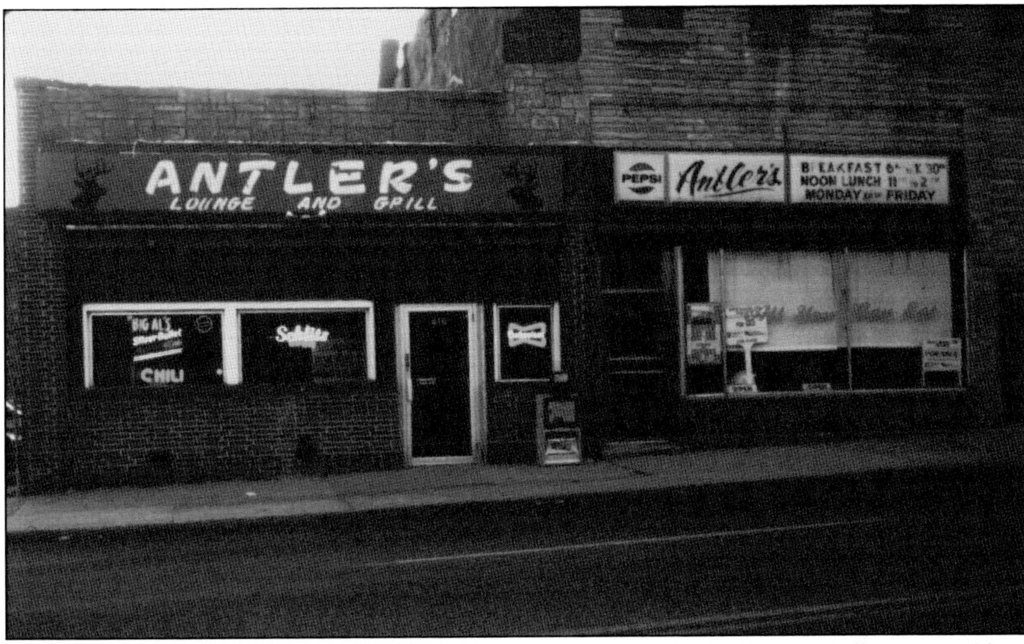

Antler's Lounge and Grill at 414 East Sixth Street was a great little diner and tap that could not keep up with a changing neighborhood. The inside of Antler's had just as much character as the outside—a mix of kitsch and history served off the grill and loaded with cheese. Antler's owner, Alfred Foggia, sold the building and retired the business in 2004. (JDL.)

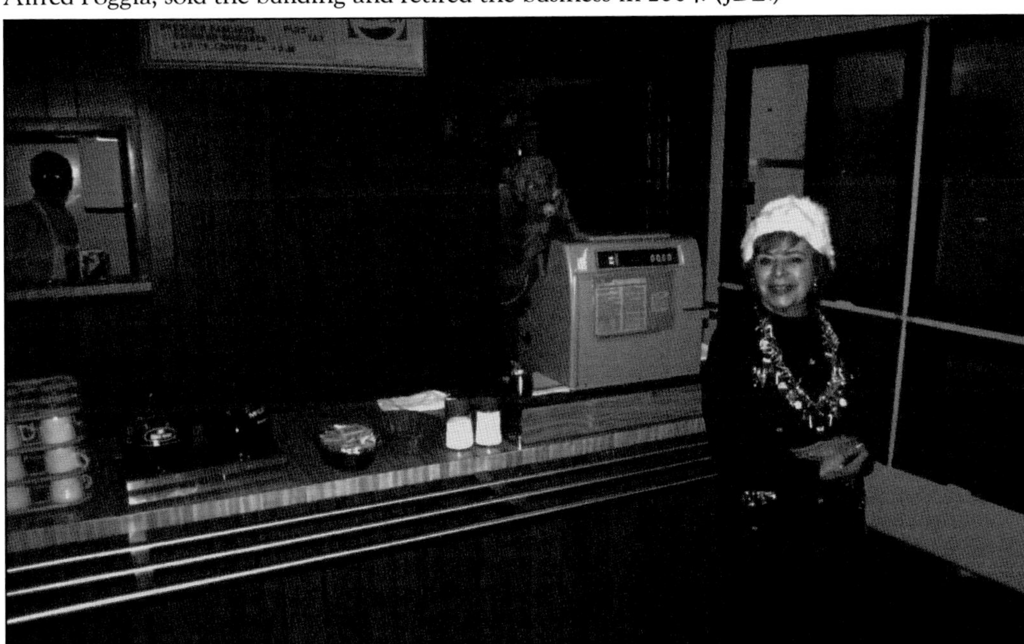

Every year at Christmas, Antler's Lounge and Grill offered a free meal to anyone who came through the door. As a way of giving back to the community, Foggia offered the traditional Christmas dinner for the homeless, the elderly, and others who might have spent the holiday alone. Staff pictured here are getting ready and taking reservations for the meal. (JDL.)

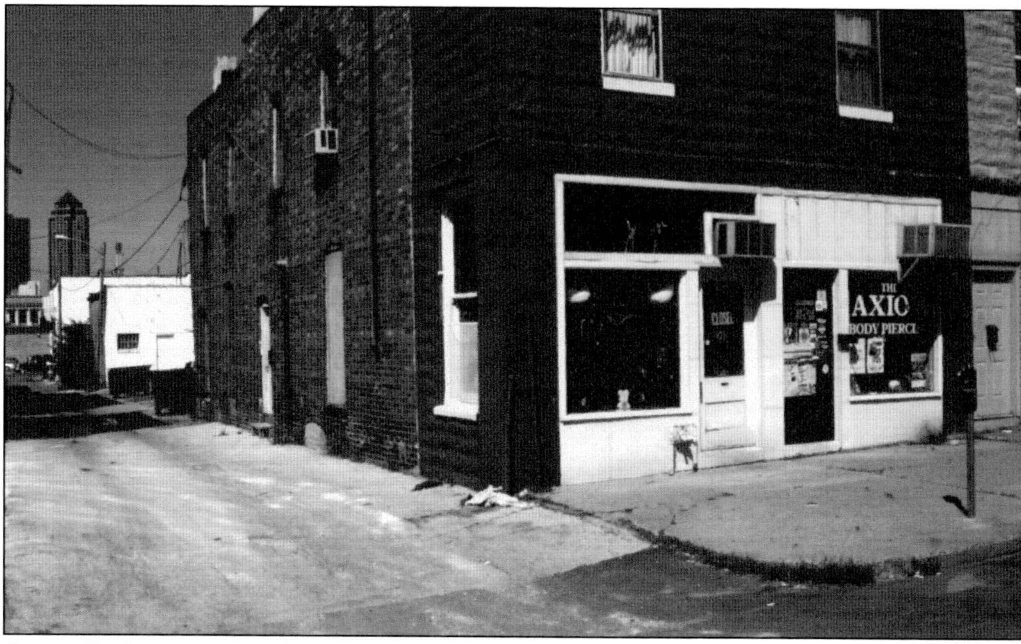

Axiom Body Piercing and Curl Up and Dye hair salon were early additions to the changing neighborhood in 2000. These stores were located on East Fifth Street between East Grand Avenue and East Locust Street. At the time, rents were cheap and the area was gaining a reputation for its diversity; several gay bars were within walking distance. This was different from the west side of the river, which had an established retail industry and entertainment district. (JDL.)

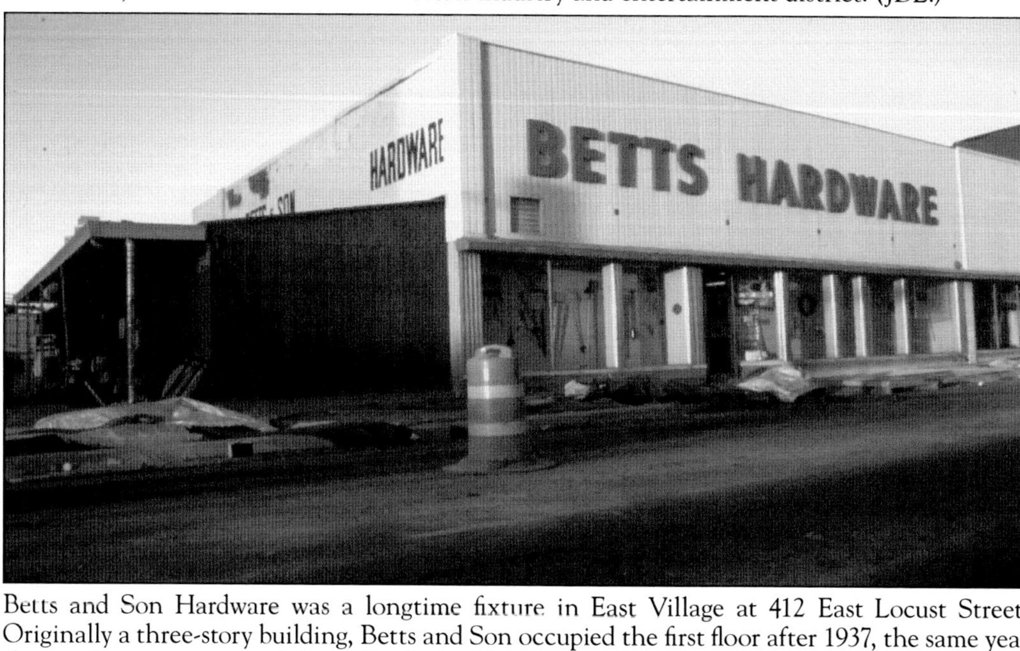

Betts and Son Hardware was a longtime fixture in East Village at 412 East Locust Street. Originally a three-story building, Betts and Son occupied the first floor after 1937, the same year the top floor was removed. In 1978, the building underwent a significant remodel, resulting in the appearance it had until it was torn down in 2000. What started as a hardware store ended with an emphasis on military surplus and paintball supplies. The business is now located on the south side of Des Moines. (JDL.)

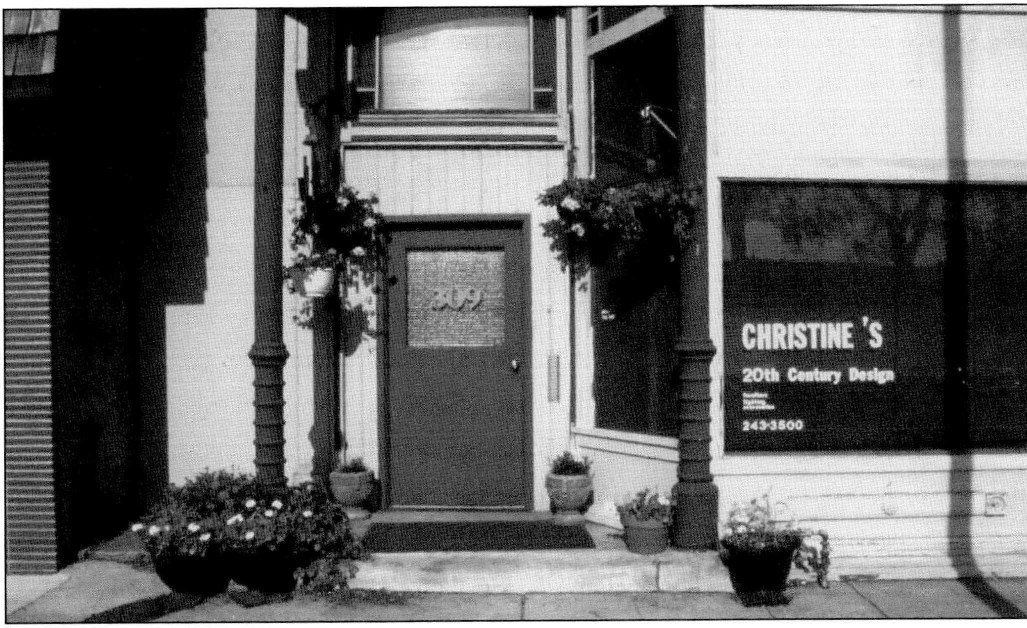

Christine Paskins owned and operated Christine's 20th Century Design—Furniture, Lighting, Accessories for more than 20 years at 309 East Fifth Street. She started the East Village Neighborhood Association and was active in the work to revitalize the neighborhood. This building is not there any more; it was torn down in 2007 as part of a larger land purchase, and now the land has a large residential and commercial building on it. Paskins died in 2008 at the age of 63. (JDL.)

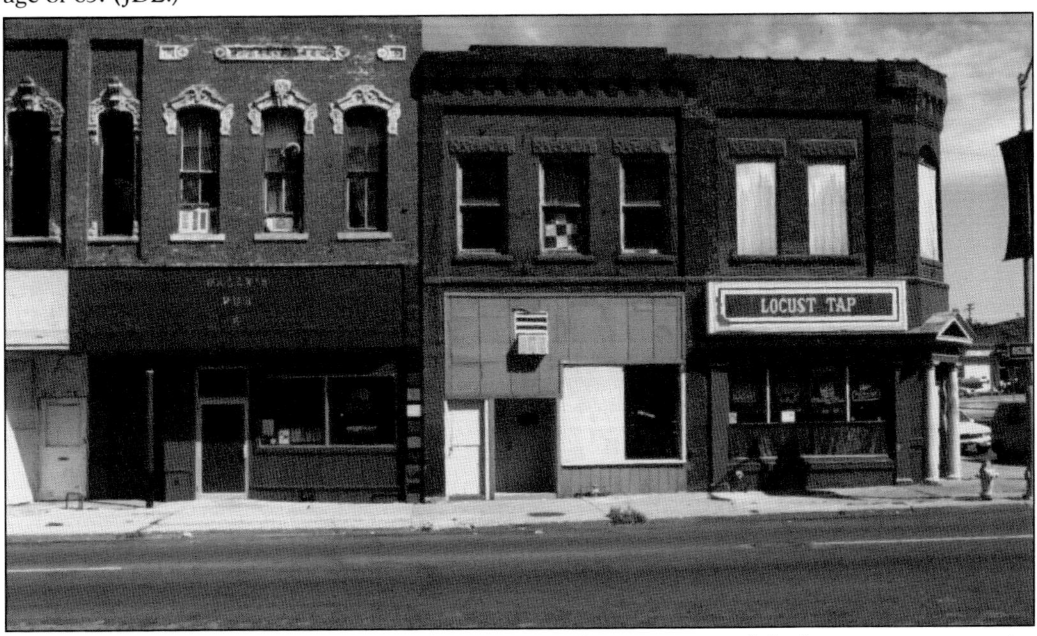

The northwest corner of East Fifth and East Locust Streets is one of the biggest success stories in East Village. This photograph, taken in 2000, shows neglected buildings and the lack of any street beautification. Locust Tap, on the corner, and the building adjacent were purchased by architect Kirk Blunck in 2003 and immediately renovated. These buildings date to 1895. (JDL.)

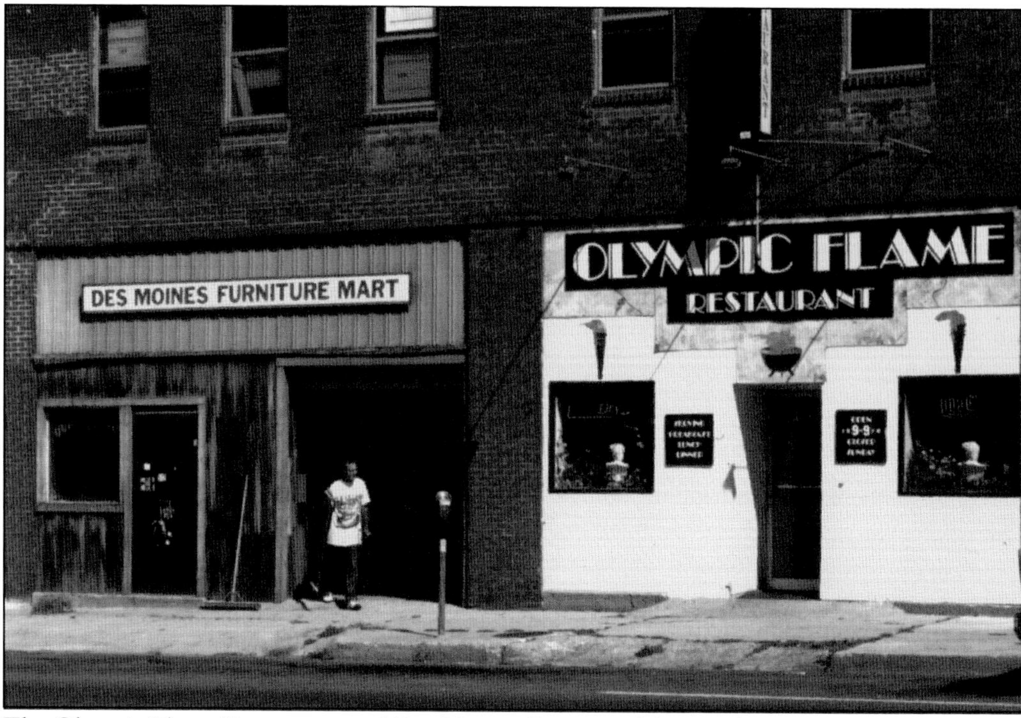

The Olympic Flame Restaurant and Des Moines Furniture Mart at 512–514 East Grand Avenue appear here prior to a building renovation in 2006. The furniture store is now gone and replaced by a sushi restaurant. Larger storefronts were added, and the two bays were updated to match business buildings on either side. There was still little attention paid to the aesthetics of East Grand Avenue, as evidenced here by the cracked sidewalks and curbs. (JDL.)

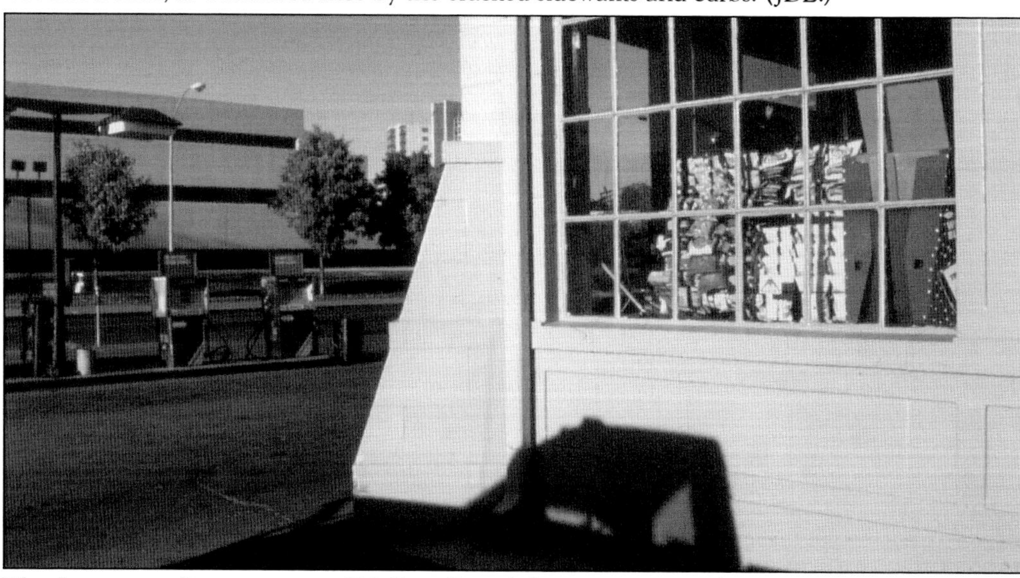

The former gasoline station at 203 East Grand Avenue was saved in 2008 from the wrecking ball after the property was purchased and planned for a parking lot. The building dates to the 1930s and is constructed of terra-cotta, a unique building material for that time. From the 1980s through 2008, the building was Don's East Grand Texaco. (JDL.)

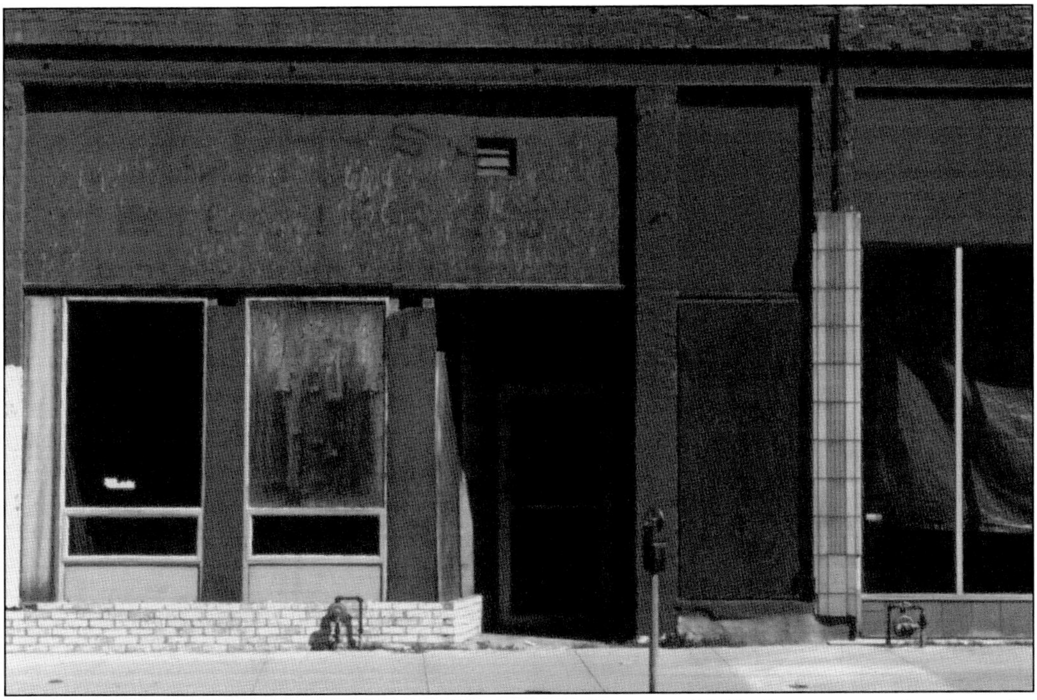

Here is a rough-looking storefront at 420 East Locust Street in 2000. One can just barely make out the sign that reads, "Al's Locust Billiards." At this time, the property was vacant and was probably vandalized or broken into since one of the windows is boarded. This property is now home to an upscale restaurant. (JDL.)

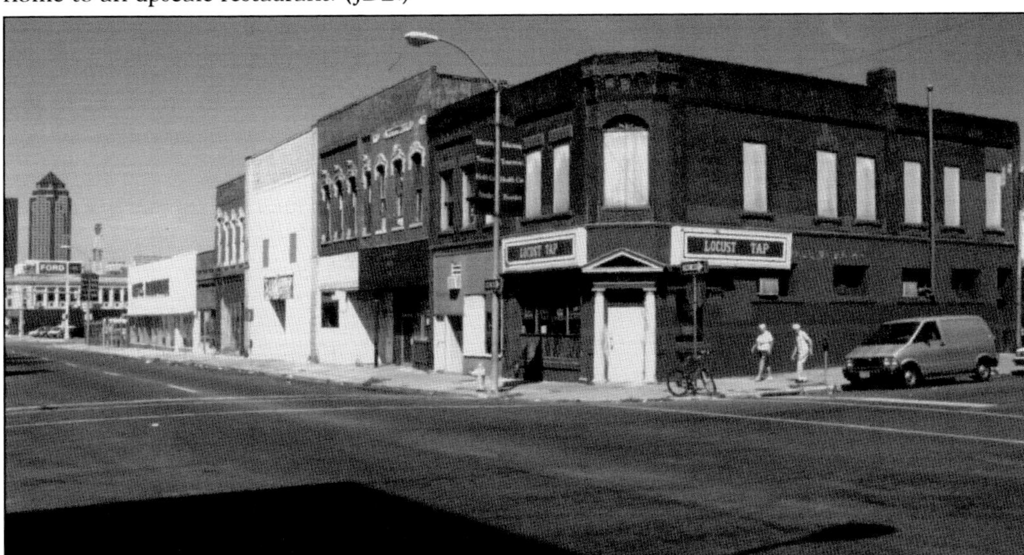

This is a better view down the 400 block of East Locust Street in 2000. The city dubbed it "the opportunity block" in a 2000 study, which stated, "While it has been agreed that every reasonable effort should be made to retain these historic structures, it is also clear this requires significant additional investment in stabilization and rehabilitation to insure their physical survival. Without that investment, they cannot survive." (JDL.)

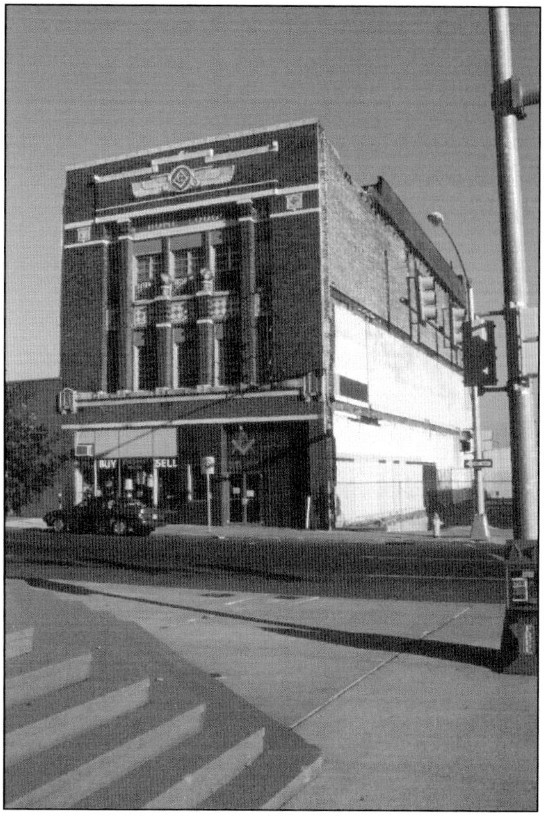

By 2000, the Masonic temple building at East Sixth and Locust Streets was a shell of its former glorious self. The adjacent building to the right had already fallen, literally. Although there are some remarkable architectural details to the facade, the interior of the building had been neglected beyond repair. It was demolished in 2001, with a new building planned for its place. (JDL.)

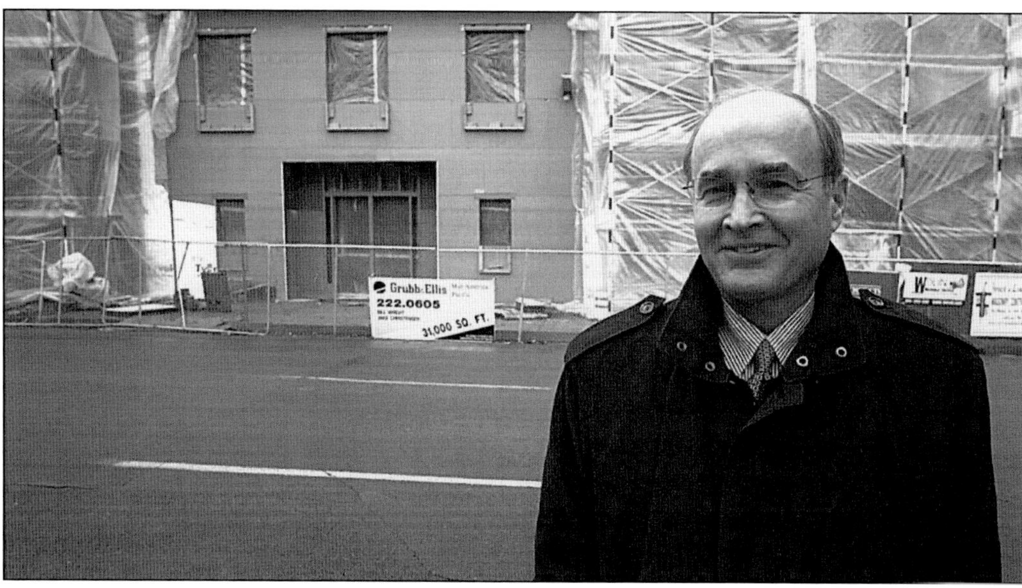

Iowa State Bank president and East Village developer John Burgeson stands in front of his new building at 601 East Locust Street. "Our Gateway plan, which was completed in 1997, recommended that we should preserve the architectural integrity of the area. We have tried to accomplish that theme. Our building is built with double-hung windows, stone sills and stone accents—the building will look like a new, 100-year-old building when completed." (DMBR.)

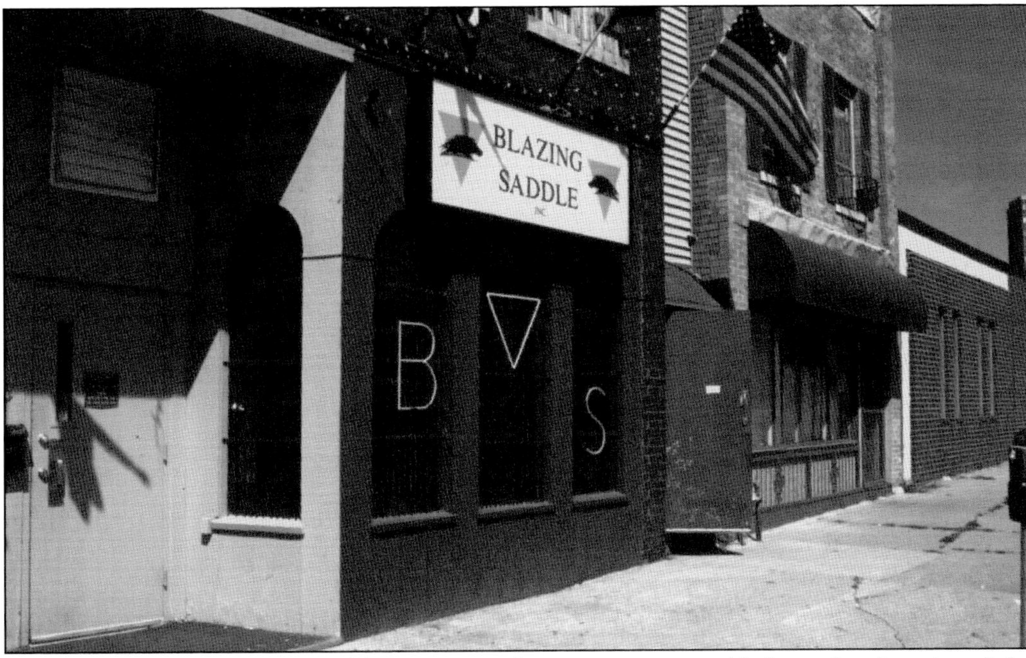

The Blazing Saddle on East Fifth Street is a front-runner to establishing the diversity of the East Village neighborhood. Owner Bob Eikleberry opened the gay bar in this location in 1992. He quickly became known for his support of the gay community and his outspoken activism for East Village. The bar has become increasingly popular among gays and straights alike, and the neighborhood has grown up around it. (JDL.)

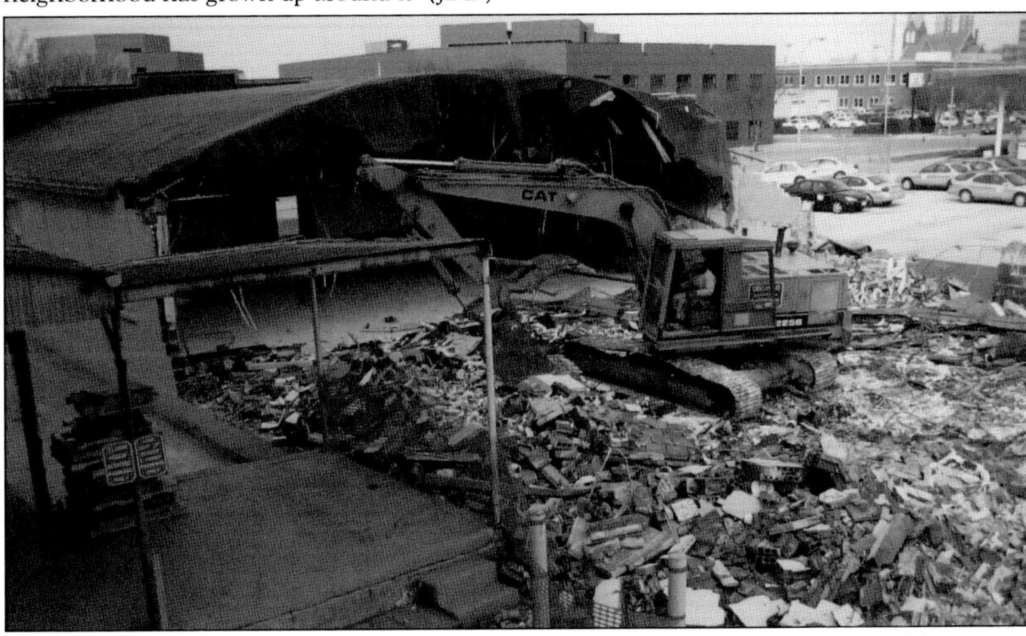

In 2004, the building that had housed the Citizen's Aid and Ombudsman's offices of the State of Iowa was torn down so that improvements could be made to what would be the new Department of Public Safety building next door. This building sat just south of the East Seventh Street and East Walnut Street corner. (SHSI.)

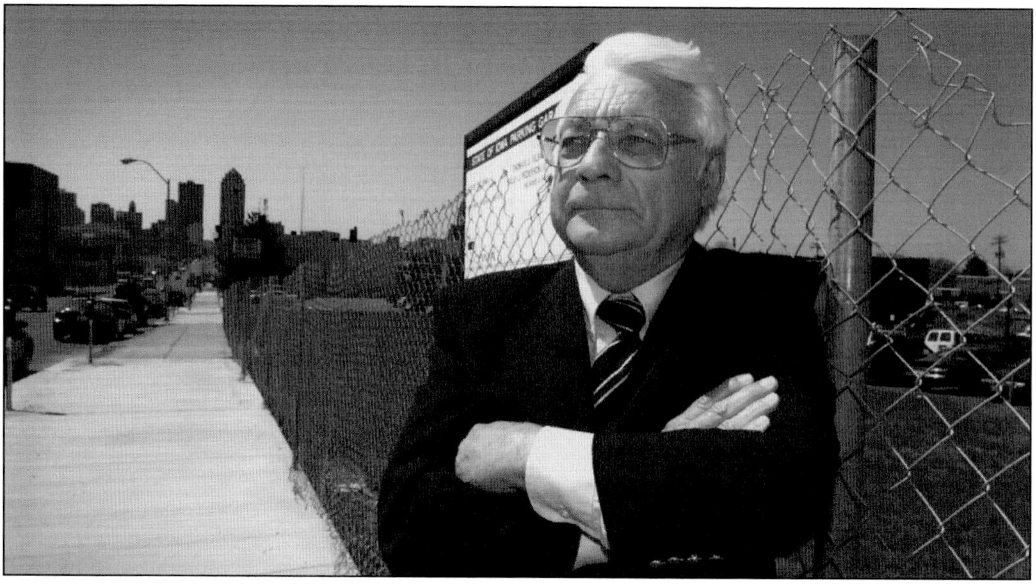

Longtime east side supporter Jim Boyt lobbied in 2000 to build a parking ramp on the corner of East Grand and Pennsylvania Avenues. He stands in front of the site prior to construction. Boyt's hope was to ease parking around the state capitol. His vision was to build a hotel in the area, something the parking ramp would have provided parking for. However, the hotel never came to fruition. (DMBR.)

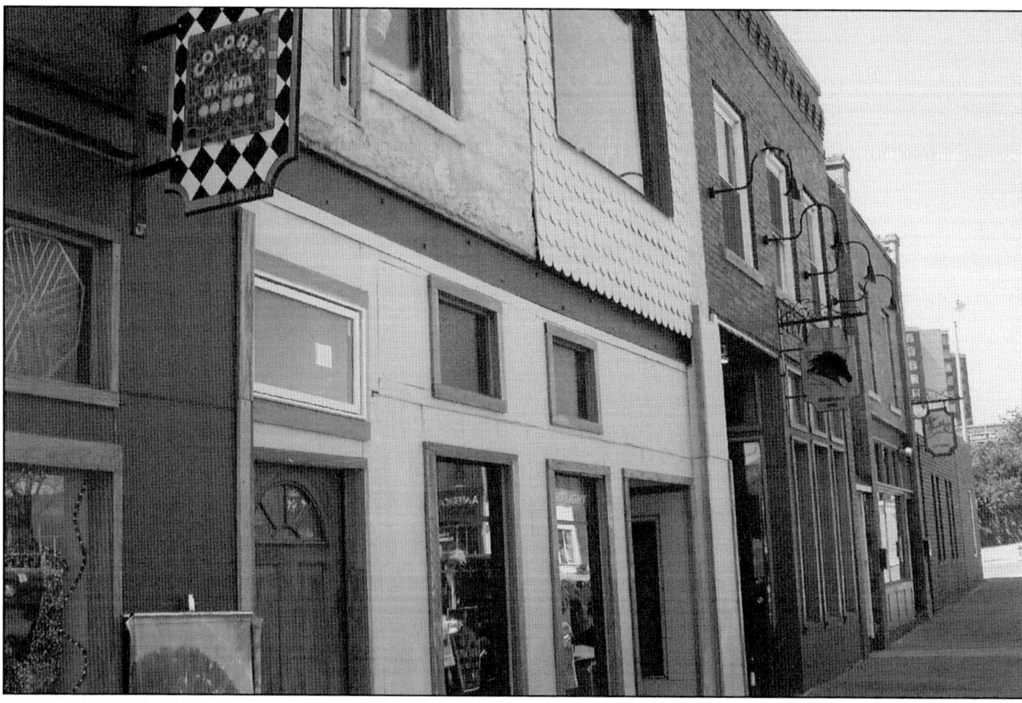

Here is East Fifth Street as it appeared in 2006. Storefronts have improved and outward signage has made its reemergence in the neighborhood. At this time, the businesses located in this small grouping of buildings include the Atlantean, Colores by Nita, the Blazing Saddle, Buddy's Corral, and an attorney's office on the corner. (Sarah Oltrogge.)

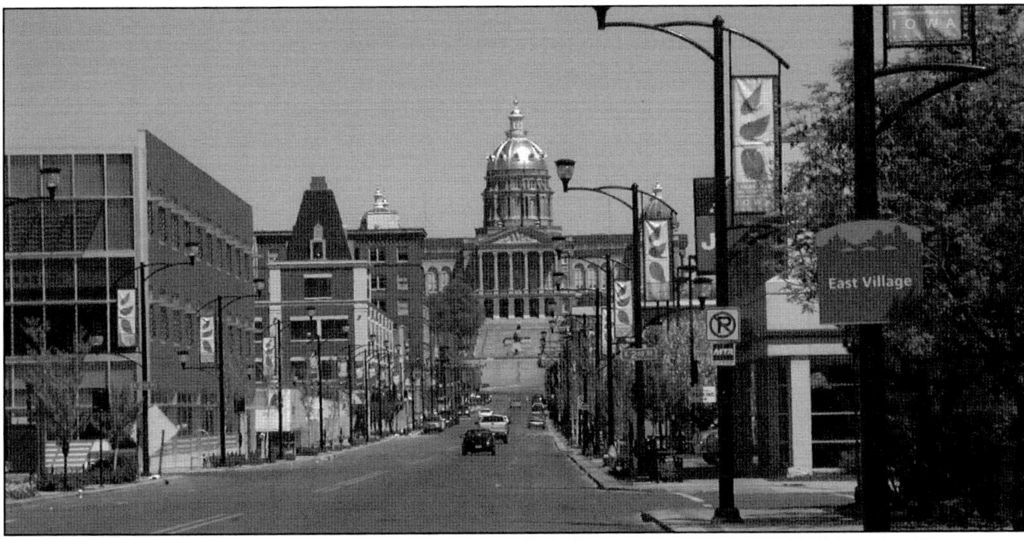

The view down East Locust Street in 2006 included new signage installed by the Downtown Community Alliance. The capitol building still stands tall in the background. The tower on the north side of the street belongs to the Soho Lofts building; the ultra modern building in the immediate foreground is where Metro Waste Authority and other small offices are located. (Sarah Oltrogge.)

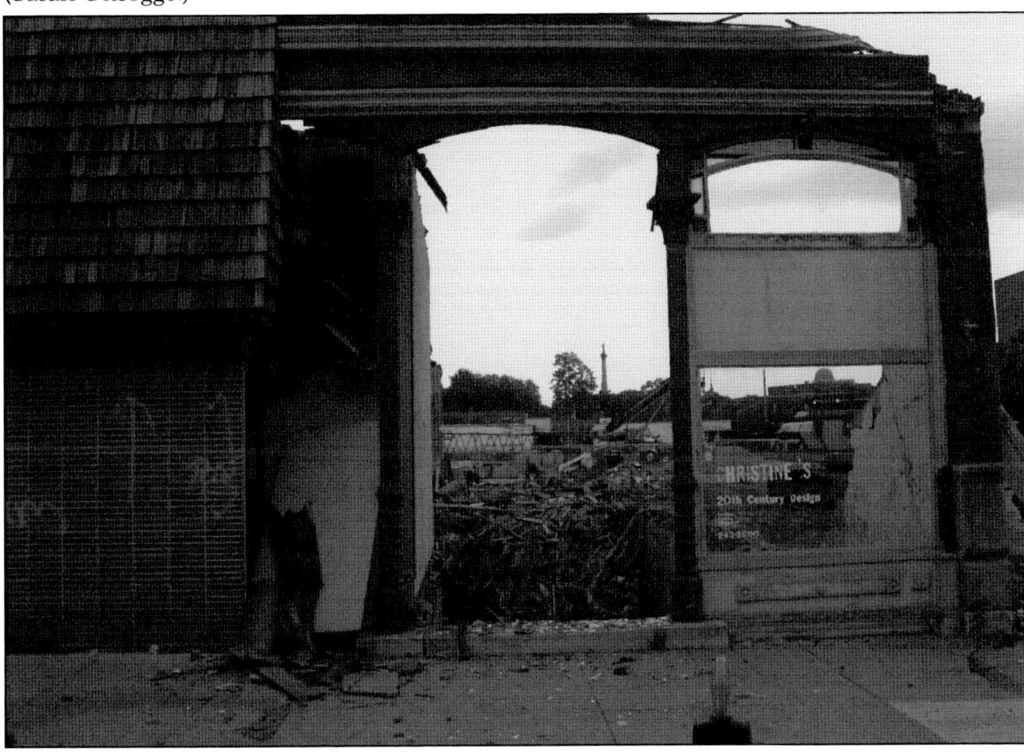

The building that had formerly housed Christine's 20th Century Designs was bulldozed in 2007. Located near the corner of East Fifth and East Walnut Streets, Christine's bordered a little-used parking lot and was prime for development. The property was purchased by S. T. Howard Development, who built e5w, a mixed-use urban loft. (Lisa Howard.)

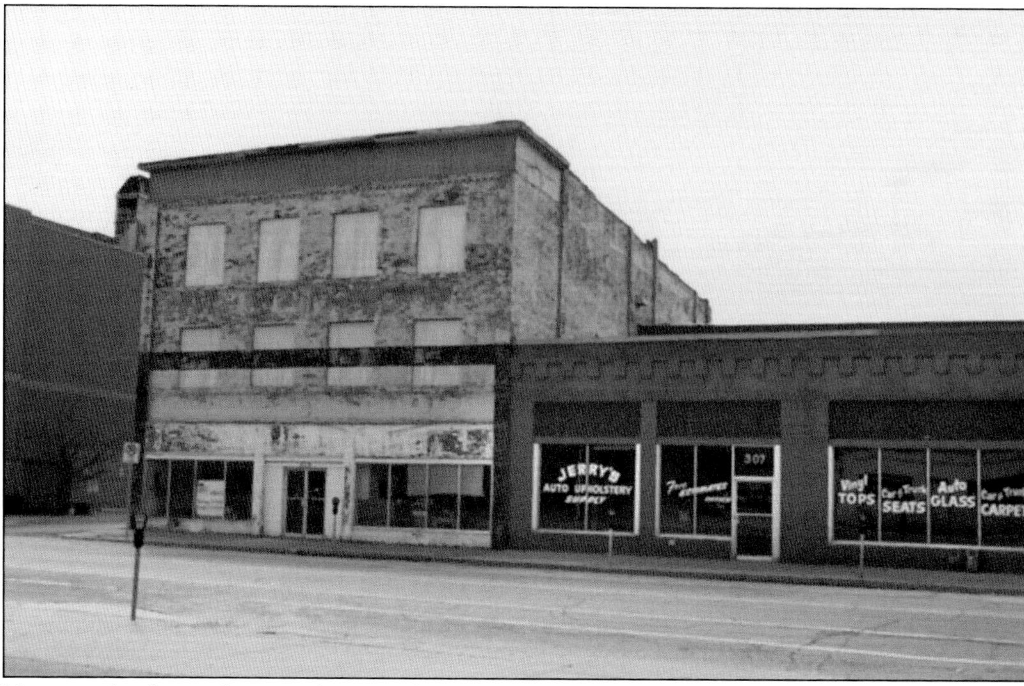

Here are the former homes of Sioux Plating Company, left, and Jerry's Auto Upholstery in the 300 block of East Walnut Street in 2008. The white building has been vacant for some time but is ripe for development. The area south of the main business district has growing interest for new development and rejuvenation. (Sarah Oltrogge.)

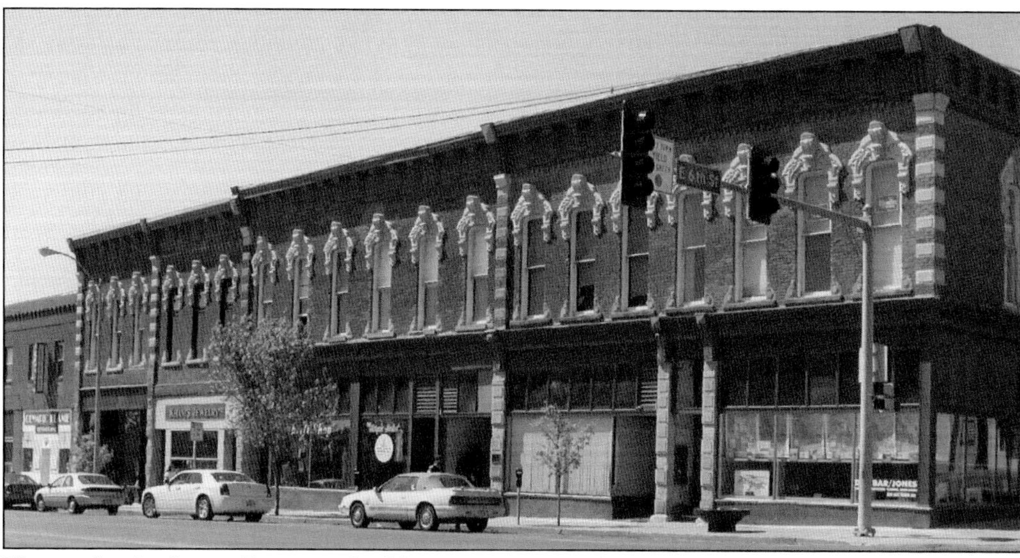

This is the Anderson Furniture building as it appeared in 2006, after it had recently changed ownership. The Bargain Basket thrift store, Kham Jewelry, and the Collector's Shop still occupied their spaces, although all moved out once updates were underway. A landscape architecture firm occupies the corner bay. (Sarah Oltrogge.)

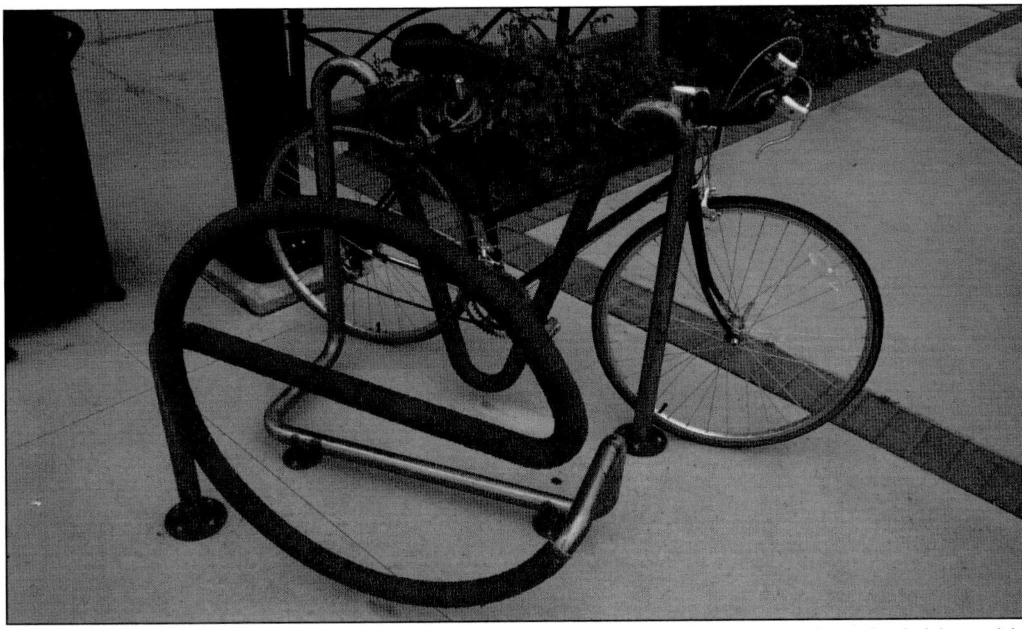

In 2005 and 2006, East Village became home to a series of bike racks made to look like public art. A first for the City of Des Moines, the "art racks" drew attention not only to utilitarian public art but also to an increasing commuter bike community. This art rack, called "ev," stands at East Fourth and East Locust Streets. (Victoria Watson.)

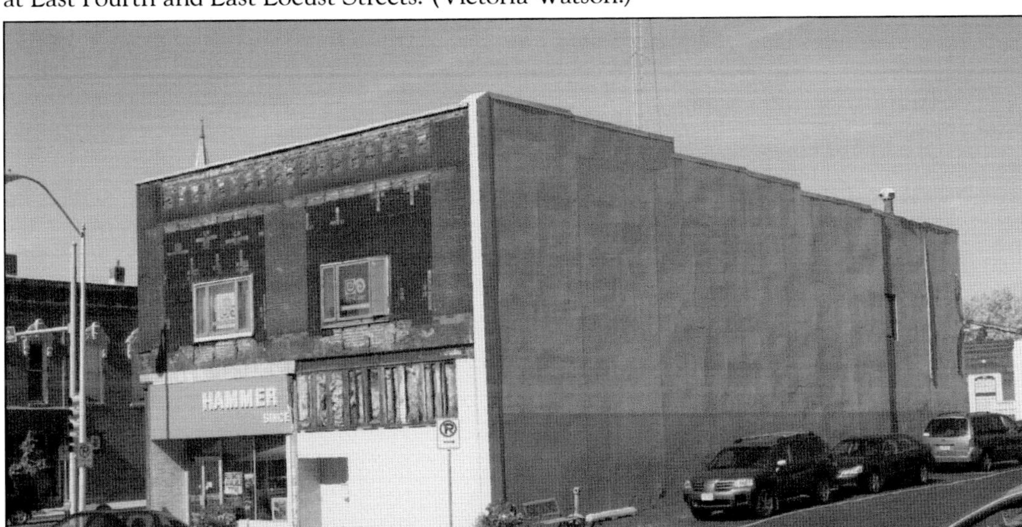

This photograph shows construction and destruction of the Hammer Pharmacy building began shortly after it changed ownership in 2007. The green siding that had been installed in the 1950s was removed to reveal the original brick exterior as well as a "ghost" advertising sign on the west wall. Today much of the exterior has been restored to its original look. (John Zeller.)

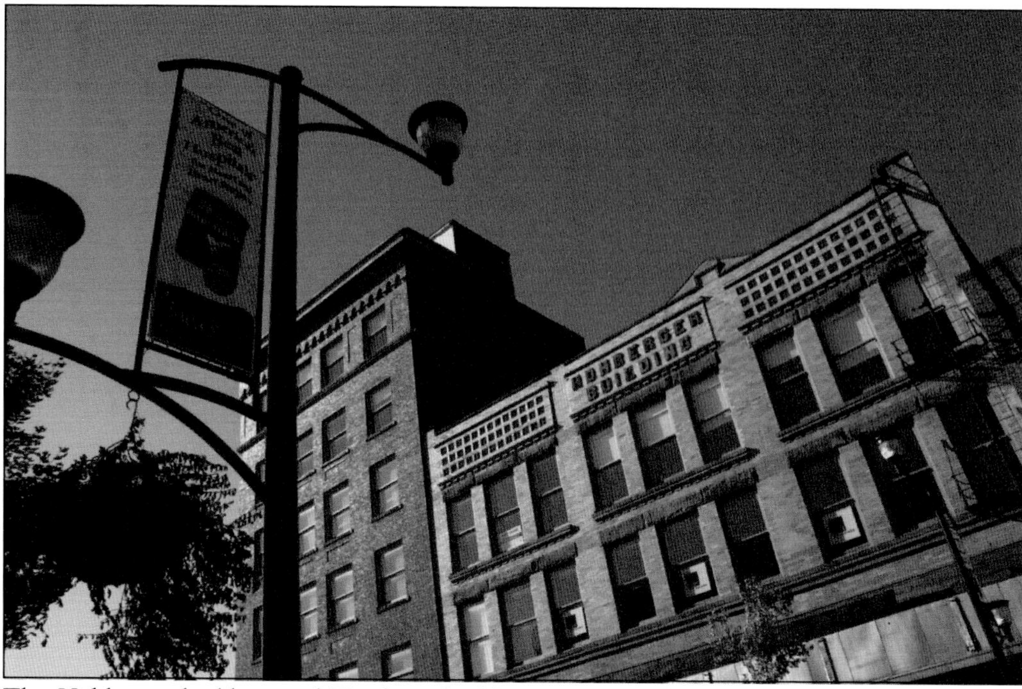

The Hohberger building and Teachout building remain linked partners in 2007. Hohberger housed the Ballet Des Moines Company, and Teachout housed small offices, studios, a retail store, and a residence on its very top floor. The two buildings were among the first to be renovated by Kirk Blunck in the late 1990s. (John Zeller.)

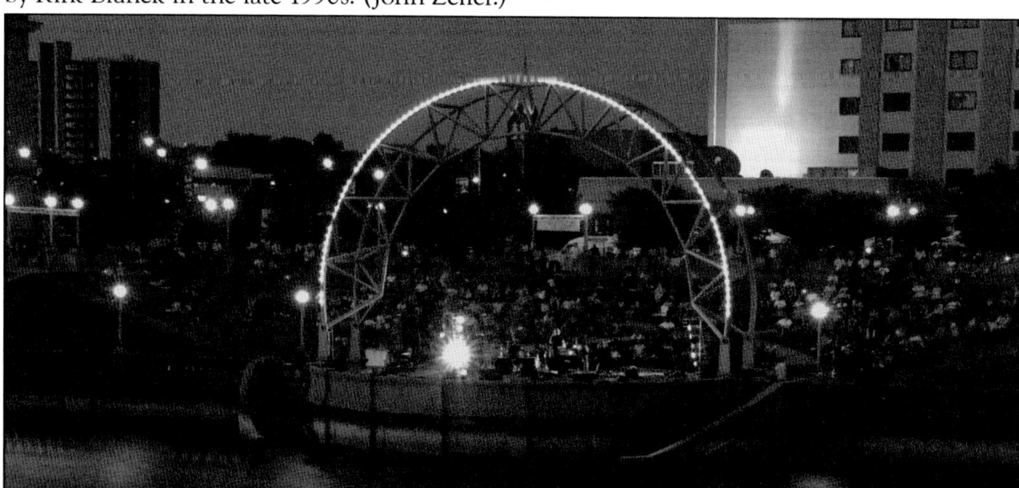

People enjoy an evening concert at Simon Estes Amphitheater. The amphitheater was constructed as an outdoor performance venue. In summer, it is popular for the Nitefall on the River and Alive concert series and has drawn nationwide touring acts. It also serves as a gathering spot for charity runs, Shakespeare performances, and private events. (Bill Nellans.)

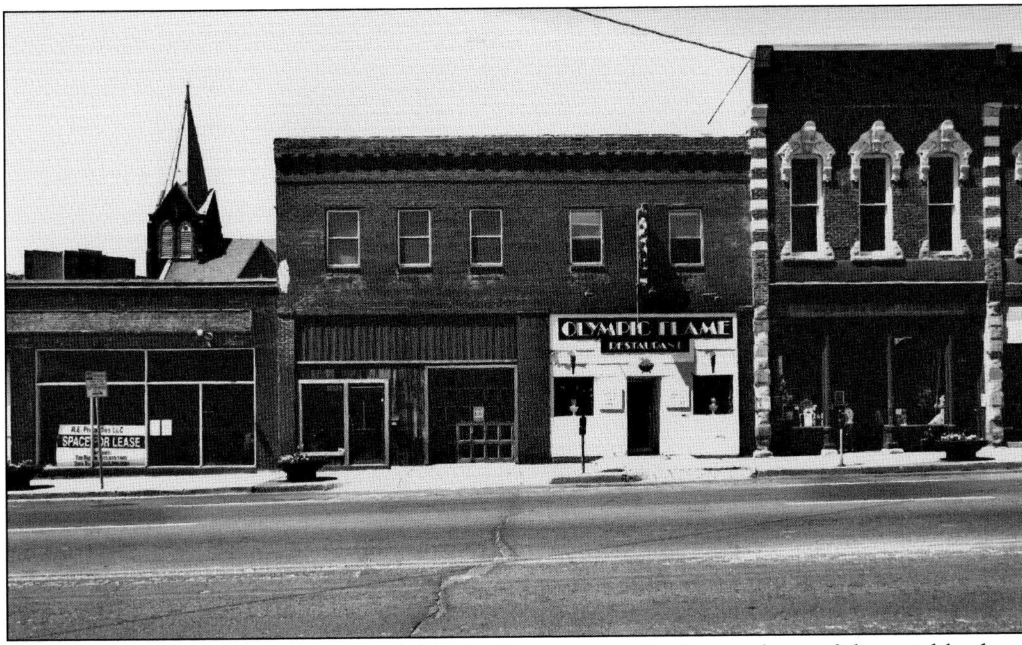

The Des Moines Furniture Mart and Aamco Transmission had moved out of the neighborhood at the time this photograph was taken in 2006. The storefronts and the streetscapes had changed little by this time, and East Grand Avenue was seeing none of the beautification effort that had taken place on East Locust Street one block south. (MN.)

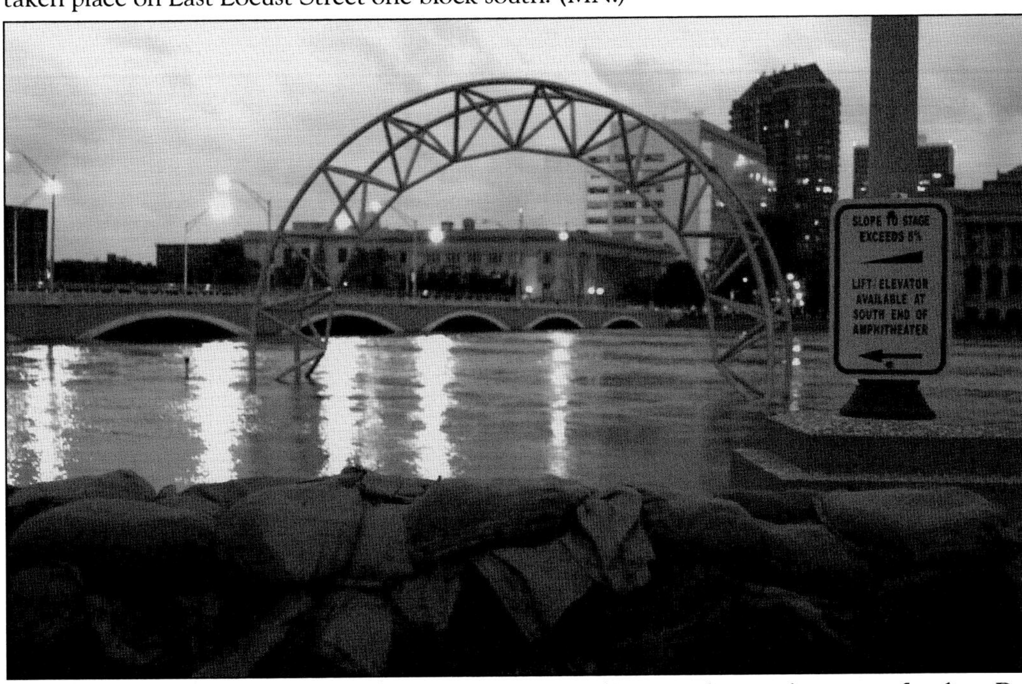

The Simon Estes Amphitheatre in East Village is underwater during the severe flooding Des Moines experienced in June 2008. The outdoor entertainment venue was unusable for weeks during and after the flood. Clean up was expeditious, however, and concerts were quickly back on the schedule. (Nicolaas Bertelsen.)

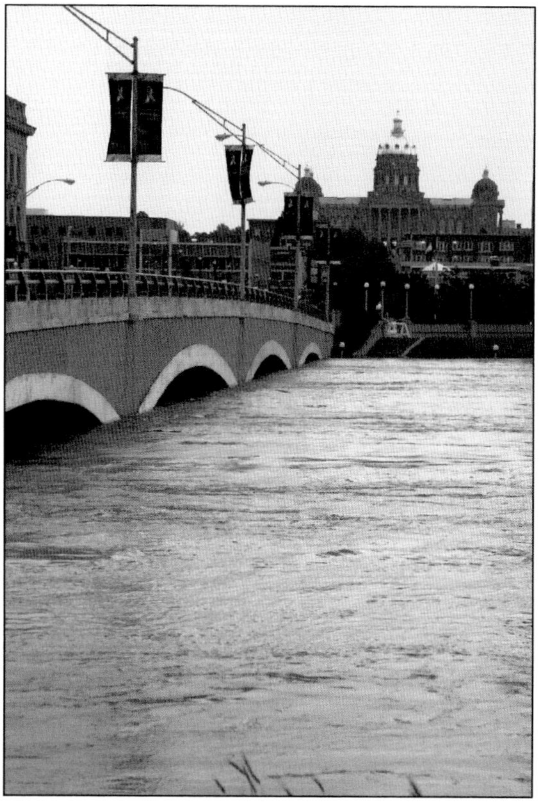

The City of Des Moines has experienced major flooding at least four times in the last century, including 1903, 1967, 1993, and 2008, when this photograph was taken. Because it sits right along the Des Moines River, East Village was put on high alert in June 2008 as over-burgeoned waters threatened the metro area. Most of the neighborhood came away unscathed, while major damage and loss occurred farther upstream when a levee broke. (Nicolaas Bertelsen.)

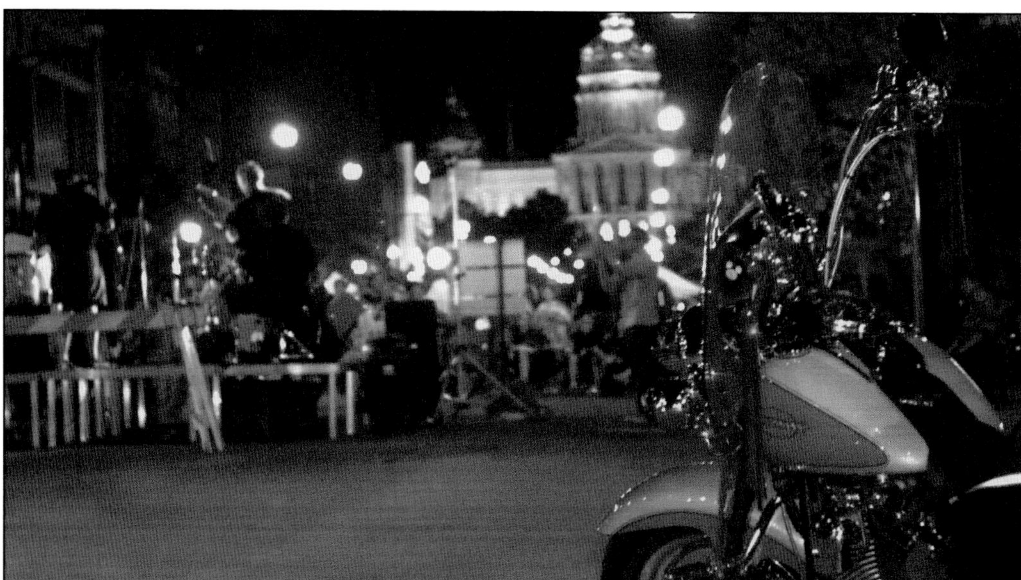

East Village Bike Night 2007 let the state capitol be the backdrop to bands, entertainment, and numerous motorcycles. As one of East Village's most popular events, bike night draws thousands of people to the neighborhood all looking to show off their bikes and admire others. Music, food, and bikes add to the recognition of the East Village as a cultural and entertainment district. (Bill Nellans.)

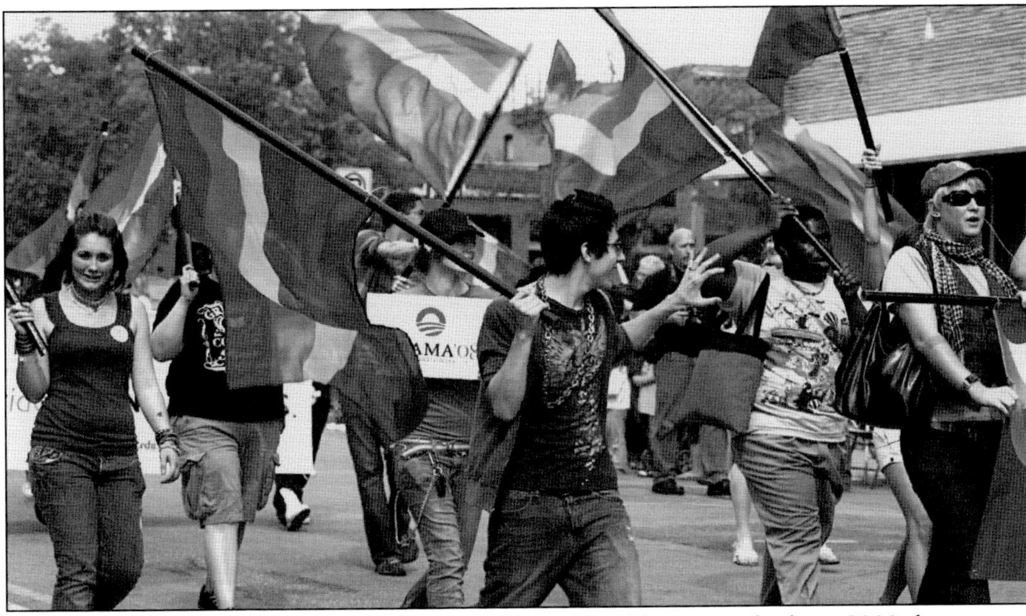

Every year, East Village hosts the Capital City Pride celebration, which in 2008 drew record attendance. The weekend includes a celebration parade from the state capitol to the river. Music, food, and educational programs are also included. The neighborhood is known for its welcoming diversity and for the numerous gay bars that reside in the vicinity. (Jeff Gitchel.)

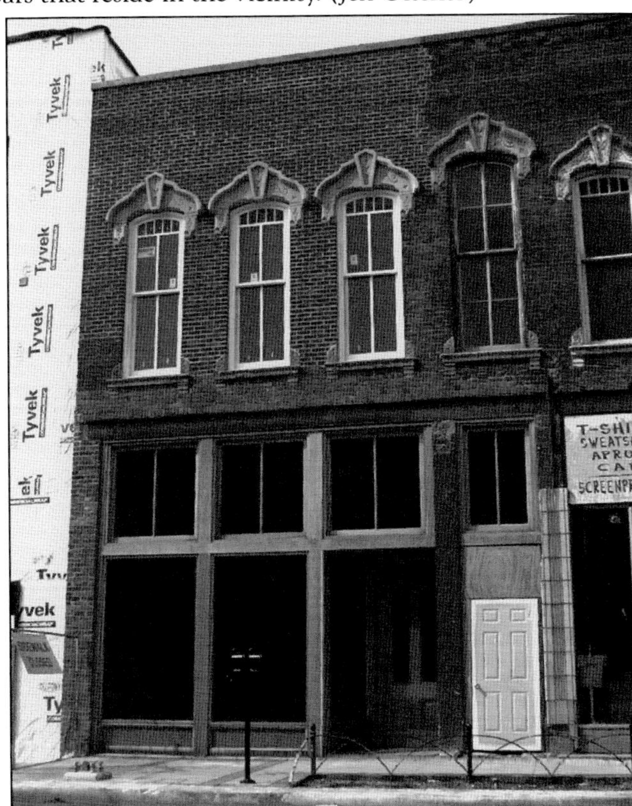

This building, which now houses an upscale restaurant, underwent incredible transformation in 2006. What was formerly a run-down adult bookstore was rebuilt from the ground up. The second story was added to match its neighbor on the right. Look closely to see the subtle variation in the brick pattern toward the roof. The window caps and windows also were custom made to provide a seamless transition from one building to the next. (Polk County Assessor.)

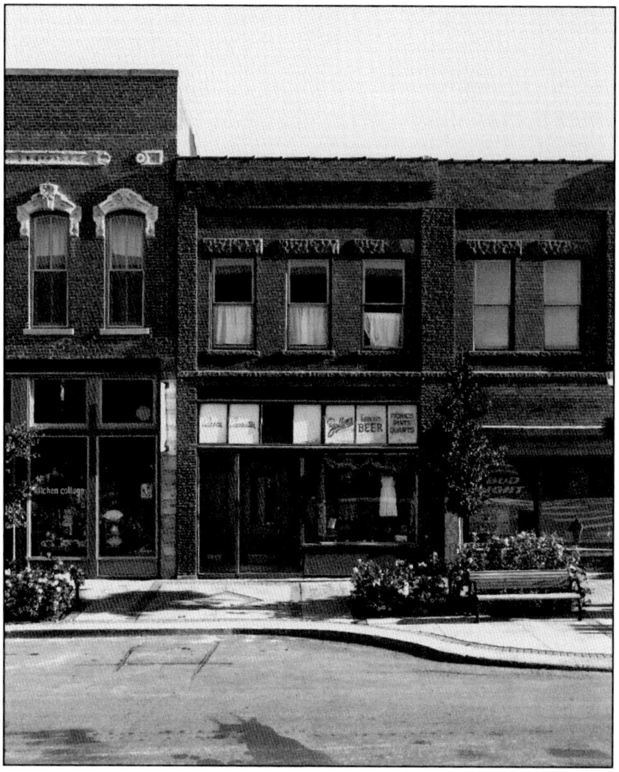

The landscaping, benches, and renovated building fronts added greatly to the East Locust Street corridor. The 2000 East Village Study Block report states, "There is no other area in the greater downtown or inner city of Des Moines that offers the same combination of small scale historic buildings and small locally-owned specialty retail, entertainment and dining businesses . . . No better opportunity exists in Des Moines to expand opportunities for an urban lifestyle associated with the assets of the East Village." (MN.)

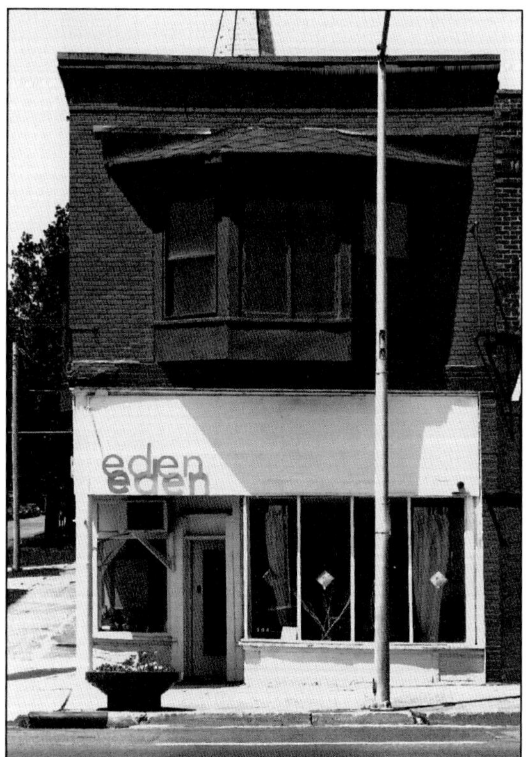

The bath store Eden is seen here as it appeared in 2006 on the corner of East Fifth Street and East Grand Avenue. The store and its products fit in well there amid the emerging upscale boutiques. The store opened in this location in 2003 and by 2008 was renovating another historic building in the neighborhood in which a second shop would be opened. (MN.)

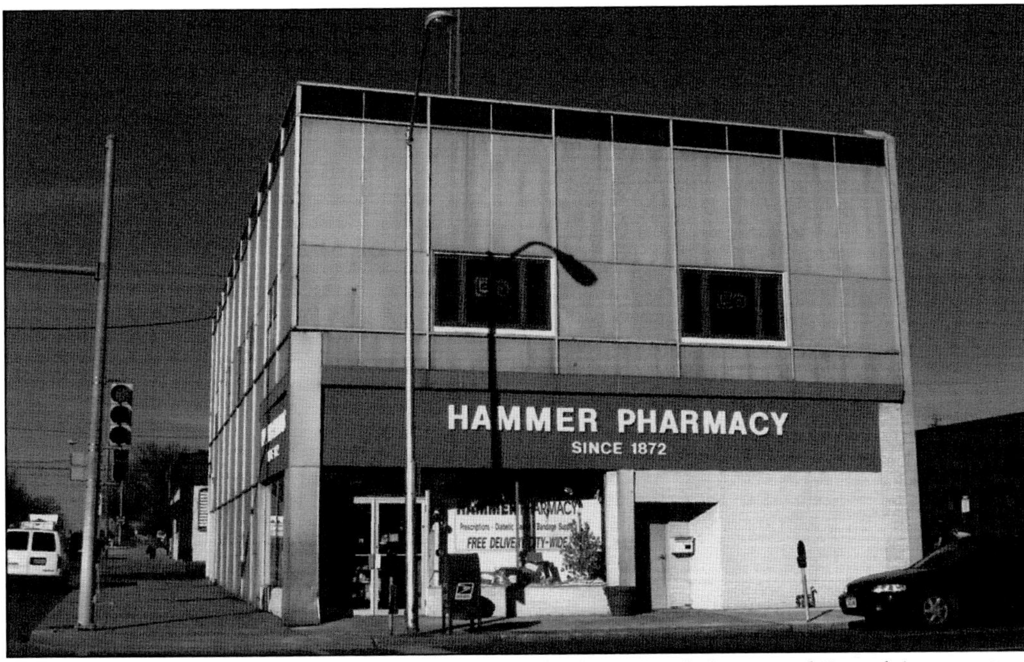

Hammer Pharmacy has been a fixture on the corner of East Sixth Street and Grand Avenue since 1872. It is the oldest pharmacy in Iowa. In the 1950s, green siding was added to its exterior. This photograph was taken in 2007 shortly before the building changed ownership and restoration work began. The building houses the pharmacy and ResCare, Inc., a support service for people with disabilities and special-needs youth. ResCare president Bill Dodds purchased the building and drove the restoration. (Polk County Assessor.)

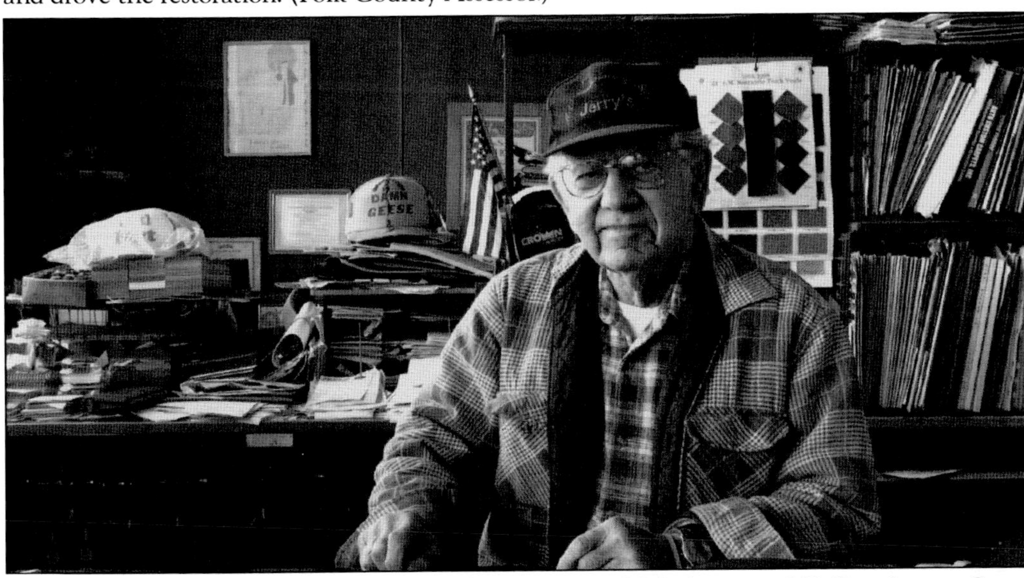

Jerome (Jerry) Geller owned and operated Jerry's Auto Upholstery at 309 East Locust Street since 1972. Photographer Matt Niebuhr spent a day photographing Geller and his shop in 2007. "Oddly to me—Jerry seemed to be more at ease with the impending changes than I expected—maybe that's the perspective you gain over 89 years of living and seeing the world change around you." (MN.)

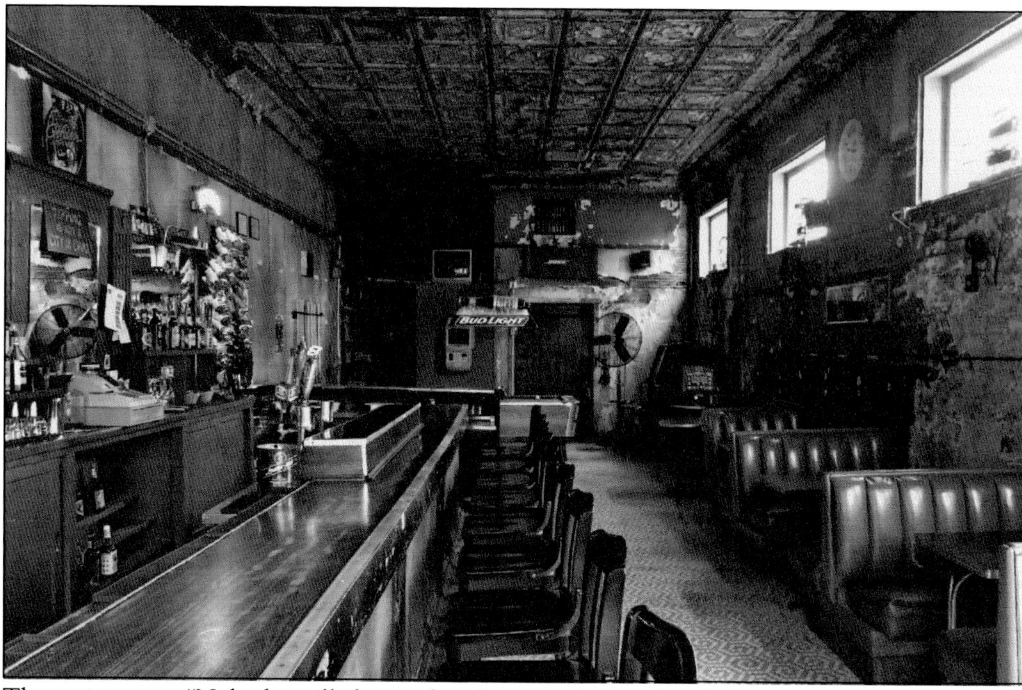

The saying goes, "Nobody really knows how long the Locust Tap has been in existence because everyone who was there at the beginning has since died." Needless to say, it is one of the oldest drinking establishments in Des Moines. The bar still has its original tin ceiling, heating system, tiles, and plaster walls, which lend to its charm. (MN.)

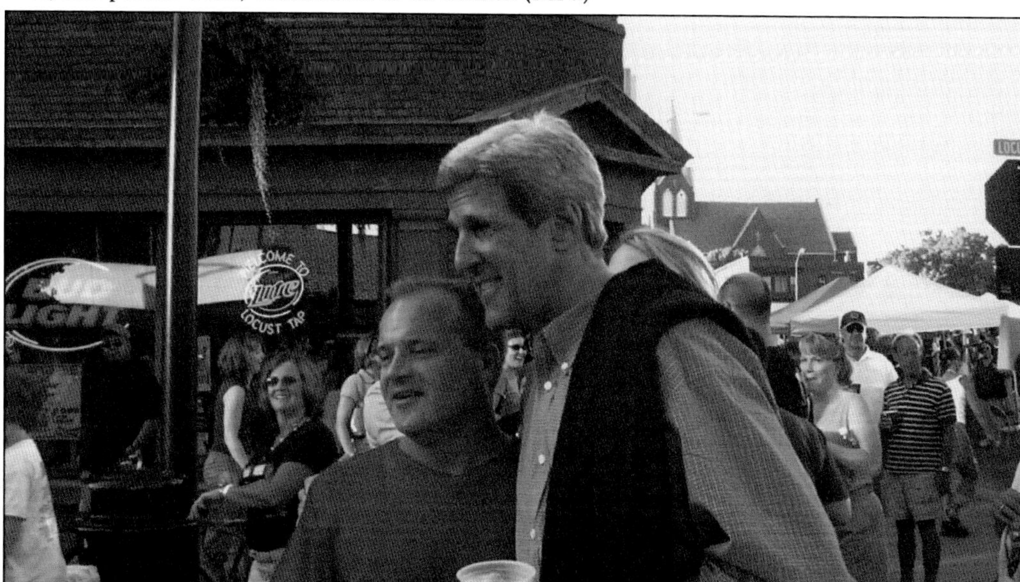

Sen. John Kerry attended the 2006 East Village Bike Night while he was in town. Although he had lost the presidential nomination two years prior, Kerry still drew fans and supporters during the event, even relaxing enough to enjoy a beer and admire the many motorcycles in attendance. The photograph here was taken in front of the Locust Tap at East Fifth and East Locust Streets. (Historic East Village, Inc.)

Started in 2005, the World Food Festival formed to highlight Iowa's diverse cultural traditions. People can taste their way around the world while enjoying traditional, ethnic entertainment. The festival also highlights Des Moines as the home of the World Food Prize, an annual honor recognizing the "achievements of individuals who have advanced human development by improving the quality, quantity or availability of food in the world." (Downtown Events Group.)

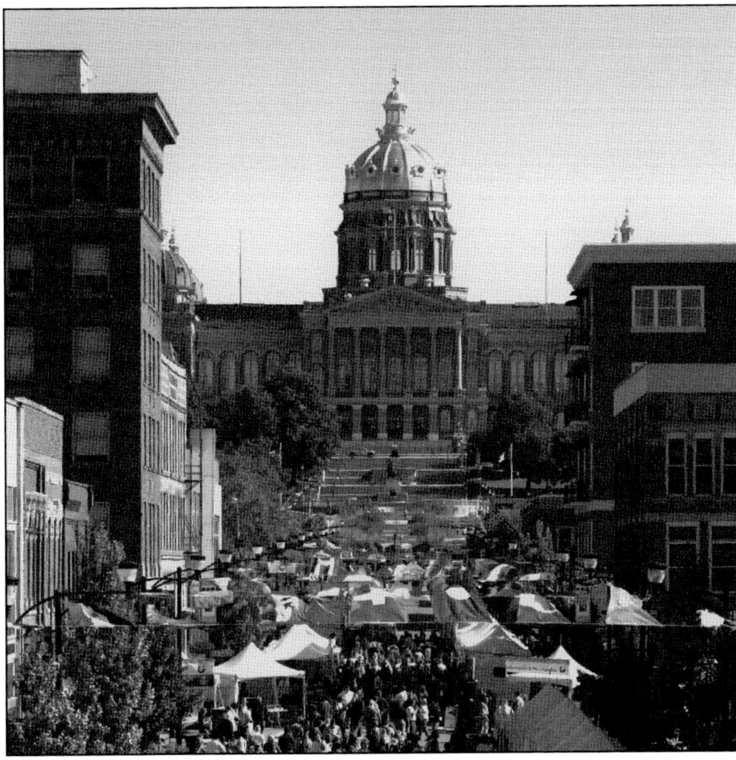

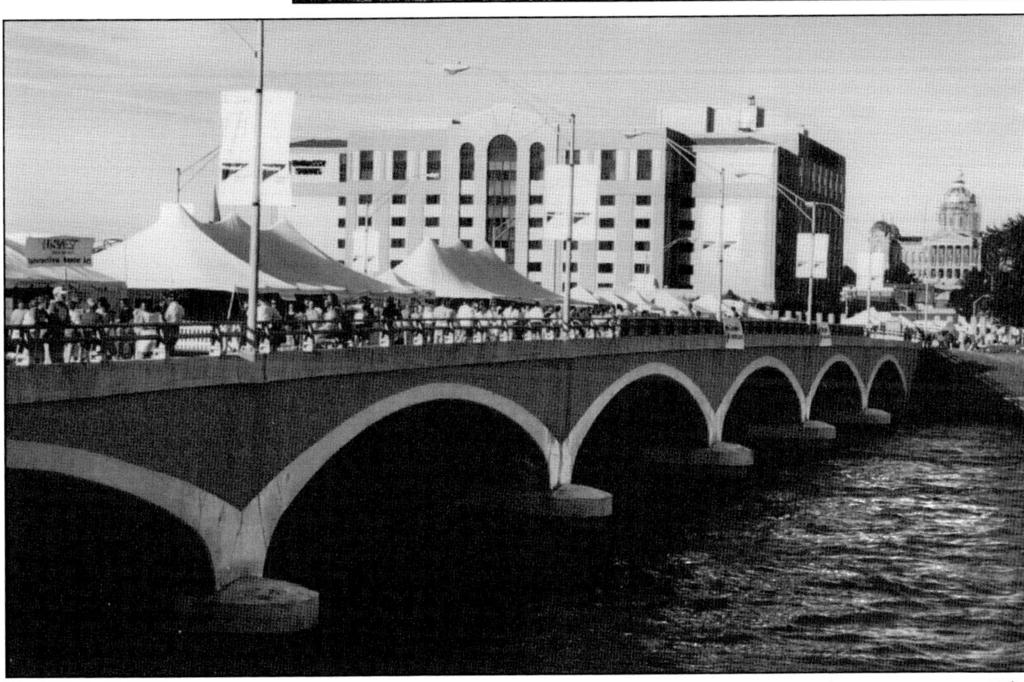

The Des Moines Arts Festival is a popular event that has earned nationwide recognition. The event did not really pick up full steam until it moved downtown and relocated from the state fairgrounds to the banks and bridges of the Des Moines River. The event draws thousands of people to the city to see the finest artists locally and from across the country. (CDM.)

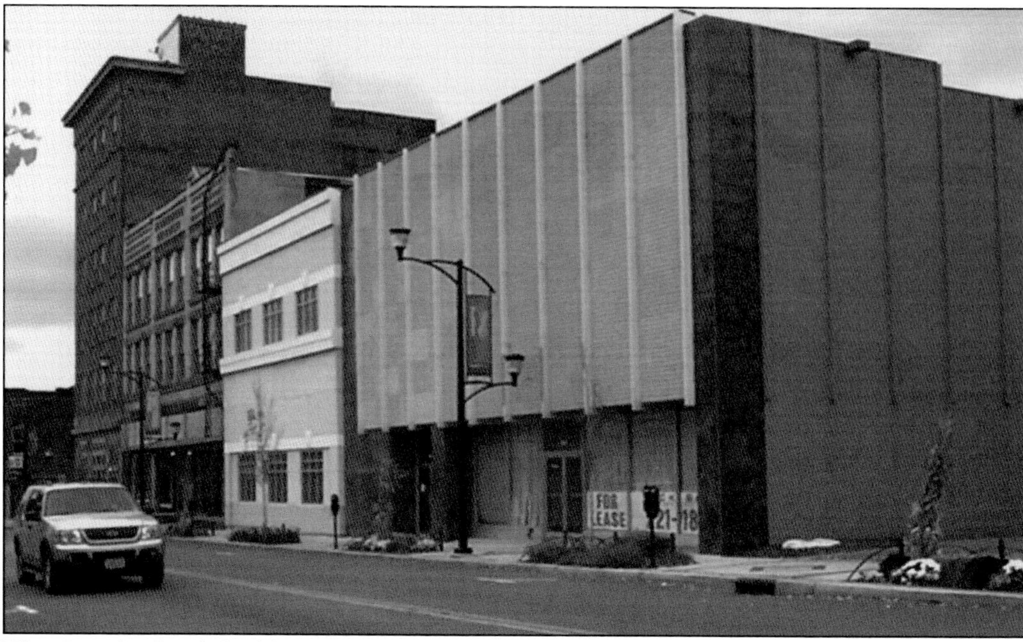

The Scandia Bank building at 510 East Locust Street is seen here prior to its purchase and renovation in 2005. The building had hardly changed since its exterior was altered in the 1960s. An architectural firm out of Dubuque redesigned the building and made it into its new Des Moines office, and added retail bays at the street level. The building had gone through varying tenants since 1990. (Durrant.)

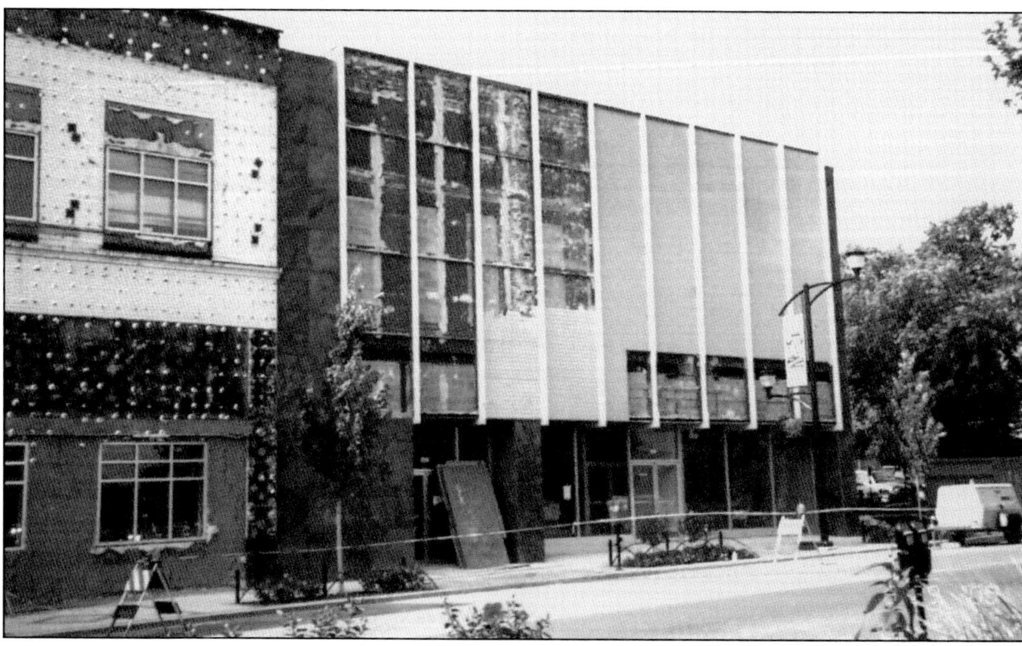

The Scandia Bank building dates to 1895. As renovation got underway in 2005, the external siding was removed to reveal the original windows and exterior. The second floor was opened up for office space, leaving the interior brick walls exposed. With its location near the busy East Locust Street and East Sixth Street intersection, the building was prime for development. (Durrant.)

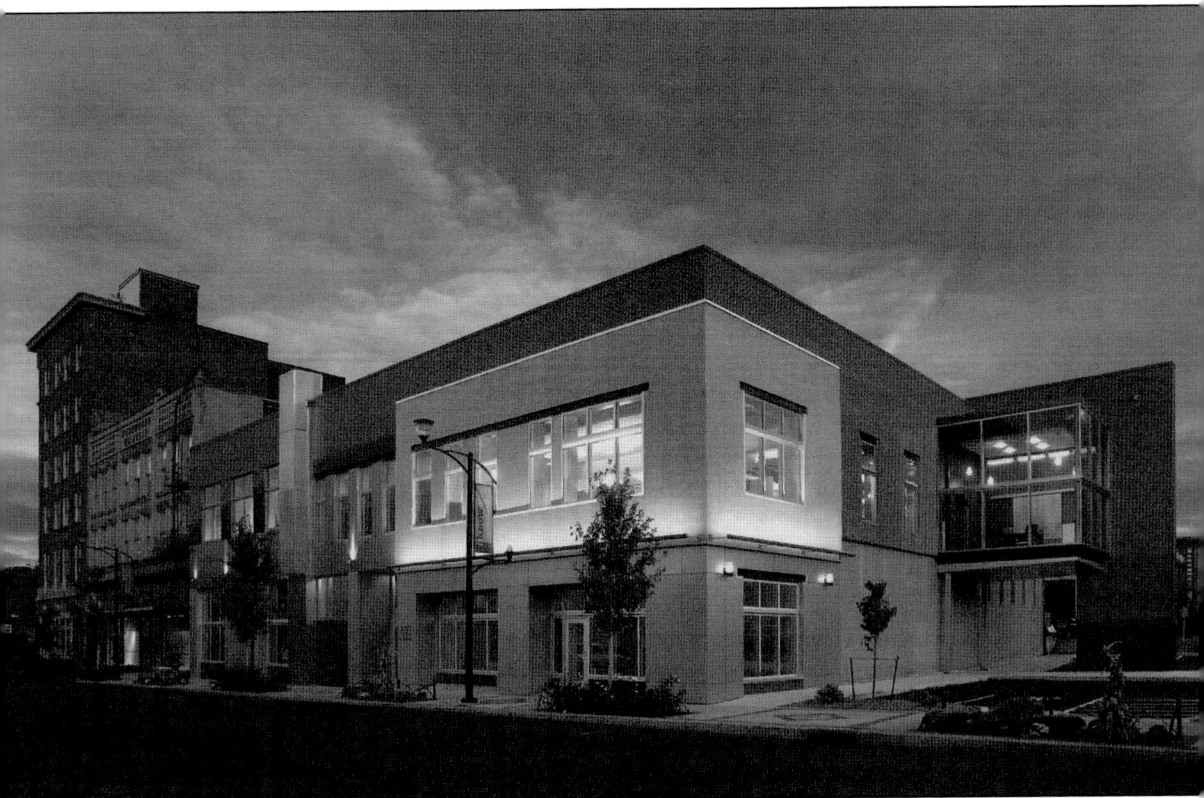

The final product of the newly redesigned Scandia building was unveiled in 2006 as offices and a new bookstore moved in. Jon Garnaas purchased the building at 510 East Locust Street in 1989. His son Luke was helping clean up properties owned by the Garnaas family when he mentioned to his dad that he should have sold the Scandia building long ago, particularly after the floods of 1993 damaged it. However, managing this property and a few others was just the start of what would become Ladco Development, Inc., in 1998. Durrant Architects and Engineers, who use the second floor of the building for their Des Moines office, handled the redesign. The exterior was brought up to date; note the glass cube second-floor meeting space above where the bank drive-through used to be. An LED light sculpture affixed to the front of the building changes colors. (Durrant.)

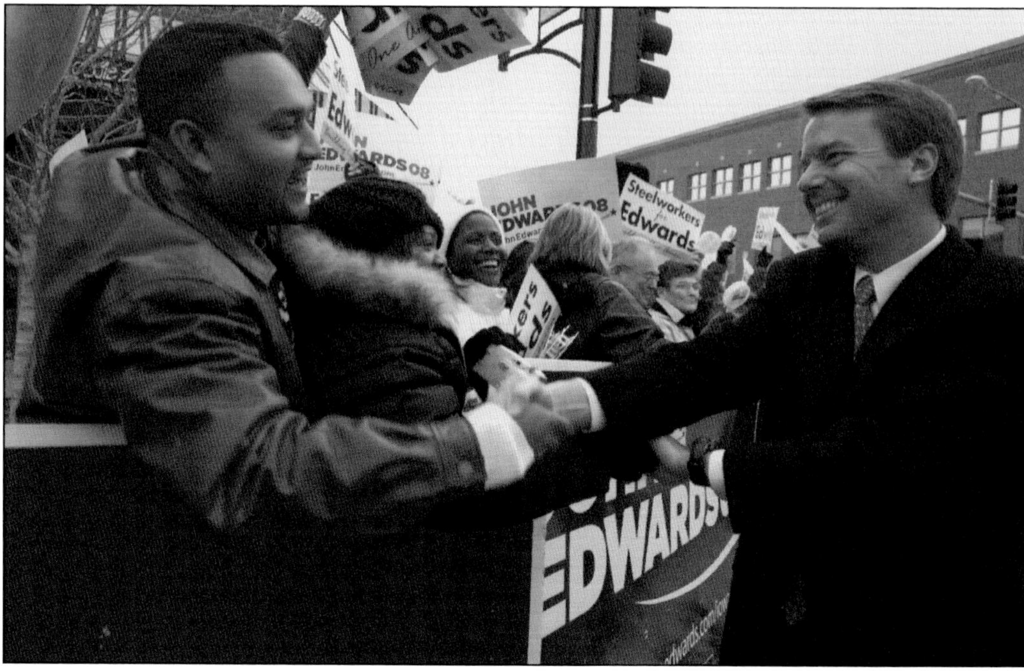

John Edwards greets supporters in December 2007 at the corner of East Sixth and East Locust Streets. He was in Des Moines taking part in a democratic candidate debate on National Public Radio, hosted at the State Historical Building. All candidates were in attendance, as well as more than 100 international media outlets and countless more supporters. (Alex Cooney.)

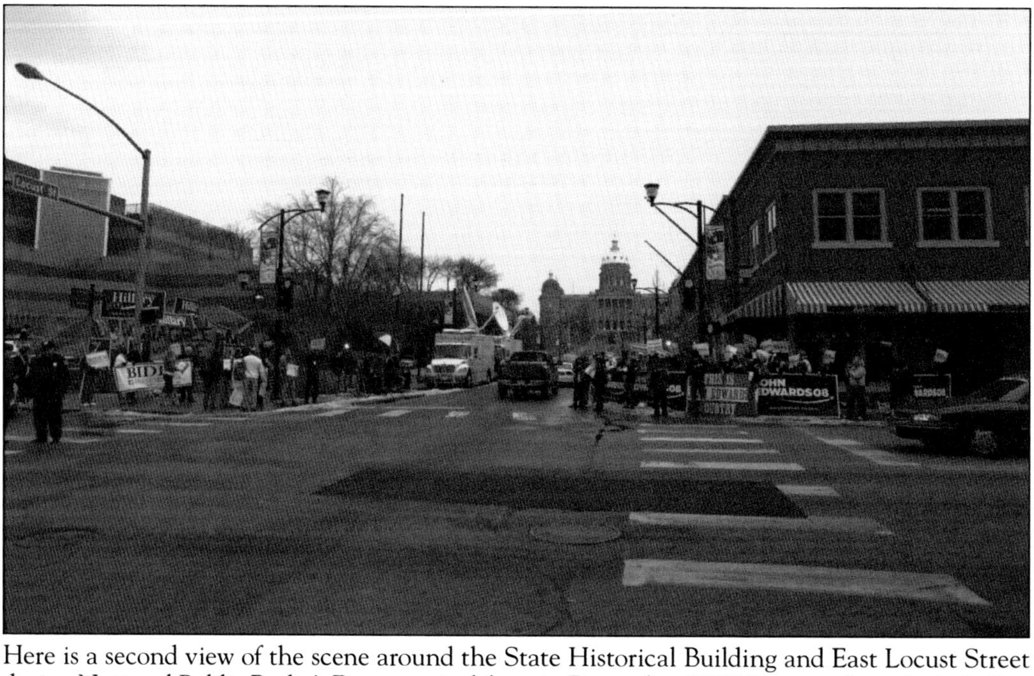

Here is a second view of the scene around the State Historical Building and East Locust Street during National Public Radio's Democratic debate in December 2007. Iowa, and particularly Des Moines, receive much attention from the candidates and worldwide media in the weeks prior to its first-in-the-nation caucuses, which are traditionally held in January. (Alex Cooney.)

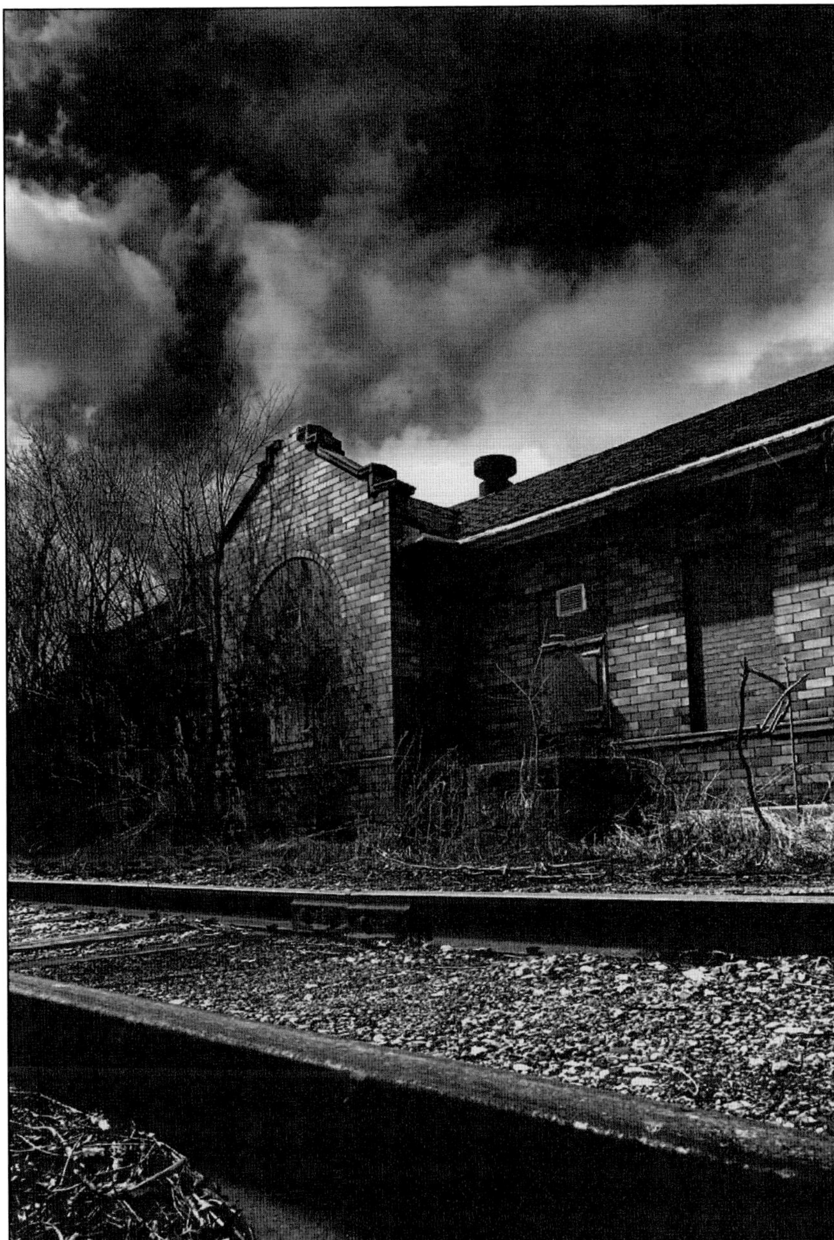

Passenger rail service in Des Moines ended for good in 1969, although many of the existing depots had already been closed. Shortly after the Des Moines Union Railway depot at 120 East Fifth Street ended its passenger service, the building went dormant and has never served another purpose. It is one of only two known passenger depots still standing in Des Moines and the only one on the east side. The building was given further study in 1983 when historian Barbara Beving Long noted, "According to railroad buff Ronald Sims, it was built for the Iowa Falls and Northern Railroad, although it may have been the Wabash depot. A 1909 map, however, shows a Des Moines Union Railway Depot on the site. To complicate matters further, a 1911 City Directory makes no mention of a depot for any of these railroads." In 2008, it was nominated as one of Des Moines's most endangered buildings for not being used to its full potential. (Jerry Ranch.)